Kiel Center Of Sanctuary For Ex-Nazis

Schleswig - Holstein Pays Them Pensions

By Gaston Coblentz

From the Herald Tribune Bureau

...small

...of the SS

More Swastikas Bloom; Bonn Purge Demanded

nd ein Staatsanwalt

kenkreuzes" / Von Rolf Seeliger

Bonn Allowed To Build Big Destroyers

6,000-Ton Warships May Carry Missiles

By Tom Lambert
From the Herald Tribune Bureau

LONDON, May 24
Germany wa...
...esday

Wer sucht unsere Mörder?

Von HEINZ LIEDKE

Shirer Says Bonn Nazis Fill Foreign Office

Nazi Law

n Verden

rang ins...

Salt L... City, April 18 (AP)
...William L. Shir...

for th...
ap...
in the
tu...
n...

THE NEW GERMANY AND THE OLD NAZIS

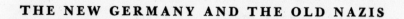

By T. H. Tetens

WHITHER HITLER?

CHRISTIANITY, HITLERISM, BOLSHEVISM

KNOW YOUR ENEMY

GERMANY PLOTS WITH THE KREMLIN

THE NEW GERMANY AND THE OLD NAZIS

THE
NEW GERMANY
AND THE
OLD NAZIS

T. H. Tetens

 Random House   New York

FIRST PRINTING

© Copyright, 1961, by T. H. Tetens
All rights reserved under International and Pan-American Copyright
Conventions. Published in New York by Random House, Inc., and
simultaneously in Toronto, Canada, by Random House of Canada, Limited.
Library of Congress Catalog Card Number: 61–7240

Manufactured in the United States of America
by H. Wolff, New York

PART ONE

The Legacy of Hitler

1 *Return of the Native*

It was long after sunset on the evening of April 23, 1957, when Kurt Lieser, a textile dealer, left one of the drab buildings in the business section of the south German town of Offenburg, in the foothills of the Black Forest. Herr Lieser— a slight man, past forty, but still young looking—paused a few moments to inhale the fresh spring air. Then at a leisurely pace he set out toward Bismarckstrasse, Offenburg's lively main street. The mild evening had brought out the crowd. Young people chatted gaily, and stuffy middle-class burghers strolled with measured steps past the neon-lighted, chrome-blinking show windows of the department stores and specialty shops. Here and there friends greeted each other with a loud and hearty *"Guten Abend!"*

As he walked along Bismarckstrasse, Kurt Lieser recognized people who thirty years before had been his classmates and playmates. Today they passed like strangers, and their rebuffs brought back the bitter realization that he could never again be an accepted Offenburger. As a "non-Aryan" he had once been driven away by the Nazis, and when he had miraculously returned alive from a concentration camp, he had not been readmitted to the community. The people of Offenburg still regarded him as a *Zugereister*—a newcomer to the town.

Kurt Lieser was pleased that the long and strenuous day was behind him. Out-of-town customers had kept him at the office much later than usual, and he had told his wife not to wait dinner for him; he would take his evening meal in a restaurant and relax with a glass of beer. As he walked down to the newspaper kiosk at the railroad station, where he always bought his favorite out-of-town paper, he had time to decide where to eat. He had a choice of the Bahnhof Restaurant, the Weinstube, or the meeting place of the town's upper crust, the Zaehringer Hof.

The food at the Bahnhof Restaurant was not to his liking and the place was *ungemuetlich*—it just didn't have the homey atmosphere that a German is accustomed to. The Weinstube radiated real warmth, but unfortunately Kurt Lieser was not welcome there. He had never seemed to receive the attention and friendly service given the other patrons. And complaints, he knew, would be useless. He would probably be told that he could go elsewhere if he was dissatisfied. Thus the choice was made simple for him. The Zaehringer Hof was a fine place, their Schnitzel à la Holstein was excellent, and the wine and the *Muenchner Dunkel* were of superb quality.

Herr Lieser found a place at a table where a local businessman and his wife were just finishing their dinner. After a short time they left with stiff formality. It was quite a while before the waiter came to take his order, but Lieser was accustomed to that. The meal was good, and afterward he relaxed comfortably over his newspaper with a beer before him. He had just glanced over the headlines on the front page when another guest appeared at his table. Herr Lieser recognized the man at once. He was Ludwig Pankratz Zind— Herr Studienrat Zind—a teacher. Standing straight and trim, Zind rattled the customary German formality: *"Gestatten?"* Kurt Lieser nodded a friendly invitation, but he got not the slightest response from the new diner. While Zind slowly moved his chair into position, his eyes wandered searchingly over the crowd, and several times he made a slight formal bow to friends sitting nearby.

As a teacher at the Grimmelshausen Gymnasium, a school "devoted to the humanities," Herr Zind enjoyed the respect not only of the small ruling clique that ran this town of twenty-eight thousand but also of the people at large. Kurt Lieser knew him as the president of Offenburg's athletic club, the *Turnverein*. He also served as an official of the bowling club and was active in other organizations.

Ludwig Zind could have filled the Hollywood role of an arrogant German officer perfectly. Although in his early fifties and of rather slight build, Herr Zind stood ramrod erect, giving the impression that he was a man of stern stuff. His long sun-tanned face showed heavy scars from his student days at Heidelberg. Under an intelligent, high forehead were hard, penetrating eyes, which betrayed a considerable degree of energy and fanaticism.

Studienrat Zind took his seat and suddenly spoke, at once haughty and studiously jovial.

"Well, Herr Lieser, what is the news in the world today?"

A little surprised to be called by name, Lieser folded his paper and shrugged his shoulders.

"Oh, just the same old story—Nasser and the Suez Canal, trouble in Jordan, and protests against the bomb-testing."

The discussion that followed between Zind and Lieser was reconstructed a year later before a court in Offenburg. The trial, which lasted three days, made headlines throughout the world and entered the annals of history as the macabre "affair Zind."

Nasser and the Suez Canal gave Ludwig Zind a welcome opportunity to reel off a whole catalogue of fixed Nazi clichés, ranging from "the shameful Treaty of Versailles" to Roosevelt's "criminal sellout at Yalta." Had Germany only won the heroic battle fought under Hitler, Zind proclaimed, the world today would be in a different shape. There would be German order and not cold war, Communism, and crime. With a German victory we would today enjoy justice and decency, and not suffer under democratic mob rule, corruption, and decadence. However, not everything was lost; history had not yet come to its end. Nasser was proof that the British lion had lost its roar and was ready to die. France was rotting away in chronic disorder, and America was too fat, lazy, and stupid ever to become a soldier nation. Make no mistake, five to ten years hence Germany will again be confronted with the *Schicksalsstunde*—the hour of destiny. For that day the Fatherland must be prepared and the youth must be ready. Look how we have come back from defeat within a dozen years. Give us ten years more and we will again be the top nation in the world.

Kurt Lieser tried to interject a few skeptical remarks about wishful thinking and miscalculations in history, about winning the battles and losing the war, and about the absurdity of another world butchery. But Herr Studienrat Zind dismissed such defeatist ideas with the sweeping statement that this was all poison, dished out daily by those licensed papers which were either sympathetic to the Communists or were paid handsomely for selling American democracy.

As the discussion—now an argument—continued, Herr Zind motioned two young men over to the table in order to let them take part in his refresher course on Nazi *Weltanschauung*. Years before, the two had been his pupils at the Gymnasium, and now they were both finishing their final semester at a university. One of the young men had introduced himself as the law student Werner Walzer, the son of Oberstudiendirektor Walzer, Zind's superior at the Gymnasium.

With this young generation in front of him, the Herr Studienrat lifted his voice to condemn everything that was "un-German." He quoted Schiller and Bismarck and the old Teutonic patriot, Ernst Moritz Arndt, in order to prove that there would be eternal war between *die Untermenschen*—the scum of the earth—and the fair Nordic race.

At this point Kurt Lieser became extremely irritated.

"Herr Zind, would you say that you believe in the superiority of a so-called Nordic race, and that you condone the prejudices and the excesses against other races and creeds?"

"Of course I do! And I will tell you frankly that there was nothing wrong with the racial laws that were introduced under Adolf Hitler. Those laws served a very good purpose!"

Slowly looking around, Kurt Lieser saw the sneering faces of guests and waiters who were excitedly following this remarkable discussion. He knew that at this moment he had to stand up and be counted. For a long time he had expected that such a day might come.

"I know you made Germany *judenrein*—free of Jews. But what about the methods? What about all the atrocities committed by the Nazis against the Jews and other prisoners? How can you justify them?"

"Herr Lieser, don't give me that! I know too well this propaganda hogwash spread by the Jews. The Fuehrer was forced to arrest the Jews because they constituted a serious threat to the security of the state. The Jews in the camps were well fed and well treated; after the war every one of them received huge sums of money. But look at me, who paid me for what I have suffered after the war?"

Kurt Lieser recognized that he was getting deeper and deeper into a hopeless argument. He tried to bring the discussion up to the present.

"What about today's sacrilegious acts against Jewish temples and cemeteries? Do you think it is right to paint swastikas on synagogues and defile Jewish graveyards?"

"What's wrong with that? These youngsters have a right to register their protest against the presence of Jews, even dead ones, on our German soil."

The foregoing exchange and that which follows is taken from reports which appeared in the German news magazine

Der Spiegel and from accounts about the Zind trial in the German press.

KURT LIESER "You as a teacher should feel ashamed of your statement. I suspect that you would even have the audacity to praise the Nazi mass murder?"

LUDWIG ZIND "In my opinion far too few Jews went into the gas chambers."

KURT LIESER "This is outrageous! Do you know that I spent the war in a concentration camp, that I was tortured and beaten, and that I almost lost my voice?"

LUDWIG ZIND "What? That means they forgot to gas you too? It is a pity that you did not go up in smoke with all the others!"

KURT LIESER "Today you would put me into a concentration camp if you had your way, wouldn't you?"

LUDWIG ZIND "Why not? And let me add this: I would not hesitate to kill you!"

KURT LIESER "And what about my wife—you would gas her too?"

LUDWIG ZIND "Of course I would! It could all be done at the same time!"

KURT LIESER "What would you do with my two children?"

LUDWIG ZIND "For my part they could stay alive. But let me tell you this: I am proud that during the war I and my men killed hundreds of Jews with shovel blows on the skull. I would not hesitate to do it again."

Kurt Lieser flew into a rage and tried to jump at the Studienrat's throat, shouting "Murderer!" A fight broke out. Zind called him a "dirty Jew" and cursed Israel.

While the waiters shoved them out into the night, Ludwig Zind yelled, "Israel is a pesthole! The day will come when the Arabs will remove it like a carbuncle!"

2 *The Zind Case*

On his way home Kurt Lieser was haunted by ugly memories. Dazed, bewildered, and in despair, he wondered whether it had been a wise decision to remain in Germany. His wife, almost hysterical with fear, could not gain a clear picture of what had happened. The only thing she could make out was that Herr Studienrat Zind would have no qualms about starting the gassing and killing all over again.

Lieser had gone through it all before, and amazingly he had survived. But what would the future bring? He was tormented by a thousand questions to which he had no answers. What kind of world was he living in, anyway? Why had he so foolishly ignored the complaints of his children, who had been frequently accosted in the streets with the too-familiar invective: *"Dreckige Judensau!"*—dirty Jewish pig.

As he tossed and turned in his bed, the long-forgotten shacks of the Sulz concentration camp came to life vividly in his memories. There they had broken him, body and spirit. How many Sulzes, how many Dachaus, Belsens, Buchenwalds, Auschwitzes, and Birkenaus had been put in operation by Germany? Could all this come back one day—the torture cellars, the death bunkers, the gas chambers, and the crematories? He relived it all. He saw himself in his striped rags, which the Germans called a "uniform," working in the stone quarry under almost inhuman conditions. Oh, yes, since he was only a *Halbjude*—part Jew—he had even been considered a privileged prisoner, and was allowed to do heavy work fourteen hours each day. As long as he could slave in the quarry he had at least been safe from the gas chamber.

When Kurt Lieser finally awoke from his nightmares late the following forenoon, he found it difficult to remember where he was. It took him some time to realize that he was in a comfortable bed in a civilized home, that it was not 1943, not 1945, but the year 1957—twelve years, fully twelve years after his liberation from the camp! And here he was, back in Offenburg, in his home town, among all the Zinds.

There was an entirely different atmosphere at the house of Studienrat Ludwig Pankratz Zind. The news about the event at the Zaehringer Hof had spread with whirlwind speed all over town. Friends telephoned the Studienrat to find out whether it was true that he had given the Jew—*dem Zugereisten*—a good beating. "Only a good tongue-lashing which he will never forget," was Zind's answer.

Wherever he went the Studienrat was again the hero of the town. His former pupils proudly recalled how in 1938 Zind, then a Nazi storm trooper, had praised his boys for their participation in the infamous "Kristallnacht." Synagogues and "non-Aryan" stores went up in flames, and the *Judenbande*—the Jewish scum—were herded together, many of them with bloody heads and broken bones. Men and women were separated and then shipped off in cattle cars to various labor and concentration camps.

"*Ja, das waren noch Zeiten!*—Those were the good old days!" commented some of his former pupils nostalgically when they met their old "prof" on the street. Such moments

were more than encouraging for Studienrat Zind, because
he strongly believed it to be of great importance to "keep
the spirit alive." Whatever our misfortunes are, we must
not lose our heads, he used to say. "History is uninterrupted
warfare; it is like a roller coaster—sometimes you're up, and
sometimes you're down." Such talks were the real strength
of the Studienrat. He was considered a leader in the community because he radiated confidence. No wonder the whole
town was buzzing with excitement over the "battle at the
Zaehringer Hof." Studienrat Zind had demonstrated again
that something could be done if the people only had the
courage to be bold.

Although the townspeople of Offenburg had an ample
supply of gossip for weeks about Zind's "victory" at the Zaehringer Hof, not a word of it appeared in the local paper. In
all probability nothing of the incident would ever have been
brought before the public had it not come to the attention of
the lively and courageous news magazine *Der Spiegel*. On
December 18, 1957, nine months after the affair at the Zaehringer Hof, *Der Spiegel* published verbatim the highlights
of the Zind-Lieser dialogue, under the caption "Israel Should
Be Eradicated."

This single page in a news magazine created unexpected
repercussions. It was not so much the fact that an anti-
Semitic incident had been recorded. That happened almost
every week in every German town. Such cases were usually
reported at the bottom of the back pages in five lines of small
print under "Miscellaneous." What made the Zind case
notable and caused the most comment was the revelation of
all the maneuvers with which the authorities—the Ministry
of Higher Education in the State of Baden-Wuerttemberg,
as well as the Ministry of Justice—had tried for several
months to hush up the case.

Suddenly, with the Zind affair in the open, hectic communications were exchanged between the Grimmelshausen

Gymnasium and the school authorities in Freiburg, between the lower court in Offenburg and the Ministry of Justice in Karlsruhe, between the Minister-President of Baden-Wuerttemberg and the federal government in Bonn. There were inquiries from the Social Democratic opposition in Parliament, denials by the officials, explanations and soothing talk from those who wanted to keep the story quiet. However, from the day *Der Spiegel* described the incident, things moved quickly. There was considerable fear in Bonn that world public opinion might be aroused by the resurgence of anti-Semitic outbursts in Germany. There were hasty investigations by the authorities, and an indictment against Zind was followed by his suspension from the Gymnasium. He was arrested, but was freed without bail a few days later. After elaborate preparations, the trial began in Offenburg in early April 1958, in the spotlight of the German and international press.

The huge wood-paneled trial room of the Provincial Court was filled to standing room only with Offenburgers. The halls and stairways of the courthouse were crowded with hundreds of townspeople who could not be admitted. Charged with having publicly approved the Nazi crimes and "slandered the memory of the dead," Zind had to defend himself before three judges and two lay jurors. When he took the stand on the first day, Zind described the development from his early days as an anti-Semitic student up to the time he became a faithful follower of Hitler. During the twenties he joined the Stahlelm (Steel Helmet), a right-wing veterans' organization, and later became a storm trooper. During the war he fought on the Eastern Front as a captain. Banned from teaching after the war, he was readmitted to the Gymnasium in 1948 as a mathematics and biology instructor.

According to the trial account in the *Frankfurter Allgemeine Zeitung* (April 10-12, 1958), Zind proudly stated:

"Without hesitation I adopted the political concepts of National Socialism and even today I regard these concepts as completely valid." Zind berated the court with long nationalistic tirades. He saw nothing wrong with his statement that Lieser "should have been gassed too." Expressions like this, said Zind, "have become as common among the great majority of the German people as the curse, 'Go to the devil.'"

Under questioning from the presiding judge, Dr. Hans Eckert, Zind admitted that an attempt had been made by the school authorities to settle the incident quietly through a proposed conciliation between Lieser and the defendant. But Zind had refused to apologize. He declared: "I would rather clean the streets than come crawling to a Jew."

Zind did not deny the accuracy of the dialogue which Lieser had testified to and *Der Spiegel* had reported. His only defense was that he had been provoked by Lieser's questions, and that he had not said it was the Jews but the Russians whose heads had been bashed in by the hundreds. However, he admitted quite freely that he was "firmly committed to the Nazi principle of fighting the Jew, a matter which was not only justified in the past, but even necessary today."

It was established during the trial that Zind had propagated his anti-Semitic bias in the classroom. Otherwise the trial produced little evidence that had not been known before. It was, however, a revelation for the international press to see Studienrat Zind in action, and to get a close look at the fraternity and atmosphere among the townspeople of Offenburg. Almost without exception, the witnesses tried to help Zind by declaring that they had no clear recollection of the incident at the Zaehringer Hof.

By sentencing Zind to one year in prison for "defaming the dead," the court declared that it believed Lieser's account of the incident, and that Zind, at certain points, had been lying. It was the first stringent sentence handed down by a German court, applying a new law designed to deal sternly with anti-Semitic hatemongers. The court branded Zind as "an intellectual arsonist," who had "severely damaged Germany's reputation abroad."

During the trial the German press reported that Zind had received an offer of a position at a school in Cairo. When the Appellate Court confirmed the one-year prison term, Zind promptly escaped to Egypt.

The remarkable thing about the Zind affair was its echo throughout the world and in part of the German press. On April 13, 1958, the New York *Times* quoted two German papers on the Zind trial. The *Frankfurter Neue Presse* said: "Herr Zind is not interesting. Interesting is the atmosphere in which the Zinds flourish. This atmosphere explains why a man whose attitude identifies itself with crime was thought fit to teach and educate a new generation. You Deputies, you Ministers, you Parliaments and trade unions, do you not realize that it is your fault?" The *Neue Ruhr Zeitung* said: "It is not Herr Zind who faced the court. Society was on trial, a society that tolerated a Zind and made it possible for him to behave as he did."

What the *Times* dispatch did not reveal was the scandal behind the scandal. The press also reported that the people in Offenburg gave their fullest sympathy to the unreconstructed Zind. When the defendant walked out of the courtroom "where the audience had been plainly on his side, women wept at the verdict and men reached out to shake his hand" (*Time,* April 21, 1958). At the courthouse Zind passed through long cheering crowds, and one reporter was told: "Whatever the court might say against him, you can rest assured that the whole of Offenburg is backing Zind" (*Die Zeit,* April 17, 1958).

Was the Zind case symptomatic of a resurgence of Nazism? The New York *Herald Tribune* correspondent Gaston Coblentz, in a report of April 12, 1958, quoted a Protestant

Church leader from Tuebingen as saying: "Elements which prudently became silent after 1945 are again insolently raising their heads. If steps are not taken, we shall have within a few years a new Nazism lacking only a Fuehrer." The same dispatch quoted the State Prosecutor in the Zind trial as follows: "There are many people in Germany who believe that the time has arrived for them to come forward again aggressively with their anti-Jewish hatred."

Alarmed about the growing wave of anti-Semitism in West Germany, the *Frankfurter Rundschau* of April 14, 1958, declared in an editorial: "There are thousands of Zinds who give unabashed vent to their feelings in the *Bierstuben*. The anti-Semitic exchanges that one overhears are downright revolting. They always end with statements like: 'Not enough Jews were gassed' or 'They should be exterminated like vermin.' " Democratic newspapers wondered how many junior Zinds had graduated from Offenburg and elsewhere.

The New York *Times* of March 15, 1958, quoted a Christian Democratic deputy of the Bundestag, Dr. Franz Boehm, as saying that "anti-Semitism has not been overcome"—a fact well known by the 30,000 Jews or "part Jews" who are still in Germany. The *Sueddeutsche Zeitung* of April 15, 1958, touched the sore spot of German public opinion by pointing out in an editorial:

The circumstances of the Zind case have brought to light that the conditions in Germany are worse than most of us dare to say. The alarming fact is that the German people are today deeply confused in their concepts of right and wrong. . . . There is widespread praise of Zind as an "upright character" who dared to stick to his opinion and would "rather clean the streets than lie low before a Jew." We wonder whether this is the voice of an oversensitive national conscience or only the conspiracy of our society standing on the principle that "one crow does not scratch the eyes of another crow."

Similar warnings were published in respected periodicals such as the *Frankfurter Hefte, Die Zeit,* and even in Dr. Adenauer's own mouthpiece, the *Rheinischer Merkur.** Unfortunately no firm steps were taken by the Adenauer administration to prevent the resurgence of anti-Semitic propaganda and vandalistic outbursts. On November 27, 1957, long before the Zind case, the important conservative newspaper *Die Welt* stated that anti-Semitism had again become a problem of "painful actuality." Pointing to a public opinion poll, the paper expressed concern over the fact that 88 percent of those questioned refused to discuss their opinions on the Jewish question. The paper mentioned another poll where "a third came out clearly in favor of the old anti-Semitic concepts."

The *Frankfurter Allgemeine Zeitung* of October 1, 1957, reported an increase of anti-Semitic activities and came to the conclusion that the "escape into hatred" is a dangerous sign in Germany, "together with many other things which are still very much alive under the surface."

On May 27, 1957, six months before the Zind affair became public, the *Christian Science Monitor* printed this dispatch from Bonn:

* The newspapers and periodicals quoted in this and the following chapters have a high standing in Germany. A survey of the German press, published in *The Department of State Bulletin* of February 23, 1953, names as the four leading newspapers:

1] *Frankfurter Rundschau,* left of center, independent, friendly to U.S. policies.

2] *Frankfurter Allgemeine Zeitung,* conservative.

3] *Deutsche Zeitung,* conservative, expresses the view of the business community.

4] *Sueddeutsche Zeitung,* independent, the most important paper in Bavaria.

In recent years *Die Welt* of Hamburg, conservative, has developed into an outstanding national newspaper. Among the leading periodicals are the *Frankfurter Hefte, Der Monat,* the news magazine *Der Spiegel,* the conservative weekly *Die Zeit,* the Catholic weekly *Rheinischer Merkur,* and the conservative Protestant weekly *Christ und Welt.*

Church and civic leaders are expressing alarm at the outburst of anti-Semitic feeling and Nazi flag-waving recently displayed in various parts of Germany.

Bishop Otto Dibelius, head of the German Evangelical Church, warned here May 24 that recent desecration of Jewish cemeteries in West Germany indicates a "regrowth of anti-Semitic tendencies. . . ."

In Salzgitter, raiders overturned about 80 gravestones and even a 20-ton memorial.

They left behind a straw dummy bearing a swastika and a sign with the note: "Germany awake—Israel perish." . . .

Nuremberg was the scene of another April 20 birthday party for Hitler when swastika flags were raised on the field where the Fuehrer used to address Nazi rallies. . . .

The editor of the Jewish weekly, *Allgemeine Wochenzeitung,* rejected as "highly exaggerated" a report by the Communist East German news agency ADN that 2,000 raids on Jewish cemeteries had been committed since the war. He placed the number at 250.

At the same time the German-language paper in New York, *Der Aufbau,* reported on June 21, 1957, a "new wave of anti-Semitism in West Germany," with Nazi-type youth groups, veterans' societies, and expellee organizations as the main supporters of the anti-Semitic hate campaign.

The Zind case only confirmed what close observers of the German political scene had been predicting for a long time: that the Nazis would come out of their hibernation as soon as it was no longer risky to demonstrate their true feelings. That moment arrived in 1955, when Germany became a sovereign state and the Allied rights of control came to an end. Since then the trend had been growing stronger toward a nationalistic revival and open manifestations of neo-Nazism.

For several years now the Bonn Republic has been plagued by periodic outbursts of anti-Semitic vandalism. Such waves occurred in 1955, in 1957, and again at the end of 1959, when the rash of swastika-daubings started on Christmas eve. The desecration of the synagogue in Cologne gave the signal for an epidemic of anti-Semitism which had its contagious effects throughout the world.

3 *"Nazism Is Dead and Buried"*

By an ironic coincidence it happened that at about the same
time the Bonn Republic was experiencing the Zind affair, a
prominent American educator and diplomat was picturing
West Germany in an entirely different light.

Early in January 1958 a distinguished audience, composed of educators, scientists, and representatives of America's political elite, assembled in one of the large lecture halls
on the campus of Harvard University. The speaker, the be-
loved and esteemed president emeritus of Harvard, Dr.
James Bryant Conant, was received with great applause. Dr.
Conant had just returned from four years in Germany, first
as United States High Commissioner and later as Ambassador to the Federal Republic of Germany. In three consecutive lectures Dr. Conant reviewed the postwar developments
in the Bonn Republic, using the most hopeful terms. He
told his audience that in West Germany he had found "a
people who had turned their backs on the German past."
Reaffirming an earlier statement that "the mood of modern
Germany is that of a people repudiating the brutality of the

Nazi rule," Dr. Conant came to the conclusion that "Nazism is dead and buried."

"Free Germany today," the speaker told his audience, "is a united nation without military ambitions and with few illusions about the catastrophe from which it has only just emerged." To his own question "Will it happen again?" Dr. Conant gave the explicit answer: "Taking all the facts available into consideration, it seems to be quite clear that the myth of the Third Reich has been destroyed. Free Germany today repudiates the Nazi past."

Dr. Conant's evaluation of modern Germany cannot be overlooked. Here was a rational, informed scientist, educator, and diplomat, who had made a careful study of all the facts and forces at play in postwar Germany. The educators and political leaders heard with great relief Dr. Conant's assurances that the Germany which had twice within one generation run amuck against the whole civilized world had finally undergone a profound change. The nation of Goethe, Kant, and Humboldt was back on the road to its highest ideals. "I predict," Dr. Conant concluded, "that the enthusiasms now germinating in Germany are not the wrong ones."

Long press dispatches in leading American newspapers emphasized the highlights of Dr. Conant's address.* A few months later the three lectures were published in book form under the title *Germany and Freedom*. Laudatory reviews spread Dr. Conant's optimistic outlook on the future of Germany to an even larger audience. Most remarkable was the New York *Times* book review of April 6, 1958, which pointed out that Dr. Conant's thesis of a new purified Germany rested on "realistic optimism." It quoted Dr. Conant's opinion that a healthy state of affairs had developed in Germany: "However closely we look for symptoms of revived national-

---

* The above quotations from Dr. Conant's address were taken from the *Christian Science Monitor* of January 10, 1958.

ism, racism, militarism, or despotism, we must admit they simply are not there." Dr. Conant's report convinced the *Times* reviewer that "those who are always seeing a new Nazism around the corner are living in the past." Certainly Dr. Conant's statements reflected the official line of the Bonn government, as well as that of the U. S. State Department.

Long before Dr. Conant made his optimistic statements on the change in Germany in 1957 and 1958, I had had lengthy discussions with State Department officials whose considerable experience in postwar Germany had made them unquestioned experts in this field. These officials admitted quite frankly the discrepancy between Washington's policy position and the actual conditions in certain areas. Their argument can be summed up as follows: It is not so much that the State Department is badly informed about the developments in various countries and especially in Germany, but it is rather a matter of evaluation and emphasis. All unpleasant events and facts which might unfavorably affect the realization of our plans are played down as much as possible. This is obviously done in order to avoid criticism which might undermine the confidence of the American people and that of our allies in the effectiveness of our policy.

The officials admitted that there were some risks involved in our German experiment. However, it was considered necessary to take the position that in the Bonn Republic we have a dependable ally and that the large majority of Germans have sincerely reformed.

The dogma of the untouchable policy position was underscored by Dr. Conant himself. In a dispatch from Cambridge, the New York *Times* reported on January 10, 1958, that Dr. Conant had criticized George F. Kennan, our former ambassador to the Soviet Union, for having advocated in his British Broadcasting lectures (December 1957) a gradual military disengagement in Central Europe and a limited rearmament in Germany. What was really startling was Dr. Conant's suggestion that on such a vital issue as the future of Germany there should be no public discussion which in any way might differ from the official State Department position. The *Times* quoted Dr. Conant as follows: "Anything that is said or done to stir up German suspicions about American intentions in Europe or American suspicions about Germany vis-à-vis the Soviet is a blow to the solidarity of NATO. Conversely, anything that can be done to quiet such suspicions will strengthen the defense of our freedom." Nevertheless, beneath the surface there is still a widespread feeling of uneasiness among the American public in regard to the future of Germany. Time and again radio and television programs have come up with the significant question: Can we trust Germany?

People often wonder where the millions of Nazis have disappeared to, all those who once hailed and faithfully served the Fuehrer. What has happened to those thousands of top Nazis in Hitler's Third Reich—the high officials in the administration, the Brown-Shirt bullies and the SS guard officers who once strutted in snappy uniforms and riding boots, with their chests covered with "lametta"? Where are the Nazi diplomats, the geopolitical strategists, and the advocates of a master race and Lebensraum? Where are the thousands of judges and prosecutors who, year after year, sent countless "enemies of the state" to the gallows and tens of thousands to lifelong hard labor, starvation, and death? What has happened to the thousands of brutes who committed the daily massacres and tortures in the concentrations camps? Where are those who supervised the extermination of millions—including women and children—in the gas chambers? Finally, where are the tens of thousands of Nazi teachers, the millions of fanatical Hitler youths, and the thousands of highly indoctrinated youth leaders who are today in the age group between thirty-five and forty-five? Have they all become thoroughly reformed democrats, so that Nazism is really "dead and buried"?

Early in 1959 the owner of an independent radio station in New York discussed the German problem in three consecutive editorial broadcasts.* "Is there any danger that the Nazis might come back into positions of power in Germany?" he asked, and answered himself unequivocally: ". . . the Nazis *are* back in positions of power in government, in industry, in banking, in the press, in education." In support of this thesis the editorial marshaled a wide array of indisputable facts and came to the conclusion:

The very Nazi leaders of the days of Hitler are back in power. Thus do we conjure up the ghosts of a nation that, only a few years ago, was dedicated to sadism, torture and murder—a national policy of calculated cruelty unmatched in the history of modern man. WMCA fears that our deeds today will haunt our children tomorrow.

What is the truth? Is Nazism "dead and buried," or are the Nazis back in power? To obtain a balanced and true picture about the new Germany it is necessary to take a closer look at the record.

* The talks by Nathan Straus of WMCA (January 2, 9, and 16, 1959) had an unprecedented response from the audience and attracted violent criticism from the German press.

4 *The Plotters*

Late on the night of January 14, 1953, the telephones rang in the homes of newspaper correspondents representing the foreign press in London. The sleepy newsmen, responding to the calls, were requested by a Foreign Office official to assemble at Downing Street by seven o'clock the following morning for an important press conference. There was little doubt that something extraordinary had happened, since it was the first time since the end of the war that a news conference had been scheduled for such an unusual hour.

The next morning shortly after seven, the head of the press division of the Foreign Office, Sir William Ridsdale, distributed a communiqué which stated that a group of seven former high Nazi officials had been arrested in Duesseldorf and Hamburg for having plotted the overthrow of the Bonn Republic. The official announcement said that the British authorities had been aware for some time that the seven men had been involved in a plot and that the arrest had been made under the authority of Foreign Minister Eden.

The ringleader of the group was a Dr. Werner Naumann, who, until the German collapse, had served as State Secre-

tary in Dr. Goebbels' Propaganda Ministry. Dr. Naumann
had been with Hitler during the very last days in the bunker
of the Chancellery in Berlin, and he was the one designated
by the Fuehrer in his testament to succeed Dr. Goebbels as
Propaganda Minister.

Arrested along with Naumann were the following prominent Nazis:

Karl Kaufmann, one-time Gauleiter of Hamburg.

Paul Zimmermann, an SS General and official of the concentration camp branch of the SS organization.

Gustav Scheel, Gauleiter of Salzburg, Austria, and designated Minister of Education in Hitler's will.

Dr. Heinrich Haselmeyer, head of the National Socialist Student League, and Hitler's "expert on race and sterilization."

Dr. Karl Scharping, a propaganda official under Dr. Goebbels.

Heinz Siepen, another district leader of the Third Reich.

The British announced that they had confiscated "tons
of material" (four truckloads), and after the first check, they
hinted that a careful examination would produce ample evidence to back up an indictment of conspiracy and high treason. The seven arrested men were described as the leaders of
a group of a hundred twenty-five important Nazis whose aim
was to infiltrate the three Rightist parties in the Adenauer
coalition. Their final goal had been "the overthrow of the
Bonn parliamentary regime."

The arrest of the plotters had a strong effect upon the
Bonn government and on German public opinion. According to a dispatch in the New York *Times,* Chancellor Adenauer was "shocked and angered." The *Times,* quoting
from the *General Anzeiger* of Bonn, a paper close to Adenauer, said that the British "had contrived the whole affair
for the purpose of warning the Americans against entering a
direct alliance with the dangerous Germans." *Times* correspondent Drew Middleton reported from Bonn that "Ger-

man public sentiment began to crystallize in defense of the seven arrested National Socialists." Leading Bonn officials and politicians, supported by the majority of the German press, opened an all-out campaign against the British, implying that they had sinister motives and telling them that they had no business poking into a strictly domestic German affair. Only a handful of democratic and conservative papers took a more critical view of the Naumann conspiracy.*

The main concern of German government officials and the press was that the British had acted "unfairly" against Bonn at a moment when Dr. Adenauer had to face a most delicate international situation. At that time the Adenauer cabinet hoped for a speedy ratification of the European Defense Community Treaty (EDC) which would restore full German sovereignty and would be the first step toward political unification of Europe. To raise the specter of a resurgent Nazi danger before world public opinion at such a moment was, in Dr. Adenauer's eyes, an unpardonable crime. The Chancellor was especially bitter because the British High Commissioner, Sir Ivone Kirkpatrick, had not consulted him before the arrest.

The British reply was polite but determined. It pointed out that the occupation authorities had been profoundly disturbed when they had found evidence of an advanced plot, instigated by a vast Nazi network spreading from Duesseldorf to Cairo, Madrid, Buenos Aires, and Malmö, Sweden. They stated furthermore that they had had to proceed with the utmost secrecy, since the plotters had close contacts with high government circles in Bonn. Acording to the New York *Times,* the British submitted evidence to the Chancellor

---

* Although this information is based upon a collection of several hundred dispatches and editorials, I have drawn chiefly on the reports from the New York *Times* of January 16 to 18, 1953. Also of special significance were several articles which appeared in the *Frankfurter Rundschau* and the *Stuttgarter Nachrichten* during the latter part of January 1953, revealing the magnitude of the Naumann plot.

which "revealed a wide-spread plot with ramifications into many political parties and other influential organizations of West Germany." Faced with the grave implications of the Naumann conspiracy, Dr. Adenauer and his Minister of Justice, Dr. Thomas Dehler, had to confirm the seriousness of the case.

After the British had convinced Dr. Adenauer that they had an open-and-shut case against the Naumann plotters, the Bonn government suddenly exerted great pressure to bring the proceedings under German jurisdiction. On March 13, 1953, Dr. Adenauer wrote a letter to the British High Commissioner asking "that the investigation and eventual prosecution of Dr. Naumann and his associates should be handed over to the German authorities." The British responded favorably to this request on March 26, 1953.

After taking over the investigation, Dr. Adenauer admitted at a press conference "the existence of a far-flung plot" and that Naumann's activities "had been financed with considerable sums by Nazi groups in foreign countries." Minister of Justice Dehler told reporters that the Naumann group had developed "a most cunning and diabolic system of infiltration" and that the conspiracy represented "an acute threat to the democratic institutions in the Federal Republic." The captured Naumann documents, he said, "gave clear proof that the aim of the group had been to fill key positions in all Rightist parties with hard-core Nazis and thereby create propaganda vehicles which later could be used for a broad neo-Nazi mass movement." According to the *Wiesbadener Kurier* of May 6, 1953, Dr. Dehler quoted from one document in which Naumann expressed the hope that, if his scheme succeeded, "the coming election might be the last of its kind."

Soon after the British had transferred the prosecution of the case to the German authorities, the lawyers of the arrested plotters began to put pressure on the federal government to suppress the case and release their clients. The *Bremer Nachrichten* reported on June 15, 1953, that the Naumann lawyers had even threatened to discuss "the true background of the case openly" if their clients were not released soon.

By the end of June 1953 Dr. Naumann and his co-plotters were suddenly released, in violation of the most rigid stipulations of German law and court procedure. A year and a half later, in December 1954, in spite of the fact that the prosecutor had brought an indictment against Naumann charging conspiracy against the constitution of the Federal Republic, the highest court quietly dismissed the case without any trial or hearing.

Even before the plotters were released, the British became suspicious about the handling of the Naumann case and leaked some of the incriminating material to a stanchly democratic German newspaper which had gained quite a reputation for its revealing articles on the infiltration of former Nazis into the Adenauer administration. During the early part of June 1953 the *Frankfurter Rundschau* published five articles dealing with Naumann's tapped telephone conversations, notes from his appointment calendar, correspondence between the plotters, and significant excerpts from his diary. The published material gave a full inside view of the scope and character of the conspiracy.

The description of the intricate structure of the plot and the background of the many people involved filled whole pages in the *Frankfurter Rundschau*.* Here it is sufficient to state the main objectives as they emerged from the confiscated material:

1] Use the democratic constitution as a façade behind

---

* Articles and editorials in the *Frankfurter Rundschau* for January, February, and June 1953; also three informative articles in the *Stuttgarter Nachrichten*, January 29-31, and an editorial, "The Spider," in the *Bremer Nachrichten*, June 16, 1953.

which a new Nazi movement could be organized, designed to take over the apparatus of the state when time and circumstances would make such a step necessary and profitable.

2] Let Chancellor Adenauer serve as a front, exactly as Gustav Stresemann did during the twenties, behind which a new German power could develop undisturbed without arousing premature suspicions.

3] Apply a new method of infiltration (*Unterwanderung*) in order to conquer the existing parties and the administrative machinery of the state from within. Avoid noisy nationalistic demonstrations, flag-waving and incidents; use the more efficient and unsuspicious procedure of working in small cells, which some day, at an opportune moment, might consolidate themselves into a broad mass organization.

The detailed plan, which the Germans soon called the "Nau-Nau" strategy, instructed former well-known Nazi leaders to stay discreetly in the background until the time was ripe for action. In the meantime the leaders were to use all their connections to bring bright and capable young Nazis, especially those trained in the Hitler Youth, into influential positions, not only in the Adenauer coalition parties but also into all other political organizations.

The Naumann documents revealed much more than a mere strategic blueprint of how to subvert a state apparatus or the existing parties from within. There was a detailed record of how Dr. Naumann had used his contacts with top industrialists and leading politicians to fill well-paid positions in the Free Democratic party with scores of young, able Nazis who once had learned the tricks of the trade in the Goebbels' Propaganda Ministry. Dr. Naumann's most devoted collaborator in this enterprise was his intimate friend, Dr. Ernst Achenbach, a former Ribbentrop diplomat who, after the war, had become a prominent lawyer in the Ruhr district. It was reported that Achenbach and Naumann had been close friends during the war when they served together in important positions under Ambassador Otto Abetz in the German Embassy in occupied Paris. It was Dr. Achenbach who, in 1943, recommended to the Foreign Office that two thousand Jews be shipped to the East as reprisal for an attack on two Nazi officers.*

After the war Achenbach aggressively defended Nazi notables in many war crime trials. In later years he became the legal counselor and political confidant of a group of right-wing Ruhr industrialists. With the financial power of the industrial giants of the Ruhr behind him, Achenbach exerted a dominating influence in the Free Democratic party, where he held the important position of Chairman of the Foreign Affairs Committee. Many of his close friends and connections, mainly young Nazi activists, had successfully infiltrated the two other Adenauer coalition parties, the ultra-Rightist German party and the All-German Bloc (Refugee party), the latter appealing chiefly to the ten million refugees from the Eastern territories.

For some time after his arrest the British kept Dr. Naumann incommunicado, because they regarded his lawyer, who was Dr. Achenbach, as severely implicated in the plot. The pro-Adenauer paper *Stuttgarter Nachrichten* of January 17, 1953, named Achenbach the *spiritus rector* behind the drive toward a neo-Nazi restoration. A lengthy British white paper on the Naumann-Achenbach plot was ready to be released in August 1953, when it was suddenly "withdrawn at the last moment on Cabinet instructions, for reasons which never have been made quite clear." † There were rumors that the British had yielded under the combined pressure of Washington and Bonn.

The confiscated material disclosed that the Achenbach-Naumann group represented a so-called *Fuehrungsring*—a

---

* The document was published in *Das Freie Wort*, Duesseldorf, May 16, 1953.
† Alistair Horne, *Return to Power* (New York: Frederick A. Praeger, Inc., 1956), p. 165.

Nazi high command—a kind of political Mafia, with headquarters in Madrid, which operated by remote control
through clever organizational schemes on different levels,
serving various purposes. This Gauleiter group met periodically in the strictest secrecy, mainly in Duesseldorf or Hamburg. Up to thirty former Nazi top officials assembled under
false names as "old friends" in hotels, where they carried on
their political scheming. Among them were the ex-Gauleiters
Kaufmann, Grohe, Florian, Wegener, Frauenfeld, and Scheel,
a number of high officials from the Propaganda Ministry,
some Ribbentrop diplomats, and top-ranking SS officers.
According to the British correspondent Alistair Horne, the
"roll calls of the ex-Gauleiters and high SS officials present
read like a page from some nightmare *Who's Who* of the
Third Reich." These Nazi leaders had either escaped the
dragnet of the victorious Allies by false identification papers
or had been released from internment after a year or two
without any substantial penalty. The aim of the group was
"to form the general staff of the 'National Opposition'" and
build "a new political party out of the existing parties of the
right." *

Besides the infiltration of co-conspirators into positions of
command within the existing parties and into government
departments and party organizations on the middle and lower
levels, another task of the *Fuehrungsring* was to organize and
direct mass organizations, such as veterans' and refugee associations, which one day could easily be used as instruments
for political action. Other fields of activities for the group
were political propaganda in foreign countries, carried out in
close contact with the Nazi headquarters in Madrid, and the
initiation of conspiracies in foreign markets in behalf of German industrial cartels.

Have the Nazi schemers—the Achenbachs, Naumanns, and
Company—accomplished what they aimed for after the Nazi

* Horne, *Return to Power*, p. 168.

collapse? Have they regained influence and power in the
Bonn Republic? The answer has been given in the affirmative
by the plotters themselves. Long before, they had captured
numerous key positions in the Adenauer administration, in
political parties, and in the Laender (state) parliaments. They
were exuberant about their successes in one of their secret
directives circulated by the Nazi headquarters in Madrid.
This lengthy document, issued in September 1950, spoke contemptuously of the total failure of the Western occupation
policy and pointed gleefully to the success of the "flexible and
smoothly-working organization which, at the end of the war,
provided the precondition for all the gains that by necessity
emerged for Germany out of the chaos of the postwar period.
. . . Five years after Potsdam, we can look back with pride at
our accomplishments. . . . Nothing happened by chance;
everything was carefully planned." *

There is considerable material available which gives con-
clusive proof that the Nazis had made preparations long before their collapse to train an army of agents, often skillfully
camouflaged as "resistance fighters." About the successful
continuation of the Nazi subversive activities, the Madrid
Circular Letter had this to say:

Even after the collapse, the National Socialist party continued to
work in a camouflaged way [*getarnt*] in dozens of seemingly in-
nocuous societies and groups, in order to keep the national outlook of the German people alive and undiluted. Just as many
small brooks go toward making a mighty stream, the various
nationalistic and radical groups in the Zonen-Reich carried out,
almost without exception, worthwhile and powerful propaganda.
Each of these groups had its special task and had to adjust its

---

* The Madrid Circular Letter gave a general analysis of the world situation
five years after the German collapse and put special emphasis on the possibilities of a German comeback. The full text of the document was printed in
T. H. Tetens' *Germany Plots with the Kremlin* (New York: Henry Schuman,
1953).

work to certain situations and circumstances. However, it was of chief importance to direct the underlying trend of the patriotic propaganda toward the same goal. The more diverse and disconnected these groups appeared on the surface, the less they were apt to arouse suspicion that they were directed and influenced by a central organization. We have placed our confidential agents, observers, and representatives for special assignments in all groups and parties, even among Communist organizations and their fronts. The greater the number of organizations controlled and influenced by us, the more effective will be the results of our work.

The effectiveness and results of this Nazi strategy of infiltration will best be shown by taking a closer look at the conditions in present-day Germany.

PART TWO
Germany Today

NOTE: *Beginning with Chapter 5 most data concerning German newspapers and other sources will be given in the notes following the last chapter. These are keyed to the text by number. Exceptions are those sources which are clearly identified in the text by name and date of publication.*

5 *The Hidden Enemy*

Surveying the entire political structure of the Bonn Republic, one comes to the inescapable conclusion that the Nazis have had a quiet comeback almost everywhere. From the Chancellery down through every cabinet office, through the parties, the parliaments of the Laender, the police, the school system, and the press, former Nazis are deeply entrenched in many key positions, as well as in the middle and lower ranks of the federal and state government.

In the Chancellery there are two influential senior officials, Secretary of State Dr. Hans Globke and the senior diplomat Dr. Herbert Blankenhorn, who have been accused by the Social Democratic opposition of having faithfully served the Nazi cause. Both men, in spite of their unsavory records, have been entrusted by Dr. Adenauer from the very beginning with the rebuilding of the new government for the Federal Republic.

Under the Nazi regime Hans Globke served as the top official in the Office for Jewish Affairs in the Ministry of the Interior. It was here that the infamous Nuremberg Laws for the Protection of the German Blood were first drafted. The man who signed the racial laws against the Jews, Interior Minister Dr. Wilhelm Frick, was sentenced to death by the International Court in Nuremberg and hanged on October 16, 1946. And the one directly involved with the formulation of these laws was Dr. Hans Globke. It was he who drafted the text of Hitler's race law and who wrote the notorious "Commentary" interpreting this Nuremberg law, which paved the way for the extermination of millions of human beings.

When the Nazis decided to carry out the mass liquidation of European Jews, Dr. Globke's direct superior, Ministerial Counsel Bernard Loesner, himself a Nazi party member, had scruples of conscience and resigned from office. His post was taken over by Dr. Hans Globke. As chief legal adviser and head of the Office of Jewish Affairs, Dr. Globke thus became a direct participant in the gigantic venture to make Germany *judenrein*.

In applying the racial laws Dr. Globke worked hand in hand with the Main Security Office, the headquarters of the SS murder organization. *Der Spiegel* of September 28, 1960, reported a case which reveals that Dr. Globke had direct dealings with the SS Colonel Adolf Eichmann. More than that, the evidence shows that Dr. Globke was a key administrator in the "Final Solution," the master plan for the extermination of the Jews. The article in *Der Spiegel* quoted the testimony of a Wehrmacht officer, Max Merten, who together with Eichmann suggested in 1943 that 20,000 Jews in Macedonia (marked for the gas chambers in Auschwitz) should be released and shipped to Palestine. It was obviously not a feeling of humanity, but rather a personal greed for money, as well as a shortage of transportation facilities to the concentration camps, that motivated both Nazis to make this suggestion.*

---

* Wehrmacht officer Merten was involved in a number of shady deals and war crimes for which a high court in Greece sentenced him to twenty-five years in prison. Under pressure from the Bonn government, Merten was set free after thirty months of detention.

According to the story in *Der Spiegel,* Merten and Eichmann reached Dr. Globke and tried to obtain permission from the Office of Jewish Affairs for the release of the prisoners. Their efforts were in vain. Dr. Globke insisted on the strict execution of the Fuehrer's order. That sealed the fate of the 20,000 Jews, who were then shipped in cattle cars to Auschwitz.

Why Dr. Adenauer could not find another man capable of setting up a true democratic civil service has never been explained. Whatever lies behind this mystery, the fact is that Dr. Hans Globke, who faithfully served the Nazi hierarchy, became one of the most powerful men in the Federal Republic.

Dr. Globke has denied that he was a member of the Nazi party. But as the *Frankfurter Rundschau* of April 3, 1956, pointed out, Dr. Globke forgot to tell the Nuremberg judges that "he once filled out an application for membership in the Nazi party." In any event, it is an established fact that his services to the Nazi regime were highly appreciated by the party hierarchy and that he was amply rewarded. On April 25, 1938, the Minister of the Interior, Dr. Frick, wrote a letter to Hitler's deputy in the Brown House in which he praised Dr. Globke as "the most capable and efficient official in my ministry." The Nazi minister gave Globke a special accolade for his "extraordinary efforts in drafting the law for the Protection of the German Blood" and for a number of similar racial laws. Recognizing his "loyalty and constant willingness to act for the Nazi cause," Dr. Frick recommended that Hans Globke be promoted to the position of a senior official. Three months later Dr. Globke was appointed Ministerial Counsel. The full text of Dr. Frick's letter was published in *Der Spiegel* on August 10, 1960.

The German press has called Dr. Globke "The Gray Eminence," "the power behind the throne," and "The Spider." *Die Welt* of October 30, 1955, described Dr. Globke as "the second-in-command in the control tower of the German ship of state." According to *Die Welt,* Dr. Globke is the "only man who has access to Adenauer at all times or who can call the Chancellor at any hour." The paper adds: "Globke's political power rests entirely on the confidence which emanates from his chief, and on his domination over the official apparatus which must be regarded as his exclusive handiwork."

Many political observers believe that Dr. Globke in his quest for power simply adopted the authoritarian principles of Hitler's Fuehrerstaat in order to establish the undisputed authority of the Fuehrungszentrale—steering center—in the Chancellery. It is possible that Dr. Globke has done more than anyone else to re-Nazify West Germany. He has been accused by the opposition of having filled many key positions with former Nazis who are only waiting for a change in the political wind. For many years Dr. Globke's past has been an embarrassing topic in the Bonn Parliament.

On July 12, 1950, the legal expert of the Social Democratic party, Dr. Adolf Arndt, speaking before the Bundestag, described Dr. Globke's record in detail. Dr. Arndt accused the Chancellor's chief assistant of having "committed mass murder with the help of legal paragraphs." As a servant of the Nazis, Dr. Arndt pointed out, Herr Globke had "trampled upon the dignity of the human race and dishonored the German name." Since that time the Social Democrats have frequently demanded the ouster of Bonn's number-one bureaucrat. In the Bundestag debate of October 16, 1951, the Social Democratic deputy Dr. Gerhard Luetkens charged that the packing of the Bonn Foreign Office with ex-Nazis "was the work of a clique, once closely connected with the SS Main Security Office, which is steered by the ineffable Herr Globke, whose role has been discussed from this rostrum repeatedly" (official record of the Bundestag, October 16, 1951, p. 6,927).

The result of Dr. Globke's clever manipulations is that as chief assistant to Dr. Adenauer he makes decisions about a great many affairs in the federal government. A full-page article in the *Deutsche Zeitung* of June 11, 1958, explained how Dr. Globke is able to wield rigid control over every ministry. The various government departments have to submit monthly reports about their activities and plans, which all end up on Globke's desk. According to this analysis, no minister can make an important decision without the approval of Dr. Globke. It is the Secretary of State who convenes cabinet meetings and determines their agenda. The *Deutsche Zeitung* described Globke as the head of a huge staff, a super-ministry led by thirty-six senior officials, which constitutes the hub of the entire government machinery. It is Globke who decides what part of the incoming mail reaches the Chancellor. Nominations for appointments to high positions in all ministries are made by Dr. Globke. The result is that every ministry is run either by dependable friends or loyal servants of Dr. Glokbe.[1] The *Christian Science Monitor* has stated that this concentration of government power in the hands of a single man has made observers "bitterly complain that Dr. Globke often has had more authority than cabinet ministers." [2] The New York *Times* correspondent Sydney Gruson gave the following appraisal: "As State Secretary of the Chancellery, Dr. Globke is acknowledged to be one of the most influential men in West Germany. He runs the Chancellor's office, and nearly all papers for the Chancellor must first go through his hands." [3] Ironically, the one-time servant of the Nazi regime today has full control over the Office for the Protection of the Constitution. Also under Globke's direct authority is the operation of a supersecret organization headed by Hitler's former spy chief, Lieutenant General Reinhard Gehlen.

In order to understand the tremendous power concentrated in the hands of Dr. Globke, we must first take a look at the world-wide intelligence network of the mysterious Bureau Gehlen. The story of General Gehlen has often been told in the European press, but seldom has his name been mentioned in the United States. The reason is, as the Washington *Post* stated on September 19, 1954, that Hitler's former intelligence chief is working as "America's number-one spy abroad." Although for many years the Soviets had made a great outcry about the number of Gehlen agents they had captured, and although Europeans could read lengthy stories about the Bureau Gehlen in their newspapers, American readers heard the following facts for the first time in 1954:

. . . Without Reinhard Gehlen's name ever being mentioned in the appropriation's debate in Congress, he spends six million dollars a year from the United States Treasury.

Thousands of agents of diverse nationalities are on his payroll, together with the elite of the old German army's counter-intelligence corps. . . .

The Central Intelligence Agency and the Pentagon appear to trust this retired German Lieutenant General more than they do any Allied statesman. . . .

Here, in brief, is the story of the ex-Wehrmacht intelligence ace.* Under Hitler, Gehlen rose rapidly in the German General Staff. In 1942 he was appointed chief of the Enemy Armies East Department. As such, he worked hand in hand with Walter Schellenberg, the notorious head of the SS cloak-and-dagger Abwehr (Intelligence Bureau).

With the German military collapse imminent, Gehlen stored his valuable archives in safe places and ordered his staff to retreat into isolated regions high up in the Alpine redoubt. Some time after the shooting stopped, Gehlen surrendered to General Patton's Seventh Army. He immediately asked for an interview with the commanding officer of the U. S. Counter Intelligence Corps. Gehlen offered the American officer his intelligence staff, spy apparatus, and the priceless files for future service.

---

* The most informative articles about Gehlen appeared in the London *Daily Express*, March 17, 1952; *Die Weltwoche*, Zurich, August 6, 1954; *Christ und Welt*, Stuttgart, August 19, 1954; and *Der Spiegel*, September 22, 1954.

It was clear that Gehlen was a "big fish." Hitler's spy chief was immediately flown to Washington, where he conducted long negotiations in the Pentagon during the summer of 1945. According to *Der Spiegel* of September 22, 1954, a secret understanding was reached to the effect that Gehlen would reconstruct an "exclusively German-staffed" intelligence apparatus, "financed with the fat dollar funds from the U. S. Counter Intelligence." His files were found "invaluable" and "all his conditions were accepted."

The Pentagon-Gehlen agreement in practice guaranteed the continuation of the all-important Abwehr division of the German General Staff. Hundreds of German army and SS officers were quietly released from internment camps and joined Gehlen's headquarters in the Spessart Mountains in central Germany. When the staff had grown to three thousand men, the Bureau Gehlen opened a closely guarded twenty-five-acre compound near Pullach, south of Munich, operating under the innocent name of the South German Industrial Development Organization. By 1950 the activities of the Bureau Gehlen had become public knowledge in Germany and all over Europe. The top secret was no longer a secret, yet "for years both Washington and Bonn refused to confirm that the organization existed." [4]

Within a few years the Gehlen apparatus had grown by leaps and bounds. In the early fifties it was estimated that the organization employed up to 4,000 intelligence specialists in Germany, mainly former army and SS officers, and that more than 4,000 V-men (undercover agents) were active throughout the Soviet-bloc countries. Gehlen's spy network stretches from Korea to Cairo, from Siberia to Santiago de Chile. "With the aid of his old and intimate friend, Secretary of State Globke, Reinhard Gehlen had access to Chancellor Adenauer at any time." [5] When the Federal Republic became a sovereign state in 1955, the Bureau Gehlen was openly recognized as the official intelligence arm of the Bonn government. Thus the

world-wide Gehlen network came under the direct command
and control of Dr. Hans Globke. There can be little doubt
that with the conspiratorial capacity of the Bureau Gehlen,
the Chancellor and his Secretary of State have at their dis-
posal a formidable instrument for the internal and external
struggle for power.

Another organization operating under the direct control
of Dr. Globke is the Federal Press Department, which in recent years has been involved in several scandals in connection
with the use of its multimillion-dollar "reptile funds." Dr.
Adenauer's Secretary of State has been charged in the Bundestag with "paying journalists 1,000 and 2,000 marks for a
political analysis." Such payments were obvious bribes, given
to newspapermen so that they would "play along with the
government line." [6] Other millions have been spent to sub-
sidize "friendly" publishers. To these sums must be added
secret funds of more than 40,000,000 marks which are earmarked for the discretionary use of the Chancellor and his
Secretary of State outside of any parliamentary control.

The opposition has been arguing for years that a man with
Dr. Globke's questionable record does not belong in such a
high and sensitive position. Yet whenever criticism has arisen,
Dr. Adenauer has gone to great lengths to protect and defend
his chief assistant by declaring that he is "indispensable."

No less dark is the picture of another high official, Dr. Herbert Blankenhorn, who for many years acted as Dr. Adenauer's adviser on foreign affairs. Like Globke, Dr. Blankenhorn had faithfully served Hitler and the Nazi hierarchy.
When Dr. Adenauer was being groomed to become the first
Chancellor of the Republic, he entrusted the ex-Nazi Blankenhorn with the task of organizing a new Foreign Office.

Long before the 1945 collapse, the Nazi diplomats had
made elaborate preparations for a quick comeback. They
organized a special Niederlage (defeat) section whose task was

to work out detailed plans of "how to overcome the catastrophe." It is disturbing to examine the maneuvers of these diplomatic cavaliers as they evaded and wriggled free from automatic arrest and gradually disappeared into previously prepared emergency shelters in such guises as "director of an orphanage" or harmless officials employed by an "Evangelical Relief Society." Most of these men had been actively involved in preparing Hitler's aggressive moves by spreading propaganda and lies among the future victims and by financing and directing "fifth columns" and espionage networks abroad. In some countries these diplomats gave all-out support to groups which organized rebellion against lawfully elected governments, as, for example, in Austria, Spain, Czechoslovakia, and Iraq. They were implicated in kidnappings, the plotting of murder, mass deportation and gassing of Jews, the killing of hostages, and looting of whole countries.*

Only a few diplomats were ever investigated by the Allies in the "Wilhelmstrasse Trial" in 1949. Many others, although severely implicated, were never prosecuted. One of these men was Dr. Martin Luther, head of the Deutschland Department, where mass murder, looting, and other crimes were hatched in an almost daily routine. Dr. Luther acted in close coöperation with the Main Security Office of the SS, and his department was also "the liaison office with the Ministry of the Interior" in which Dr. Hans Globke acted as the Referent for Jewish Affairs.[7] Numerous documents show that diplomats such as Horst Wagner, Karl Klingenfuss, Franz Rademacher, Werner von Grundherr, and others, participated in the "liquidation of the Jews." †

* These statements are based on intimate knowledge of the captured German Foreign Office files which I examined during 1946-48 as an investigator for the U. S. War Crimes Commission.

† Some of the incriminating evidence was presented in the "Wilhelmstrasse Trial" in 1949, and later in a German court in proceedings against the diplomat Rademacher. Gerald Reitlinger, in *The Final Solution* (p. 26), calls the

As early as 1949 the *Neue Zeitung,* the official American paper in Germany, warned of the preparations being made by the Ribbentrop clique to recapture the Foreign Office. The advice was not heeded by Dr. Adenauer. When the Chancellor, in 1950, ordered the establishment of a new Foreign Office, Herbert Blankenhorn presented him with the nucleus of the discredited Ribbentrop group. The Chancellor must have known that Blankenhorn, Ribbentrop's close confidant, was himself implicated in the crime of deportation and mass murder. On April 22, 1952, the Swiss newspaper *Die Tat* reported that in the trial against Rademacher certain documents and a photograph which implicated Blankenhorn had not been introduced in court as evidence although they were in the prosecutor's files. According to *Die Tat,* the picture "showed Herr von Blankenhorn in his diplomatic uniform visiting the Warsaw ghetto together with other high Nazis." It was pointed out that the Bonn Foreign Office had put pressure on the court not to introduce the picture and the incriminating documents.

The uninterrupted attacks by a few democratic papers against the reactivation of the old Ribbentrop group were soon echoed by the Social Democratic opposition in the Bundestag. The fact that the old Nazis had infiltrated a department as sensitive as the Foreign Office became a constant cause of embarrassment to Dr. Adenauer. In the Bundestag debate of October 22, 1952, the Chancellor became so irritated by the mounting criticism that he lost his temper and threatened some German newspapers with court proceedings if they did not cease what he termed "unjustified" attacks against certain diplomats. However, in spite of these threats, a German journalist, Michael Heinze-Mansfeld, continued

---

Bureau IV A 4b, in the Main Security Office, "the hub of the entire spider's web of deportation and massacre." Reitlinger also points to the large-scale forgery of foreign bank notes and documents organized by the Security Office in the Sachsenhausen camp.

to publish evidence exposing the Nazi diplomats in the Bonn Foreign Office.*

Public indignation mounted when the director of the Bavarian Radio Network, Wilhelm von Cube, a fighting democrat, denounced the impossible situation in two broadcasts. Von Cube proved in a detailed analysis that no fewer than 85 percent of the leading officials in the Bonn Foreign Office had been Nazi party members and had served the Hitler cause.

Because of these protests the Bundestag took matters in hand and appointed an investigating committee. After many hearings, concerning only the twenty diplomats named in the *Frankfurter Rundschau* articles, the committee issued its final report, consisting of a hundred printed pages. The report confirmed the fact that many Ribbentrop diplomats had gained dominating positions in the Bonn Foreign Office because they were able to act as a closely knit organization. The report stated that the group had placed their members in key positions and that they had done their utmost to whitewash one another by exchanging affidavits—*Persilscheine*—which were supposed to prove that they had all been "resistance fighters."

The report called for the retirement or the ousting from the Foreign Office of Dr. Werner von Grundherr, Dr. Werner von Bargen, Dr. Kurt Heinburg, and Dr. Herbert Dittmann, who was then chief of the Department of Foreign Service Personnel. It recommended that the former Nazi officials, Drs. Wilhelm Haas, Peter Pfeiffer, Wilhelm Melchers, Hans Schwarzmann, Werner Schwarz, Alois Tichy, and Truetzschler von Falkenstein, be prevented from assuming diplomatic missions abroad and that they be prohibited from serving in the Department of Foreign Service Personnel.

* In a series of six articles, "You Have Returned, You Ghostly Creatures," Mansfeld reviewed the sordid past of a number of prominent Bonn diplomats *Frankfurter Rundschau*, September 1-6, 1951).

The committee complained about the outright lying and falsification of facts practiced by the accused diplomats. It was established that the Foreign Office officials had elaborately conspired to protect Dr. Rademacher (accused of participation in the mass killing of Jews) in order to prevent the implication of other diplomats. Dr. Rademacher, who in one case was clearly proved to have arranged the killing of 1,500 Jews in Belgrade, drew a prison sentence of only three years and eight months. The court allowed him to remain free while his appeal was pending, thus creating a welcome opportunity for him to flee. Promptly Rademacher escaped to Argentina, the haven of so many war criminals. There the Nazi periodical *German Honor* was jubilant and called Rademacher's escape an "extraordinary feat of rescue from the clutches of the Jewish jackals."

In the Bundestag debate of October 23, 1952, Dr. Adenauer admitted that 66 percent of the diplomats in higher positions were former Nazis, but, he added, he could "not build up a Foreign Office without relying on such skilled men." The recommendations made in the Bundestag report were completely ignored. The vital Department of Personnel is still dominated by former party members. For many years the director of the official diplomatic School for Foreign Service was the ex-Nazi Dr. Peter Pfeiffer, a man closely connected with numerous conspiratorial affairs. At the end of the Tunisian campaign, in 1943, Dr. Pfeiffer closed his last telegram with "Long live the Fuehrer! Sieg Heil!"

In 1958 Foreign Minister von Brentano appointed two former Nazis as his top assistants. He made Dr. Albert-Hilger von Scherpenberg, a son-in-law of Hjalmar Schacht, State Secretary, assuming that the public had entirely forgotten a sensational kidnapping case in which this man had been involved twenty-five years before.

In February 1935 the Swiss authorities arrested the journalist Dr. Hans Wesemann and charged him with the kidnapping of Berthold Jacob, the publisher of an anti-Nazi newsletter, who was then known as a particularly well-informed expert on German secret rearmament. Wesemann, playing the role of an anti-Nazi, had lured Jacob from France to Switzerland, offering him "important information." With the help of two Gestapo specialists Jacob was doped and then brought over the German border in an automobile. Under mounting evidence Wesemann finally broke down and admitted several kidnappings for the Gestapo. He named as his closest contact man in London the diplomat Hilger von Scherpenberg—today a State Secretary in the Bonn Foreign Office.

The other man elevated by Foreign Minister von Brentano is the ex-Nazi Dr. Herbert Dittmann, who has been severely implicated by the vast evidence regarding the mass deportation and liquidation of millions of Jews in the East. The Bundestag report sharply censured him for his constant lying as a witness and declared him no longer fit to be employed in the Foreign Service. In spite of this verdict, Dr. von Brentano appointed him Undersecretary of State. In 1960 Dr. Dittmann was appointed ambassador to Brazil.

Attached to Globke's empire in the Chancellery is the Federal Press Department. Since 1952 (with a brief interruption in 1955) the Press Department has been headed by Felix von Eckardt, who during the Nazi rule was one of the most successful script writers on nationalist and Nazi topics in the state-controlled motion picture industry. A Bismarck film written by von Eckardt was chosen by Dr. Goebbels as "Film of the Nation," an equivalent of the American Oscar.[8] Herr von Eckardt's deputy in the Press Department is Dr. Werner Krueger, a former Nazi who once had been trained in Dr. Goebbels' Propaganda Ministry. Under Krueger's rule dozens of former Nazis have taken up important positions in the Press Department.

When Herr von Eckardt served temporarily as Bonn's dip-

lomatic observer at the U.N. in 1956, a Dr. Edmund Forschbach, also a former Nazi, acted as Dr. Adenauer's press chief.
The American newspaperman Theodore Kaghan, who interviewed the Chancellor at that time, described Forschbach's
nervousness when Nazism was discussed in the interview.
Forschbach felt uneasy because it had been revealed in the
German press that he "had played a leading role, back in
1933, by lining up German Catholic student organizations
behind Hitler." He had also appeared in the first complete
Nazi Reichstag "wearing a smart SA uniform and looking
resplendent in the ideological trappings of the Thousand-
Year Reich." [9]

Kaghan, who served for several years as a high public affairs
official with the U. S. High Commissioner in Germany, had
first-hand knowledge of the conditions in the Bonn Republic.
In his articles he described how even those friendly toward
Adenauer say that the Chancellor is "too closely surrounded
with ex-Nazis." Kaghan quoted *Der Mittag*, a right-of-center
newspaper as saying: "We simply cannot understand why
former prominent Nazi politicians must be in the first row
again. . . . There is no excuse."

When Chancellor Adenauer formed his second cabinet
after the 1953 election, it was presented to the world as a team
of stanch democrats. However, the record showed a number
of his ministers either as members of the Nazi party and the
SS or as extreme nationalists who had served the Hitler cause
in important positions. Ministers Theodor Oberlaender,
Emanuel Preusker, and Waldmar Kraft had been officers in
Hitler's Elite Guard. Dr. Gerhard Schroeder, a party member, served the Nazis as a legal adviser and storm troop leader.
As Minister of the Interior he now has control over the police
and is responsible for the internal security of the Bonn Republic.

Former New York *Times* correspondent Delbert Clark
reported that the record of the Minister of Economics, Dr.

Ludwig Erhard, "was one of full co-operation with the Nazi regime." He was "adviser to Nazi Gauleiter Buerckel in the Saar, and chief of the Hitlerite Institute for Industrial Research." [10] Dr. Fritz Schaeffer, the Minister of Finance (later Minister of Justice), praised Hitler in glowing terms as the "savior of the Reich." Delbert Clark described Schaeffer as "a clever and highly dangerous character." Under United States occupation Schaeffer was appointed Minister-President of Bavaria. However, mounting evidence soon revealed that he had been a Nazi collaborator, and in 1946 he was removed from office and banned for several years from all political activities.[11]

The Minister of Transportation, Dr. Hans Christoph Seebohm, served the Nazi regime as an economic adviser in Silesia and in occupied Czechoslovakia. Dr. Seebohm is known all over Europe as an ultranationalistic troublemaker. *Der Spiegel* of March 23, 1960, published a two-column profile which depicted Seebohm as the "prototype of the eternal Nazi." His rabble-rousing Sunday speeches have become a controversial topic in the European press and have frequently been a source of uneasiness to Dr. Adenauer. As leader of the Rightist German party, Dr. Seebohm has openly expressed his deep reverence for the swastika and has viciously attacked the Western powers. On September 15, 1951, he addressed a mass meeting of the Sudeten Germans at Stuttgart in which he denounced the "monstrous crime the victors had committed against Germany, Europe and the whole world."

Another cabinet member, Dr. Hermann Schaefer, served during the war as an important official in Reichsmarschal Goering's Armaments Office.

Of all his cabinet members, the Minister for Expellees, Dr. Theodor Oberlaender, caused the Chancellor most chagrin. As a high Nazi official and officer of the SS (he was Reichsfuehrer of the German Alliance in the East), Dr. Oberlaender had used the Nazi press to demand the expulsion and extermination of the Slavic peoples and the rapid colonization of the vast conquered territories by the German master race.[12] For years German democratic papers had charged Dr. Oberlaender with packing the ranks of his ministry with former Nazis.[13] In 1959 Oberlaender was the center of a storm that finally forced his resignation in May 1960. He was blamed for the mass murder of thousands of Jews and Polish intellectuals who had been liquidated in July 1941 when a special SS task force under his command occupied the Polish city of Lemberg (Lvov).*

With a cabinet of such background, it comes as no surprise to hear that the ministries are studded with former high-ranking Nazis. The excuse has often been heard that qualified applicants with a solid democratic record were not available. This has been vehemently denied by democratic critics. In the case of the Foreign Office, there was a list of more than a thousand applicants, men of democratic principles with diplomatic and foreign-language experience. Dr. Blankenhorn chose to hire his old Ribbentrop associates.

The Ministery for Expellees, once headed by Oberlaender, is still known as a haven for former high-ranking Nazis. The personal assistant to the minister is today Dr. Wolfram, a former SS officer. The fanatical race propagandist Werner Ventzki, ex-mayor of Lodz, serves as director of a department. Head of the press office, Dr. Schlicker, was a storm troop leader.

Many ex-Nazis have found shelter in the Ministry of Transportation under Dr. Hans Seebohm. One of his department

* At that time Dr. Oberlaender was an SS officer and a member of the notorious Abwehr. According to *Die Zeit* of Hamburg, he was an expert "for the treatment of other races" and the political officer of the Einsatz (terror) Nachtigall unit. Oberlaender's unit entered Lemberg on June 30, and remained in the city six days. According to Reitlinger and other sources, 7,000 people were killed, chiefly between July 2 and 4. Oberlaender does not deny that he was in Lemberg in those days, but says that during his stay "not a single shot was fired" (*Die Zeit*, October 9, 1959).

chiefs is Werner Kreipe, owner of the Nazi *Blutorden* (Order of the Blood—the highest Nazi party decoration), who once served as chief of the General Staff in Goering's Luftwaffe.

The senior civil servant in the Interior Ministry is State Secretary Ritter von Lex, a former Nazi and intimate friend of Dr. Globke. The *Deutsche Zeitung* of April 22, 1959, pointed out that it had become a habit of senior officials to bring into their department scores of officials who had worked with them during the Hitler regime.

For many years the Ministry of Justice has drawn criticism in the Bundestag. The courts, with a few notable exceptions, are to a large extent run by former Nazis. It has been charged that hundreds of Hitler's court functionaries are today in important positions, as prosecutors and presiding judges. Miscarriages of justice and favoritism toward ex-Nazis have become so routine that it is necessary to review this situation in a special chapter.

The new German Wehrmacht is directed by the young, aggressive Christian Democratic politician Franz-Joseph Strauss, whom *Time* magazine once labeled "the man to watch." The British press has called Strauss "the most dangerous man in Europe." The senior civil servant in the Defense Ministry is State Secretary Dr. Josef Rust, a former colleague and intimate of Globke. *Die Welt* of Hamburg reported on September 8, 1956, that "of thirty-eight newly appointed Generals in the Bundeswehr, thirty-one were members of the General Staff of the old Wehrmacht." These are the same Generals who served under the banner of the swastika and whose "responsibility for Hitler's rule is so heavy and so unmistakable." [14] The British correspondent Brian Connell has reported that "most of the leading members of the new German Defense Ministry were recommended to Adenauer by General Gehlen." [15]

There are active Nazi conspirators in the Ministry of All-German Affairs, which some years ago was instrumental in organizing a Nazi-type movement in the Saar in order to bring this French-controlled territory *"Heim ins Reich"*—Home to the Reich.[16] The outright Nazi character of this Pan-German organization was clearly revealed when *Der Spiegel* published the record of the ex-Nazi official Dr. Eberhard Taubert, who in 1955 attracted attention with his anti-Semitic statements.[17]

Another early Nazi fighter and anti-Semite is Dr. Theodor Sonnemann who served the Hitler regime as an ideological propagandist for total war in the German high command. In several books Dr. Sonnemann denounced the British as the "arch enemy" and the Jews as the inventors of lies in the atrocity propaganda against the German Reich. His books were acclaimed in the Nazi press.[18] Today this friend of Dr. Globke serves as State Secretary for Agriculture in the Adenauer government.

Dr. Gustav A. Sonnenhol, who joined Hitler's Brown-Shirts and the Nazi party as early as 1930, had a similar career. Later Dr. Sonnenhol became an SS officer attached to von Ribbentrop's diplomatic staff. According to the *Frankfurter Rundschau* of November 22, 1951, Dr. Sonnenhol boasted after the war that "it had been an honor to have served as a member of Hitler's SS." This Nazi record was no hindrance to the old fighter who, in 1950, was appointed head of the Information Office for Marshall Plan Aid in the Adenauer administration. A few years later Dr. Sonnenhol became the senior adviser to Vice-Chancellor Bluecher in the second Adenauer cabinet. While in this position he wrote a memorandum in which he advocated that Germany exploit the cold war to the utmost and make sure that no agreement should be reached between the United States and the Soviet bloc. According to the *Hamburger Echo* of March 27, 1954, the Sonnenhol memorandum aroused much criticism in England.

Even in the highest office of the land, that of the President, Nazis occupy positions of trust. The administrative head of the presidential office is a former Nazi official, Dr. Manfred

Klaiber, and his right-hand assistant is the ex-consul Luipold Werz, who once belonged to the SS security division.

The conditions in the administration of the Laender, county districts, and municipalities are even worse. In many of the smaller towns the old Nazi burghermasters have been re-elected.

In industry and banking the ex-Nazi *Wirtschaftsfuehrer* are back in power and position. The Krupps, Flicks, Rechbergs, and Reemtsmas have rebuilt and expanded their empires, and the Nazi banker Hermann Abs has greater influence with Dr. Adenauer than he ever had under Adolf Hitler.

That the Nazis have had a successful comeback in the Bonn Republic has been admitted even in the German press. Unfortunately, however, the general public in those countries which have aided in Germany's postwar recovery are shockingly unaware that the men who once faithfully served Hitler have quietly returned to key positions in the government.

6 Dr. Adenauer's Two Miracles

There are two "miracles" which Dr. Adenauer has often named as the foremost achievements of his postwar leadership. In talks with foreigners he seldom forgets to mention the fact that Nazism has completely disappeared and that the new Germany rests on a stable, democratic electorate, with the majority of voters flooding his Christian Democratic Union (CDU). This is an imposing picture, almost as impressive as the *Wirtschaftswunder*—the economic miracle—which in every national election has turned out to be the Chancellor's drawing card.

But what has happened to the more than 20,000,000 people who in 1933 voted enthusiastically for Hitler and his nationalistic cause? By what device did a "people that elected Hitler and joyously followed him on his mad career become overnight miraculously anti-Totalitarian?" [1]

In the last free election before Hitler came to power the Nazis rallied almost 12,000,000 votes behind their aggressive racial and militant program.* In addition to these, there were

---

* There were two elections in 1932: on July 31 the Nazis polled 13,800,000 votes for the swastika ticket; a few months later, on November 6, they suffered a loss of 2,000,000 votes.

3,000,000 ardent nationalists, chiefly officers, bureaucrats, and veterans of World War I, voting for the German National party under Hugenberg, who at that time had concluded a close alliance with Hitler. In the March 1933 election the Catholic Center party (4,200,000) moved over to the extreme Right, and Herr von Papen engineered the Hitler-Papen-Hugenberg coalition, which then polled nearly 25,000,000 votes. Of these, 17,300,000 were for the Nazi ticket alone. At that time all middle-of-the-road parties had completely disappeared and only the Left with its 12,000,000 votes (Social Democrats, 7,200,000; Communists, 4,800,000) had remained intact.

In order to understand what has been going on in the Bonn Republic we must consider briefly the three phases of Germany's postwar political development. The first period (1945-47) was notable for the systematic sabotage by most parties of the Allied denazification program. The second period (1948-52) was characterized by attempts to use the licensed parties as vehicles for Nazi propaganda, and to bring ex-Nazis into administrative positions. The third period (1953 to the present) is marked by the quiet and gradual Nazi infiltration as a consequence of secret talks between high-ranking ex-party members and spokesmen of the leading government party, the Christian Democratic Union.

During the two years following Germany's collapse, all political activities were under the strict control of the occupying powers. They licensed the newspapers and decided who was to be allowed to enter politics, first on the local and later on the regional level. The idea then was that the Germans had "to learn democracy."

The second period saw all the parties in wild competition, making extreme nationalistic appeals to 50,000,000 people who had just gone through a severe attack of the German (swastika) measles. It soon became evident that the German politicians were as shrewd as ever, but that unfortunately the Western powers had learned very little from the bitter experience of two world wars.

The third period produced the rapid growth of a Christian Democratic mass party from 7,000,000 to 15,000,000 votes, all within the brief span of eight years.

How did this "miracle" come about? Was it the result of a democratic enlightenment campaign conducted by Dr. Adenauer, Dr. Globke, and the conservative-Rightist cabinet? There was no evidence of such a campaign during the period of 1950-52. On the contrary, there were alarming reports in the Adenauer press of a continuous decline of the CDU position and of landslide gains by the extreme Rightist parties in all regional elections. After a severe defeat in a local election in Bremen, the pro-Adenauer *Rheinischer Merkur* hoisted the following storm warning on October 12, 1951:

The decline of the CDU in Northern Germany, which first became visible in the state elections of Schleswig-Holstein and Lower Saxony, has now become alarmingly clear with the election returns from Bremen. The Socialist Reichs party has attained almost the same strength and, in some local arrangements with the BHE [Refugee party], even more votes than the CDU. The latter fact is the significant hallmark of a development in which nationalistic slogans have created conditions similar to those in the late years of the Weimar Republic. . . . There is an unmistakable trend toward the radical Right. . . .

This statement shows that the CDU leaders were seriously concerned about the future of the Adenauer coalition. If the Chancellor wanted to stay in power and proceed with his plan for unification of Europe, he would first have to secure a safe continuation of his coalition. Some time in 1951 the Adenauer high command came to the conclusion that they had to stop any further trend toward the Right and find means by which as many votes as possible could be channeled into Adenauer's CDU. The most effective way to do this was to apply the time-honored device of "the stick and the carrot." The stick was used against the Socialist Reichs party (SRP) which had become the center of the neo-Nazi movement. At the request of the Bonn government the SRP was soon declared anticonstitutional and was outlawed by the Federal Court in Karlsruhe. At the same time, liberal use of the "carrot" was made in order to lure the homeless neo-Nazi voters into the ranks of the CDU. In the state of Lower Saxony all parties scrambled wildly to pick up the almost 370,000 votes of the outlawed SRP. According to press reports, "all parties had opened their arms to embrace the homeless Nazi votes, especially the declining CDU." [2]

The election returns in 1953 made it quite obvious that a large section of ultra-Rightist and neo-Nazi voters had shifted their support to the CDU. In Lower Saxony, where the Christian Democrats had polled only 17 percent of the total vote in 1949 (and had suffered further losses in 1952), the returns suddenly went up to more than 33 percent of the popular vote. The CDU's success was even greater in Schleswig-Holstein. Whereas in previous elections the Christian Democrats could barely gain 16.5 percent of the popular vote, in 1953 they polled 47.1 percent of the total returns in this state. It was clear that whole blocs of voters had suddenly shifted to the CDU.

How such political deals were made possible can best be shown by examining the situation in Schleswig-Holstein. To begin with, this northernmost state, almost exclusively Protestant and a stronghold of the Nazis, had been a poor hunting ground for the CDU. Then the neo-Nazi movement was strengthened by the influx of refugees from the lost territories in the East. The Prime Minister of the state was Dr. Walter Bartram, a Nazi who had joined the party in 1937 and who, after the war, had become a member of the CDU.

In many towns of Schleswig-Holstein the Nazis had recovered their old positions. Government officers, former party officials, and top-level SS and army officers had banded together in various organizations which wielded a strong influence in the state. They had a large following in every town and village. According to press reports they had developed a state-wide machine which had worked in behalf of the neo-Nazi SRP.[3]

A report in the *Frankfurter Rundschau* described how a group of former Nazi officials, SS officers, Hitler Youth leaders, and the ex-mayors of several cities and towns had formed an Alliance of the War Generation. This supposedly nonpolitical organization worked in close contact with a Gauleiter group in Hamburg (connected with the Achenbach-Naumann circle) and with the Bruderschaft, a nation-wide network of important Wehrmacht and SS officers. According to the *Frankfurter Rundschau,* this ex-Nazi organization had "to a considerable extent infiltrated the regional Rightist parties and had thereby gained a great deal of influence." [4]

With the outlawing of the neo-Nazi SRP, the Alliance and its followers were confronted with a basic problem: where would they find a political home in which they could work undisturbed and undetected? They did the most logical thing—they joined Dr. Adenauer's Christian Democratic Union. Of course they had the choice of joining one of the three other Rightist parties, but that would only have produced evidence in support of the old charge that they were using the tactic of infiltration, and it could have resulted in the outlawing of another Rightist party. Also there was this important point: the three Rightist parties had all their key positions filled with ex-Nazis, whereas the CDU still had an undetermined organizational structure. The CDU could use organizers, ward leaders, speakers, district leaders, and so on. Under these circumstances the best solution for the Nazi action groups was to infiltrate the CDU state organizations quietly and gradually.

There is little doubt that the weakness of the CDU in

1952 gave the neo-Nazis their great chance. Dr. Adenauer's party badly needed the votes, especially in Schleswig-Holstein. Support from every political machine and bailiwick was welcomed, provided the votes were brought in. Those who worked for the victory of the party in power could expect to be rewarded with the spoils. The following case may serve as an illustration. Among those who joined the CDU at that time was a Dr. Menzel who under the Nazis had functioned as the deputy mayor of Eckernfoerde. He had joined the Nazi party as early as 1931. After the war Dr. Menzel was a member of the four-man board that ran the Alliance of the War Generation, which supported the SRP. It was probably around 1952 that Dr. Menzel and his followers joined the CDU. Very soon afterward he became a prominent member of the State Assembly of Schleswig-Holstein. In 1955, when he was Deputy Leader of the CDU, he was nominated for the important cabinet post of Minister of the Interior.[5]

During the last few years Schleswig-Holstein has been almost constantly in the news. In 1955 the Association of Former Internees and Victims of Denazification, an active Nazi group, held a mass meeting outside Neumuenster. Several provocative speeches were made, and the chairman of the group boasted of his "intimate collaboration with the Office for the Protection of the Constitution." [6]

On December 16, 1957, the *Frankfurter Allgemeine* reported that Minister-President Kai Uwe von Hassel had dismissed from his cabinet the Minister of Welfare, Hans-Adolf Asbach, charging him with having "allowed the infiltration of former high-ranking SS officers and Nazi leaders."

In 1958 the election of former SS General Heinz Reinefarth to the Schleswig-Holstein State Assembly provoked comment throughout Germany. Reinefarth is known as the "butcher of Warsaw" because of his merciless dealings with Polish freedom fighters. When the *Frankfurter Allgemeine* criticized Reinefarth as unfit to sit in a parliamentary body, the diocesan paper of the Lutheran Church in Schleswig-Holstein rushed to the General's defense by accusing the *Frankfurter Allgemeine* (a pro-Adenauer paper) of having disturbed the domestic peace and given "aid and comfort to Red propaganda." To which the paper retorted that it is neither disturbance of the peace nor Red propaganda to chase unsavory characters out of public life. Said the paper: "People with an evidently black record do not belong in our parliaments or in important political positions." *

A New York *Times* dispatch of January 17, 1961, mentioned that Schleswig-Holstein was plagued by "growing scandals" and that there were widespread charges that the state "had become a haven for former prominent Nazis."

Developments in certain other states—for example, Lower Saxony and North Rhine-Westphalia—were not much different from those in Schleswig-Holstein. In Catholic Bavaria the teachers, local priests, and burghermasters were those on whom the CDU relied most heavily in order to build up its new party organization. Yet the teachers and the burghermasters had been the backbone of the Nazi movement throughout Bavaria. Dr. John D. Montgomery, a senior research official in the U. S. Military Government, found that "most of the older teachers had been thoroughly orientated in Nazi philosophy" and "showed the greatest resentment against the occupation." Yet Dr. Montgomery reports that "in the Bavarian schools 11,000 out of 12,000 teachers, who had been dismissed because of Nazi affiliations, were reinstated by 1949." [7]

In the following years Adenauer's party did even more to console the "old fighters" of the shattered Thousand-Year Reich. In May 1951 the Bundestag passed a law whereby, under Article 131 of the Bonn Constitution, those civil serv-

---

* The *Frankfurter Allgemeine* of January 7, 1959, used a strong German expression: "*Leute mit nachweislich erheblichem Dreck an ihrem Stecken gehoeren nicht . . .*"

ants who had been dismissed during the occupation had to be reinstated in administrative jobs. "The re-employment proceeded so rapidly that within less than a year 139,471 had been readmitted to public service, and by September 30, 1953, this figure had increased to 163,577." [8]

It was unfortunate for the German people that all parties, including the Social Democrats (and their late leader, Kurt Schumacher), who used nationalistic appeals from the very beginning were neither restrained nor reprimanded by the occupying powers. At a time when the German masses needed sane and sober leadership in order to find their way into a new future, they were exposed to waves of nationalistic intoxication. In the race for nationalist popularity, Dr. Adenauer proved himself to be an astute campaigner. In his earliest speeches he expressed open contempt for England, and he depicted the British as the true enemies, because they tried to hamper the economic resurrection of West Germany by dismantling the industries on Rhine and Ruhr. The New York *Times* of August 14, 1949, quoted the following passage from Dr. Adenauer's election oratory:

A nation like Germany, with one of the front seats in mankind's history, has a right to think along nationalistic lines. . . . The foreigners must understand that the period of collapse and unrestricted domination by the Allies is over.

On March 25, 1949, long before he was elected Chancellor, Dr. Adenauer caused consternation among the Allies when he declared in a speech in Berne, Switzerland, that the German people had never surrendered to the Allies, implying that they were free from all obligations. The German military leaders who surrendered in 1945 had "no mandate from the German people to submit to the terms of unconditional surrender." In the same speech he opposed Allied confiscation of German patents and denounced the Oder-Neisse line by declaring: "This frontier we shall never recognize!" The

Chancellor's official biographer notes that "Adenauer's Berne speech caused a political sensation far beyond the frontiers of Switzerland; almost everywhere it was received with stormy indignation." [9] And at a mass meeting in Berlin in 1950, Dr. Adenauer embarrassed the Allied representatives present when he led the crowd in the singing of "Deutschland ueber Alles," which was played at his request.

From the beginning Dr. Adenauer announced that his platform was to free Germany from the consequences of defeat, to gain back full sovereignty for the Fatherland, and to build it up again as a strong partner in a new alliance. A program like this was bound to have a considerable effect upon millions of Germans who had just lost their Fuehrer and the dream of becoming the master race of the world.

Many of these homeless nationalists were already members of existing mass organizations, such as veterans' societies and refugee associations, all under the leadership of former Nazis and Wehrmacht officers. The Christian Democrats could hope to win the support of these millions of ultranationalists and neo-Nazis only if they were willing to make concessions to the huge Rightist bloc that is known as the "Invisible Party." [10] The CDU was willing to make such concessions and to pay a price.

There were secret talks late in 1952 between leading members of Dr. Adenauer's cabinet and Dr. Werner Naumann. These negotiations were suddenly disrupted when the British arrested the ex-Nazi leader and several of his co-conspirators. The confiscated Naumann papers revealed that Naumann had conducted negotiations with Bundesminister Waldemar Kraft (also an ex-Nazi) and with the Minister of Justice, Thomas Dehler. According to *Der Spiegel,* there also had been a meeting between leading ex-Nazis and the late Bundestag Speaker, Herman Ehlers, in the fall of 1952. The purpose of all these negotiations had been to persuade the former Nazis into "positive collaboration" with the CDU.

The following facts seem to be noteworthy. First, the negotiations always took place a year or so before the elections to the Bundestag. Second, preceding an election year, certain bills were pushed through the Bundestag or promises were made which satisfied to a large extent the special interests of ex-Nazi officials, former SS and Wehrmacht officers, and the families of convicted war criminals. Dr. Adenauer promised that he would make every effort to free the "poor devils of war criminals." *

There were millions of expellees, once ardent followers of Hitler, who had lost their homes and who often found themselves in economic straits. To these people, who had to look for jobs, bigger pensions, and a new status, the CDU as the party in power had much to offer. There were other even more important issues, such as special decrees and statutes which originally had been introduced by the occupying authorities in order to keep the Nazis out of federal and state government offices. There were the 400,000 men of Hitler's Waffen SS, an organization which had been declared "criminal" during the Nuremberg War Crime Trials, who looked forward to rehabilitation. If the party in power could remove such onus, if a law could be enacted that would open the doors for the SS to enter the new Bundeswehr as officers and noncommissioned officers, such an act would be well remembered on election day.

Months before the election in 1953 many CDU speakers began addressing veterans' and refugee associations, praising Dr. Adenauer for his persistent efforts to rescue Germany from defeat and for having "restored the honor of the German soldier." In June 1953 Dr. Adenauer visited the prison

---

* New York *Times,* June 25, 1952. In a press conference on February 19, 1952, Dr. Adenauer stated: "We Germans are exceptionally deeply interested in the treatment of war criminals, both for psychological reasons and sympathy with those who, though sentenced, have in our opinion not committed any war crimes at all."

in Werl, where he shook hands demonstratively with war criminals who had been sentenced to death and whose sentences were later commuted to life imprisonment. He assured them that the Bonn government was doing everything to obtain their release.

On August 7, 1953, a CDU member of the Bundestag, former Colonel Hartmann, acted as the official representative of the Adenauer party at a mass meeting of former members of Hitler's Waffen SS. In his speech, according to a report in the *Wiking-Ruf*, the newspaper of the Waffen SS, Hartmann condemned the defamation of the Waffen SS, saying that they had been "as an organization, and in their conduct as soldiers, always honorable." The spokesman then stated:

The CDU believes in giving equal status to the claims of the Waffen SS along with those accorded to other units of the regular German army. Dr. Adenauer's visit to the prison at Werl is intended to make it clear to the whole world that the last of the so-called war criminals must be set free immediately. The Chancellor has made this a prerequisite of his policy, which is aimed at wiping out the Nuremberg concept of collective guilt. . . . The Bonn government has done its utmost to gain all advantages from the present situation and the soldiers of the Waffen SS should be appreciative of the fact that the Chancellor, in the formulation and execution of his European policies, is paying close attention to the record of common sacrifice [by the Waffen SS] in a great cause.

Needless to say, Dr. Adenauer's attitude was appreciated by Hitler's Waffen SS veterans. The *Deutsche Soldaten Zeitung* of August 27, 1953, reported that one of the Waffen SS leaders, General Herbert Gille, recommended to all former Elite Guard members that they give their votes only to a political party which "has worked constructively in the interest of Germany."

As a result, millions of former Nazis, who had not voted

in 1949, gave a vote of confidence to the Adenauer policies in 1953. The returns made it obvious that the negotiations with the Naumann clique, the generous patronage to ex-Nazis, and the emphasis on "restoration of the German honor" had the desired results. Whereas the vote of the SDP and the Rightist parties showed no unusual fluctuation, the returns for the CDU brought an upsurge from 7,300,000 to 12,400,000 votes.

The nationalistic appeal to the unreconstructed Nazis not only shocked Germany's neighbors in Switzerland, France, Holland, Britain, and Scandinavia, but it was also noted with some apprehension by critical observers in the United States. An expert in the field of Nazi infiltration and propaganda, Professor James H. Sheldon, gave the following analysis of the CDU election returns:

The West German elections show primarily a vote of confidence for "a strong man." Some early commentators on the Bonn returns seemed jubilant over the relatively small vote secured by the official neo-Nazi parties. Any encouragement to be derived from this aspect of the matter, however, is strictly skin-deep. The facts are that the Pan-Germans, neo-Nazis and ultranationalists succeeded in invading the parties of the Adenauer coalition to such an appalling extent that they are now much nearer to the control of power in West Germany than before. . . . In other words, what happened in the German elections on September 6th is about the same as what has happened to "reform" parties in scores of American municipal elections where the "corrupt" machine has adopted the cynical philosophy that "the best way to lick 'em is to join 'em." [11]

To back up his analysis, Mr. Sheldon was able to quote excerpts from an official U.S. intelligence report which stated:

Although the German voters on September 6th have banished the extremist parties of the right and the left from the Bundestag, they now must prepare themselves to seeing the basic democratic constitutional principles endangered by the authoritarian forces which exert their influence inside Adenauer's party. . . . There cannot be any doubt that the nationalist, revisionist and authoritarian tendencies at the policy-making level of the CDU-CSU will be strengthened by the very strong increase in votes received by the party from obviously rightist extremist circles. . . .

The foregoing report may serve as an illustration of the United States' policy dilemma. The intelligence officials took note of the realities and pointed to the alarming increase of the "authoritarian forces which exert their influence inside Adenauer's party." Yet our policy position required us to advertise the façade and ignore the facts. An official Washington statement hailed the CDU victory as a "clear repudiation of all anti-democratic extremist groups both of the Right and the Left." [12]

Preparations for the 1957 election were similar to those of 1953. After lengthy confidential negotiations, an invitation was sent out in January 1957—nine months before the election—to a large group of top Nazi leaders for a secret meeting with one of Dr. Adenauer's closest advisers, the Bundestag's president, Dr. Eugen Gerstenmaier. Had not *Der Spiegel* gotten wind of this extraordinary exercise in "togetherness," the outside world would not have heard a word about it. *Der Spiegel* of February 6, 1957, reported that the organizer, Carl Cerff—a former SS officer—admitted that it was intended "to keep the meeting secret," because these were "confidential talks which were not for the ears of the public and press."

Among several dozen participants were former Gauleiters and deputy Gauleiters led by Dr. Werner Naumann, SS Generals Paul Hausser and Sepp Dietrich, several leaders from the Hitler Youth and the Labor Front, and, finally and most important, top officials from the Nazi Propaganda Ministry, such as Hans-Schwarz van Berk, former editor of *Der Angriff* and *Das Reich,* the former Goebbels assistant, Helmut Suendermann, today one of the most aggressive neo-

Nazi publicists, and Dr. Robert Ernst, once a Goebbels expert for the United Europe propaganda in France.

The meeting dealt with reconciliation and the recognition of "the good sides of the Nazi regime," as well as appropriate steps "to end all defamation." There was a speech by Dr. Naumann in which he praised the Bundestag's president for his "courage and understanding." Dr. Gerstenmaier in turn paid his compliments to Werner Naumann by stating: "It is regrettable that such a talented Secretary of State had the misfortune to serve under such a bad Propaganda Minister." To prove his good intentions, Dr. Gerstenmaier assured the illustrious assembly of former Nazi officials that "a new Naumann case would be impossible."

There was a lengthy discussion about the rehabilitation of the SS which, according to Dr. Gerstenmaier, could only come about by using the necessary patience. Admonishing his listeners to moderation, Dr. Gerstenmaier pointed to an earlier statement, that with "due regard to foreign public opinion" it would not be wise to have SS officers above the rank of Colonel admitted into the new Bundeswehr.[13]

There was little doubt among the observers in Bonn that Bundestag President Gerstenmaier would never have negotiated with the Naumann group unless he had had the prior consent and backing of Dr. Adenauer.* However there was considerable difference of opinion as to whether it was sound politics for democratic leaders to work with the unregenerate followers of a regime which had the most appalling criminal record in history. The outcome of the 1957 election dispelled these doubts. The negotiations, coupled

---

* The Chancellor is known to have a propensity for this type of secret negotiation. Long before Bonn had opened official relations with the Soviets, Dr. Adenauer authorized some of his closest advisers to conduct secret meetings with the Kremlin. In October 1958, for instance, it was discovered that the Minister of Finance, Dr. Fritz Schaeffer, with Dr. Adenauer's consent, had conducted top secret talks with high officials of the Pankow regime as far back as 1956.

with Germany's spectacular economic progress, again attracted more followers to the CDU. This time the CDU polled 15,000,000 votes as against the 12,400,000 of the 1953 election.

Some German and many foreign observers have pointed out that the rapidly progressing restoration and renazification will inevitably end in another catastrophe. As early as 1954 the German papers reprinted press comments from London charging that Dr. Adenauer was served by 190 more General Staff officers than Hitler had in 1936. The Bonn correspondent of the *News Chronicle* was quoted as saying that Dr. Adenauer was "surrounded by arrogant nationalists and defenders of the past, such as the Bundesministers Schroeder, Oberlaender, Kraft and Preusker, by men like Globke, Abs, and Professor Grewe, who all had served Hitler, and by Dr. Werner Best [an ardent Nazi], who had obtained an important position in the intelligence network of the Bonn Republic." [14]

Dozens of statements like the foregoing could be quoted. Not long ago a highly respected CDU politician, Professor Walter Hagemann, director of the Institute for Publizistik at the University of Muenster, was ousted from the ranks of the Christian Democrats for having opposed German atomic rearmament and for having criticized Dr. Adenauer's autocratic habits in running the CDU. In May 1958 Professor Hagemann published an article in the Munich weekly *Die Kultur* under the heading: "We Are Again Threatened with Dictatorship." The article charges that "as once in the past, a single man has become the undisputed master over a huge mass party; a new Fuehrer mythos has been created and the capacity for critical judgment of millions of voters has been almost erased." Recalling the slogan, "The Fuehrer is always right," Professor Hagemann concludes that "at the end of this road there will again be a liquidation of the democratic order." [15]

7 The Termites

Early in the afternoon of October 7, 1952, a scheduled air-
liner coming in from Madrid touched down on the runway
of the modern Rhine-Main Airport outside of the West
German city of Frankfurt. Among the debarking travelers
was a tall, slender gentleman with a distinguished bearing.
The traveler took his place in a long line of people who were
waiting before German officials for a routine check of their
passports, and when his turn came he submitted an Italian
passport showing his picture and the name "Enrico Larcher."
The pasport identified Signor Larcher as a dealer in art and
a resident of the city of Milan.

A stocky German official slowly looked through the passport. Then, fixing his eyes on the elegant traveler, he
asked politely and calmly in German:

"Sir, are you an Italian citizen? Is this passport a genuine
identification?"

"Of course it is!" came the slightly indignant answer,
spoken in German but with a strong foreign accent.

The German official did not seem to be satisfied. He
beckoned Signor Larcher into an adjoining room.

Obviously acting on a tip, the official told Signor Larcher that he would have to undergo a thorough examination of his papers and his luggage. Ignoring the art dealer's protestations in German and Italian, the customs officers found the evidence they were looking for after a few minutes of searching. Documents revealed that Signor Larcher was not an Italian art dealer, but was rather a key figure in an international ring promoting Nazi infiltration.

The gentleman was really Eugen Dollmann, born in Regensburg, Bavaria, who had become well known to the security services of almost all European governments. Only eight months earlier Herr Dollman, alias Larcher, had been in the headlines all over Europe in connection with deportation proceedings in Switzerland. At that time the Swiss authorities had discovered the true identity of the "Italian art dealer." During World War II, Eugen Dollmann was known as the dashing SS Colonel who had played a prominent role as the top agent of Hitler and Himmler in Italy and "whose talent was more for conspiracy than for serious politics." [1]

The investigation by the Swiss authorities established the fact that the former Elite Guard officer had lived under a false name for several years in a fashionable villa in the Swiss lake resort Lugano. From there Dollmann made frequent trips to Germany, Austria, Italy, Spain, and Cairo. The Colonel's home in Lugano had been the center of lively traffic by mail and courier with far-flung places in the world. According to press reports, Dollmann's outpost in Switzerland was closely tied to the international Nazi headquarters in Madrid. [2]

Enough facts are known about the center in Madrid to show that it functions as a Nazi party organization in exile. It has been reported that the Madrid center has its own financial department, sustained by a huge treasure chest which the Nazis shipped to neutral countries before the German collapse. [3] There is a special department for German affairs, departments for Africa and Latin America, and also a unit known as the International of Nationalists. The latter is a propaganda organization with branches all over Europe and groups operating in the Western Hemisphere and on other continents. On May 29, 1951, *Times* correspondent C. I. Sulzberger confirmed the existence of this group which had revived the Fascist International in various countries "from Malmö to Tangier and from Rome to Buenos Aires." The Washington *Post* of May 6, 1956, reported on the close contacts between right-wing radicals in Germany and the center of the Nazi International in Madrid:

Observers in Bonn have traced the increasing activity of former Nazis who travel between Germany and the main centers of the International—Spain, Sweden, Switzerland, Egypt and Argentina. They often work for import-export firms and agencies and for German motor manufacturers. They are able to tap "buried" Nazi assets abroad, which may be providing the main financial backing for Nationalist activities inside Germany.

The names most frequently in the news in connection with the underground work of the Madrid Nazi center are the anti-Semitic, rabble-rousing Dr. Johann von Leers, the SS Colonel Otto Skorzeny, and the German Luftwaffe ace, Hans Ulrich Rudel. It is a well-known fact that Franco has taken the Nazi plotters to his bosom. When, in 1959, a delegation of the Nazi Condor Legion visited Madrid, Franco greeted his old civil war allies with the words: "Please regard Spain as your second fatherland." [4]

In January 1952, German and Swiss newspapers reported an extraordinary concentration of former high SS officers and ex-Nazi officials in Cairo. They were in close contact with influential Egyptian army officers and with the fanatical Arab plotter and Hitler's friend, Haj Amin el Husseini, the ex-Grand Mufti of Jerusalem. The *Basler Nachrichten* of January 29, 1952, mentioned the former Nazi SS Colonel Dollmann as one of those who had conferences with the Egyptian plotters in the Grand Mufti's headquarters, Villa Aida, in Heliopolis, a suburb outside of Cairo. The papers hinted that it was Dollmann and his co-conspirators in Madrid who had set the fuse of an anti-British plot in Cairo which, a few months later, resulted in the explosion that ended with the ousting of King Farouk.

Although the local police regarded the Dollmann arrest as "of great importance," someone in a high position in Bonn must have judged the affair from quite a different point of view, almost as an unfortunate accident that had to be remedied as quickly as possible. Despite the fact that the German law punishes the forging of passports and the use of false documents with long prison terms, Herr Dollmann did not suffer any great inconvenience. He might have been released without any trial had not the *Frankfurter Rundschau* given the case considerable publicity. Under these circumstances Dollmann appeared before a lower Magistrates Court a week after his arrest and was sentenced to two months' imprisonment for forgery.

The mild sentence given to Dollmann, the pressures to quash the prosecution against the Naumann plotters, the toleration of the activities of such important Nazis as Colonel Skorzeny and Hans Ulrich Rudel, give rise to the suspicion that high officials in Bonn had some secret ties with the Nazi center in Madrid. There are indications too that the Bonn Foreign Office and West German industrialists coöperated with the Nazis in Madrid in furthering a scheme to push the French and British out of the Near and Middle East. In most Arab countries the ties to the active Nazis were not interrupted with the collapse of the Third Reich. Many of the Nazi experts who had escaped the Allied dragnet were later hired by the Egyptian government as military, financial, and technical advisers. The official government Central

Planning Staff in Cairo under Dr. Wilhelm Voss and General Wilhelm Fahrembach was instrumental in arranging the armaments deal with the Soviet bloc.[5] It is significant that the Nazi group in Cairo reportedly had closer ties to the Bonn Foreign Office than the West German ambassador, Dr. Guenther Pawelke.[6]

Also revealing was the case of Dr. Fritz Dorls, the leader of the Socialist Reichs party, which had been outlawed in 1952. This same Dr. Dorls, whose party had been exposed by the highest Federal Court as subversive, was, after his conviction, secretly hired by the Bonn Foreign Office for delicate assignments in the Arab countries.[7]

In 1959 Dr. Adenauer was asked in a BBC television interview whether there was a resurgence of anti-Semitism and Nazism. He flatly declared: "Anti-Semitism was a characteristic of National Socialism; both together have disappeared." [8] Nine days before this interview the Roman Catholic Bishop of Limburg, Monsignor Walter Kampe, wrote an editorial in his diocesan paper, entitled "The Nazis in Our Midst." Monsignor Kampe spoke of "the existence of several underground organizations among the old-guard Nazis," through which they have created "a network of information and mutual assistance over the whole of Germany . . . whose influence is felt everywhere in all parties, in the administration of justice, in all professional organizations, among the expellee associations, and throughout our civic and economic life." Bishop Kampe then stated:

There are enough hot irons that nobody dares to touch because people deep in their bones feel a fear of the secret power and the brutality of the Nazi goon squads. It requires a certain courage to break that spell. What is missing is an organizational banding together of all the anti-Nazi forces in order to build a firm wall against the subversive attacks which undermine our not sufficiently stabilized democratic society.[9]

In a lengthy survey on the neo-Nazi and militaristic right-wing organizations, the *Frankfurter Hefte,* in its November issue of 1957, gave the following figures:

In the Federal Republic there exist today 46 political associations of this character. The Nazi-militaristic wing is served by 30 newspapers, 68 Rightist book and magazine publishers, and 120 former Nazi publicists. In addition there are approximately 50 nationalistic youth organizations.

A little later, in a series of articles, "Panorama of the Extreme Rightists," the *Frankfurter Allgemeine Zeitung* for December 18, 19, and 21, 1957, made a survey of the organizational structure of the neo-Nazi movement, "whose immediate aim is not to score political results [at the ballot box], but to cultivate *Weltanschauung.*" The *Frankfurter Allgemeine* named several dozen neo-Nazi organizations, their leading publications, and the gallery of would-be Fuehrers.[10] When the flourishing Socialist Reichs party was outlawed in 1952, the authorities soon discovered that within a few months the Nazis had set up more than sixty *tarn* organizations—camouflaged substitutes—in the state of Lower Saxony alone.[11]

The neo-Nazis have succeeded in channeling the movement into dozens of innocent-looking organizations. At present most are eager to keep their overt activities within the limits of the so-called "democratic legality."

Behind the façade of the Bund Deutscher Jugend (Association of German Youth—membership 22,000) for instance, was a well-trained secret saboteur and assassination squad which had been labeled the Technical Emergency Service. This guerrilla army was composed of several thousand former Wehrmacht and SS officers, and was secretly provided with weapons, money, and training facilities by U.S. agencies, the Bonn government, and a few large West German business concerns. In 1952 the U. S. High Commission was quite chagrined when the Minister-President of the State of Hesse, August Zinn, publicly charged that this organization had drawn up blacklists of prominent politicians who were marked for assassination in case of an "emergency." Enough evidence was produced to show that a large-scale political murder plot had been hatched in the best style of the "free corps" in the early twenties.[12]

A dispatch in the New York *Times* of October 10, 1952, stated that the plotters had "betrayed U.S. trust" and that the American officials had been unaware of what was going on:

United States authorities said they felt that the guerrilla training program was not in itself wrong, though possibly unwise. They said what most concerned them was the proclivity of the Germans involved for engaging in political activities that possibly had degenerated into a conspiracy against political and government leaders.

Similar illegal activities were discovered behind other Nazi organizations, such as the Freikorps Deutschland, the Bewegung Reich, and scores of smaller groups. It is significant that most of these plotters, including those of the Bund Deutscher Jugend, never had to stand trial.

How many stanch Nazis are today politically active in Germany? Since the Bonn government flatly denies that Nazis are still active in German politics, overtly or covertly, it is difficult to obtain figures based on official surveys. There is, however, a considerable amount of evidence—press reports on arrests of Nazis, the discovery of illegal organizations, public opinion polls, and the circulation of Nazi publications—which permits one to draw realistic estimates of the strength of the Nazi underground. As early as 1951, when figures were still reported, an official survey found that more than thirty illegal Nazi organizations were operating in West Berlin alone, all of them made up of former Nazi party officials and SS officers. According to the *Frankfurter Rund-schau* of November 12, 1951, this "illegal" NSDAP [National Socialist German Workers' Party] had a membership of at least 200,000.

In 1951, only two years after the Socialist Reichs party was founded, it polled 367,000 votes for its thinly camou-flaged platform, in the State of Lower Saxony. (This was 11 percent of a total of 3,393,000 ballots cast.) Here is a vivid description by an American observer who saw the SRP in action:

The Sozialistische Reichspartei is the closest thing to a Nazi party Germany has seen since war's end. The speakers talked a straight Nazi line. It went down well. The audience shouted and enthusiastically stamped at attacks on the U.S. and its "Kaugummi" (chewing gum) soldiers. . . . The SRP line: Germany lost World War II only through treason; atrocity charges are Allied propaganda; Dachau's death chambers were built after the war on American orders . . .

The party's brain is Count Wolf von Westarp, 45, one-armed former newspaperman and SS officer. But its loudest mouthpiece is former Major General Otto Ernst Remer. . . . Typical Remer blast: "Rather than have our women and children overrun by the Russians. . . . it would be better to post ourselves as traffic policemen, spreading our arms so that the Russians can find their way through Germany as quickly as possible. . . . [and] pick the [British and American] lords and ladies out of their silken beds!" [13]

Among the leaders of the SRP was a Dr. Franz Richter, than a member of the Bundestag. It was discovered that "Dr. Richter" was a former Nazi party official whose real name was Fritz Roessler—and no "Dr." at that. Richter-Roessler, like many other Nazis, had used false identification papers in order to avoid arrest by the Allies. Nobody really knows how many tens of thousands of party officials and Nazi war criminals are today living under false identities. In the early years of the Bonn Republic it was estimated that as many as 120,000 people were hiding behind false fronts which had been carefully prepared before the Nazi collapse. Frequent appeals by the Bonn government, guaranteeing immunity from prosecution, have not brought a change in this situation.*

In the past the Adenauer government has argued that the few unreconstructed Nazis represent no danger to the democratic order. But, as we have seen, the Nazis are there in great numbers; they are active in all parties and civic groups and they constitute an ever-present danger. After the banning of the Socialist Reichs party in 1952, the Nazis boasted that they would come to power again "through the back door" by infiltrating all existing institutions and by capturing key positions in political parties, the state, and the economy with the help of a "small, well-trained totalitarian group." This new type of fascist struggle for power was termed "the cold revolution, a revolution carried out quietly from the top." [14]

In 1952, when five functionaries of a secret Adolf Hitler Action Group were sentenced for anticonstitutional activities in West Berlin, it became known that the leader of the group, Schlockermann (alias Schroer), once a prominent official in Hitler's headquarters in Munich, had given the following directive: "Act inconspicuously! Infiltrate all Rightist organizations and make them ready for the final asault." [15]

A rally of the Deutsche Reichs party in 1956 was addressed by such prominent Nazi propagandists as Wilhelm Meinberg, once Hitler's representative in the Prussian State Council; Adolf von Thadden, a fiery young agitator; and Herbert Freiberger, an astute tactician and former Hitler Youth leader. Herr Meinberg told the audience that some day the

* Professor Friedrich Grimm, a prominent lawyer for leading Nazis, estimated in 1952 that there were still at least 80,000 people in Germany who preferred to live under false identification papers (*Frankfurter Allgemeine*, September 9, 1952).

Germans would build a monument for Der Fuehrer and his dead paladins; youth leader Freiberger predicted the failure of Adenauer's policies; and Herr von Thadden elaborated on the forces which change the course of history: "We are convinced," he said, "that against an inert, lazy majority, an iron-willed minority has to rise as the challenger. History has never been made by majorities, only by dynamic minorities." [16]

In 1958 five hundred Hoheitstraeger—top men in the Nazi elite—held their annual rally in the city of Mainz. Among the speakers was a former SS Colonel Julius Zuchbold, once the Nazi mayor of the resort town of Bad Pyrmont, who was one of the leading SS tyrants in occupied Czechoslovakia. Applauded by the frantic laughter of the assembled Nazi elite, Colonel Zuchbold quipped:

As an SS officer, I had my place on the list of war criminals that had been prepared by the Czechoslovakian government. I preferred to go underground because I wanted to spare the Czechs the unesthetic view which an overweight man with such a tremendous paunch as mine would have presented from the gallows.

The speaker followed this sample of wit with a broadside against the Bonn "system," criticizing it for its slowness in granting well-deserved pensions. He topped this attack with a thinly veiled threat:

We do not intend to go to sleep. We will stay alert and exploit all the rights and privileges which the democratic system offers to us. Yet we will be a power whenever we decide to become a power.

The confident mood of the ex-Nazis was aired by Kurt Wilbertz, a lawyer and national chairman of the Association of Former Internees and Victims of Denazification, who boastfully announced that the "new tactic" (the infiltration of other parties) would be crowned with success. The speaker then declared: "It is high time that our friends in the Bundestag and the State Assemblies move from the back benches into the front rows." [17]

Nobody can predict when and under what circumstances such Nazi ambition will again become a factor in German politics. But extreme German nationalism has fewer obstacles to overcome in its return to power than were present during Hitler's rise. The belief is that for the present, and as long as Adenauer stays at the helm, the comeback of an overt Nazi party is blocked by the decisions of the Federal Court and by an election law which says that only those parties shall be admitted to the Bundestag which either gain 5 percent of the total votes returned or directly elect three candidates in the districts. These roadblocks may be adequate for the moment, but they are not sufficient to deal with Nazism as a long-term disease.

During the first decade of the Bonn Republic the neo-Nazis have scored considerable propaganda achievements. Twelve years ago they set out with a rousing cry to free all war criminals, not only those serving their time in Germany but also those convicted in Russia, France, Holland, and the other countries in Europe. They put the Adenauer administration under heavy pressure to gain official support in forcing the Western powers to yield to their demands. Today almost all war criminals have been set free. At the moment of this writing only three leading Nazis are held in Spandau and a handful in France and Holland.* The probability is that they also will be released in the near future.

* According to an AP dispatch of May 10, 1958, the last four of the 1,500 Nazi war criminals held in Landsberg prison were finally released. Now the Rightist press demands the immediate release of the last three major war criminals in Spandau—Rudolf Hess, deputy of Der Fuehrer, Baldur von Schirach, one of Hitler's youth leaders, and Albert Speer, Hitler's munitions czar. A committee of ex-Nazis was formed to promote the Nobel Peace Prize for Rudolf Hess. Claims to the prize were based on Hess's personal courage in flying to England during the war and attempting to talk the British into a negotiated peace (*Der Fortschritt*, December 19, 1957).

Having scored these successes, the Nazis have become bolder in their program:

They foster the spiritual preparation of the youth for a return to the Nazi ideals.

They have encouraged the belief that Nazism was "a good idea" and that Hitler failed only because he was "stabbed in the back by traitors."

They relentlessly attack the democratic forces in Germany by using the labels "traitor" and "collaborationist" loosely against true democrats.

They demand full reparation for all the hardships suffered by Nazis and SS men who were interned after the war, and by expellees who were driven from their homes in the Eastern territories.

They propose the end of all restitutions and reparations to Jewish and other victims of Nazi persecution.

They advocate the "restoration of German honor" which was "besmirched and trampled upon by the victorious Jewish-Bolshevik war coalition."

They have launched an active fight against the Western "war-guilt lie."

They call for mass rejection of the "big Western lie about alleged Nazi atrocities."

They have started counterpropaganda which condemns the "war crimes committed by the Allies" and "the shameful postwar crime of Nuremberg."

They insist on the return of the "stolen territories" in the East, including the Sudetenland which they want incorporated into a restored German Reich.

They support a foreign policy in the East with the aim of turning the present cold war to Germany's fullest advantage.

They demand an end of all legal measures imposed by the victorious Allies against former Nazis and SS men, and an unrestricted return of these to public office and the ranks of the new German army.

This neo-Nazi propaganda is broadcast through the ultra-Rightist press, from the highbrow neo-Nazi monthlies with a few thousand subscribers to the fire-eating expellee weeklies with circulations up to and above 100,000.* According to the *Sueddeutsche Zeitung* of April 18, 1959, the various expellee papers alone, weeklies and fortnightlies, have a combined circulation of more than a million. Also of great influence are several Rightist publishing houses which carry on a thriving business with an ever-increasing flood of war memoirs. On the best-seller list are books by former Nazi leaders, such as the writings of Rudolf Hess, Foreign Minister von Ribbentrop, and the party "scholar," Alfred Rosenberg. There are self-justifying reports by ex-Gestapo officials and former Wehrmacht commanders. A booklet published in huge editions had the significant title *Hitler Acquitted*.

In 1956 the conservative *Stuttgarter Nachrichten* reported that a "tidal wave of fascist literature is flooding the Federal Republic." [18] The outpouring of neo-Nazi books and pamphlets had reached such alarming proportions that in order "to combat this upsurge, an anti-fascist committee of German writers, educators and booksellers has been organized on a nation-wide basis." The group, the Gruenwald Circle, took its name from a suburb of Munich where many of its founders live. Among its leading personalities are Hans Werner

---

* Among several dozen militant Rightist monthlies and weeklies these are most often mentioned: *Nation Europa, Der Reichsruf, Der Ring, Wiking-Ruf, Deutsche Soldaten Zeitung, Deutscher Aufbruch, Die Deutsche Freiheit, Der Freiwillige, Der Stahlhelm, Der Notweg, Deutsche Stimmen, Deutschland Brief, Deutsche Gemeinschaft, Der Volksbote, Der Sudeten Deutsche,* and *Suchlicht.* The rabble-rousing paper *Die Anklage* is at present defunct and its publisher has been sentenced to a two-year jail term. The Nazi monthly *Der Weg,* published in Buenos Aires, had 16,000 subscribers in Germany on its mailing list. It is now defunct.

Richter, a Bavarian writer, Dr. Rudolf Pechel, chief editor
of the South German Radio, and Juergen Aggebrecht, director of the North German Radio Network. According to a
New York *Times* report, the committee found that twenty
publishing houses, about thirty book guilds, and forty-five
periodicals "were solely devoted to dissemination of Rightist
radical material." [19] Its specialists, says the report, "compiled
a list of 200 book titles, published in the last two years, which
fit the classification of pro-Nazi or neo-Nazi."

The effects of this propaganda are clearly reflected in the
various public opinion polls. Two highly respected public
opinion institutes (the Emnid Agency and the Institute for
Demoskopie) found that the great majority of the German
people still believe that Nazism "was a good idea badly carried out." In 1953 the Reaction Analysis Staff of the U. S.
High Commission in Germany reported that only 24 percent
of the population regarded themselves as actively opposed to
Nazism.[20] Only a third of the population considers Germany
responsible for the war. In 1953 only 17 percent were in
agreement with denazification measures, 23 percent considered them "wrongly executed," and 40 percent opposed them
as "harmful and undersirable." [21] In 1955 a poll taken by the
Emnid Agency revealed that 14 percent of the electorate
would still vote for Hitler. Public opinion polls in 1958
showed that 42 percent of the population still regarded Hitler as "the greatest statesman of all times," and the Swiss newspaper *Die Weltwoche* came to the conclusion that "60 percent of the population in West Germany are of questionable
political morality." [22]

On the basis of these polls only a quarter of the population
of West Germany can be safely counted as democratic. There
are at least 7,000,000 to 8,000,000 (16-18 percent of the population) who must be regarded as fanatical supporters of old
Nazi concepts. The great majority in the middle are still
favorably inclined to the Nazi past.

There is even the danger that a new Nazi party might legally come into power again. At the beginning of 1958 Bonn canceled the Allied occupation law which had banned the Nazi party and all its affiliates. The basic law of the Federal Republic is no barrier to a Nazi comeback, because once a willing court interprets a new political shift as in "accord with the democratic procedure," everything will be legal.

The neo-Nazis are obviously aware of such opportunities. In 1958 the former Nazi official, Wilhelm Meinberg, chairman of the Deutsche Reichs party, ridiculed Bonn's efforts to minimize the Nazi strength. He contemptuously remarked that "when our opponents one day realize that they know very little, it will be too late." [23] This is exactly what happened to the Weimar Republic—the democratic factions were badly mistaken about the nature of Hitler's ambitions until the very day he came to power.

The Nazi underground, as well as the conspicuous neo-Nazis, must be regarded as well-trained political shock troops. In recent years they have even come out in a show of strength by reviving the old Brown-Shirt tactics which marked Hitler's ascent to power. On several occasions the neo-Nazi parties have brought out uniformed goon squads to rough up opposition speakers, disturb meetings of other parties, or create anti-Semitic outbursts. Such incidents are seldom reported in the foreign press. An exception was a big rally of the German party in West Berlin where Transportation Minister Hans-Christoph Seebohm gave a high-pitched nationalistic speech before ten thousand fanatical followers. The turbulent meeting showed all the old-style Nazi trimmings: shouting of anti-Semitic epithets, uniformed strong-arm bouncers, beating up of political opponents, and threatening of foreign correspondents.[24]

Similar disturbances were reported during the election campaign of 1957, when groups of Rightist hooligans disrupted meetings.[25] A year later, young students were severely beaten by neo-Nazis at a meeting in Hamburg, "with the police in the role of passive onlookers." [26]

The political stability of the Bonn Republic is slowly being undermined by millions of unreconstructed *Ehemaliger* —"old fighters"—who at present give lip service to democracy, but are deeply committed to long-term plans for a Nazi comeback and a new strong leader. They dream of a military establishment with supermodern weapons, and of a Germany-dominated Europe, free to throw its weight, "at the right moment," either to the East or the West in order to regain for Germany the status of a great world power.

8 *The Honorable SS*

The cobblestones echoed with the strutting steps of six thousand men of Hitler's Waffen SS, who marched with military precision through the narrow streets of the historic town of Verden. On this bright autumn day in 1952 they were staging a rally to honor the "great tradition" of the Waffen SS.*

They did not sport their black uniforms or the emblem of skull and crossbones. Their jackboots did not pound to the arrogant tune, "Today We Own Germany, Tomorrow the Whole World." Yet, barely seven years after the war, the SS was marching again, completely ignoring defeat, Allied occupation, and their own infamous record.

In 1946, after carefully probing the most notorious acts committed by Hitler's so-called "Elite Guard," the International Military Tribunal at Nuremberg declared the entire SS a "criminal organization." A few years later, and with Germany still under Allied occupation, thousands of former

* The following account of the Ramcke incident was taken from many German and foreign-language newspapers, among them *Die Zeit*, October 30, *Die Welt*, October 28, and the *Daily Mail* (Paris), October 27, 1952.

members of the SS were back as police officials, administrators, judges, teachers, and burghermasters. With the planning of a European army for NATO, Hitler's Waffen SS felt the time was ripe to regain lost territory. They insisted on "rehabilitation" and full pensions, and they demanded that former SS men be admitted into the ranks of the newly created German army.

It was chiefly for this purpose that the ex-SS men had assembled for their first reunion in the town of Verden. Led by the SS Generals Herbert Gille and Felix Steiner, several thousand officers and men gathered under the traditional banners of such divisions as Gross Deutschland, Viking, Das Reich, and the Death's-Head. There were also several hundred men, each standing six to seven feet tall, who rallied under a poster bearing the initials L.A.H. Inquiring newspapermen were informed that the abbreviation stood for "Leibstandarte Adolf Hitler," the guard regiment for the protection of Der Fuehrer. Here was the cream of the sworn community of *Treuegefolgschaft*—loyal followers—of Adolf Hitler. They had all gathered for two days in Verden under the pretext of conducting a "search for missing comrades" and to exchange reminiscences of the old "happy days." Their leader, SS General Gille, had assured the Bonn authorities that the SS men would not indulge in noisy, nationalistic provocations. Indeed, in his speech Gille pledged the support of the Waffen SS to the Bonn Republic and declared that "they were ready to do their duty for the Fatherland."

This first public rehearsal for rehabilitation would probably have worked out according to plan had not an unexpected event changed the whole program. The guest speaker, short and stubby paratroop commander Major General Hermann Ramcke, was scheduled to "convey the greetings" of the Fallschirmjaeger (paratroopers), another tough Nazi outfit. Unfortunately Ramcke did not follow the script too closely. Instead of bringing greetings from the paratroopers, he attacked the Allies with an avalanche of denunciations.

"Who are the war criminals?" was Ramcke's inciting rhetorical question. "Certainly not the men who were put on the blacklists by the Allies during the Nuremberg Trials. Things are changing fast, and the time will soon come when the members of the Waffen SS will again have the first place on history's honor list as the defenders of Europe." There was a deafening roar which took minutes to subside.

"Listen," Ramcke shouted, "the real war criminals are those who created the Versailles Treaty and enslaved the German people . . . they are those who bombed to rubble our towns and cities like Dresden . . . they are those who dropped the atom bombs on Hiroshima and Nagasaki . . . and they are those who stabbed us in the back when we were defending Europe against the Bolsheviks."

According to the New York *Times*, Ramcke's words were received with "clamorous applause by the assembled veterans." He then proceeded to name the "real" war criminals: Roosevelt, Churchill, Eisenhower. When he mentioned Eisenhower, many in the crowd joined in shouting *"Der Schweinehund! Der Schweinehund!—*the dirty swine." Thus ended the first step toward rehabilitation "with an explosion unmatched in the furor over the emergence of German veterans' groups in politics." [1]

When, in 1952, General Ramcke raised the question, "Who are the real war criminals?" he was promptly answered by two historians, working independently in London and Paris, who almost simultaneously brought out two thick volumes containing the infamous record of Hitler's SS.[2] The facts about this crime machine were clearly established during the many months of trial procedure before the International Military Tribunal at Nuremberg during 1945 and 1946. The evidence was obtained from thousands of top secret German documents captured by the Allies. These documents and records have been printed in dozens of volumes.* In addition, the Allied armies found the torture tools, the gas chambers, and the human furnaces which the SS had used in the liquidation of millions of men, women, and children.

In the concentration camps the swift-moving Allied troops found corpses and bodies mingled by the thousands and tens of thousands—corpses dead for days and bodies almost dead. Photographs were taken which were introduced as evidence during the trials, together with the sworn affidavits. Here is the report of an American correspondent who saw the inferno with his own eyes immediately after the Nazi collapse and who saw it again when the films were run off in the courtroom:

The camp at Leipzig is first; and then we see Penig and Nordhausen and Hadamar and Dachau and Belsen and Mauthausen and Buchenwald and half a dozen more. And they are all alike, for the impression we get is an endless river of white bodies flowing across the screen, bodies with ribs sticking out through chests, with pipestem legs and battered skulls and eyeless faces and grotesque thin arms reaching for the sky.

To many of us in the press gallery, these bodies are no strangers. We have seen them before and also smelled them, and it is queer how many of us imagine we smell them again. . . . There is no end to the bodies, tumbling bodies and bodies in mounds, and single bodies with holes between the eyes, and bodies being shoved over cliffs into common graves, and bodies pushed like dirt by giant bulldozers, and bodies that are not bodies at all, but charred bits of bones and flesh lying upon a crematory grate made of bits of steel rail laid upon blackened wooden ties.

* According to the New York *Times* Magazine of September 12, 1954, there were "38,000 affidavits, signed by 155,000 people; several tons of Alfred Rosenberg's records; 485 tons of the German Foreign Office papers, and the complete files of Heinrich Himmler, containing horrifying reports of the systematic mass slaughters committed by the Gestapo."

Now another body is shoved over a cliff into an open ditch by a bulldozer which the British called into use because there were so many dead lying around they were a menace to the living. And this body is not quite buried by the dirt, and it shines white here and there, a bony leg sticking out and one arm outstretched.[3]

The SS ran more than three hundred concentration camps; in the occupied East were several of the largest death factories. How many millions were liquidated through torture, beatings, bullets, gassing, starvation, and exhaustion? The figures available are truly staggering. In one death factory alone, Auschwitz-Birkenau, between 4,000,000 and 5,000,000 people were exterminated in the gas chambers. Here is an excerpt from the testimony given by Rudolf Hoess, a Nazi party member since 1922, who joined the SS in 1934 and was appointed Commandant of Auschwitz on May 1, 1940:

I commanded Auschwitz until December 1, 1943, and estimate that at least 2,500,000 victims were executed there by gassing and burning, and at least another 500,000 succumbed to starvation and disease, making a total of 3,000,000. This represents about 70-80 percent of all persons sent to Auschwitz, the remainder having been selected and used for slave labor in the camp industries. . . . I was ordered to establish extermination facilities at Auschwitz in June 1941. At that time there were already in the General Government three other extermination camps: Balzek, Treblinka and Wolzek. . . . When I set up the extermination building at Auschwitz, I used Cyclon B, which was a crystallized prussic acid which we dropped into the death chamber from a small opening. It took from three to fifteen minutes to kill the people in the death chamber, depending upon the climatic conditions. We knew when the people were dead because their screaming stopped. After the bodies were removed, our Special Commandos took off the rings and extracted the gold from the teeth of the corpses. Another improvement we made over Treblinka was that we built our gas chambers to accommodate 2,000 people at one time, whereas at Treblinka their ten gas chambers only accommodated 200 each. The way we selected our victims was as follows: we had two SS doctors on duty to examine incoming transports. The prisoners would be marched past the physicians who would make spot decisions as they walked by. Those who were fit for work were sent into the camp. Others were sent immediately to the extermination plants. Children of tender years were invariably exterminated, since by reason of their youth they were unable to work.[4]

In his long affidavit Rudolf Hoess admitted the gassing of "400,000 Hungarian Jews alone in the summer of 1944." But there were hundreds of thousands of Jews and other nationals shipped from all over Europe to the improved plants in Auschwitz-Birkenau. The wife of a Hungarian Jewish doctor, who served as a nurse in a lice-infested barrack, provides us with the following account:

I have the figures only for the months of May, June and July, 1944. Dr. Pasche, a French doctor of the Sonderkommando, in the crematory, who was in a position to gather statistics on the rate of the extermination, provided me with these:

May, 1944	360,000
June, 1944	512,000
From the 1st to the 26th of July, 1944	442,000
	1,314,000

In less than a quarter of a year the Germans had "liquidated" more than 1,300,000 persons at Auschwitz-Birkenau! [5]

Auschwitz was a death camp used chiefly for the extermination of Jews in East and Southeast Europe. But we must add to the Auschwitz total the "production" figures of the other camps, such as Treblinka, where each of the ten gas chambers accommodated "only" two hundred victims. With the crematories going full blast day and night, one must conservatively figure the total "output" of the gas chambers in the neighborhood of nine million.

With the gas chambers running at peak production most of the time, the corpses were often piled high outside the crematories. In order to overcome these bottlenecks, corpses by the thousands were burned in open pits.[6]

The man in charge of arresting and transporting the Jews to the various death factories was the SS Colonel Adolf Eichmann who played a major role in implementing Hitler's "Final Solution." As head of a special department in the SS Main Security Office, Eichmann organized large-scale man hunts all over Europe. For him the mass killing of Jews was a businesslike affair. The SS commander of Auschwitz testified that he received this order from Eichmann: "Without pity and in cold blood, we must complete the extermination." A witness before the Nuremberg court testified that a few months before the German collapse Eichmann boasted to his SS friend Dieter Wisliceny: "I will jump into my grave laughing, because the fact that I have the death of five million Jews on my conscience gives me extraordinary satisfaction." *

Captured by the Americans, Eichmann remained unrecognized. Like many others before him, he escaped from an internment camp with false identification papers. Postwar rumors reported Eichmann as living in Argentina, being a police official in Nasser's Egypt, and having been seen in the British protectorate Kuwait. In May 1960 an announcement by Israeli Prime Minister Ben-Gurion that avengers had captured this number-one butcher in Argentina caused a world-wide sensation. The abduction of Eichmann created a temporary rift between Israel and Argentina. Eichmann's trial before an Israeli court has dramatized for the world the inconceivable horror of Hitler's "Final Solution."

How many Jews and non-Jews perished in Hitler's extermination camps? We know from the correspondence between Hitler's assistant, Viktor Brack, department chief in the

* IMT (Nuremberg Trials record), III, 288, and Affidavit C.

Fuehrer's Chancellery, and Heinrich Himmler, Reichsfuehrer of the SS, that in 1941 there was "a total of some
10,000,000 Jews" in Nazi-conquered Europe. Of this number,
2,000,000 to 3,000,000 men and women were considered well
able to work. The rest were earmarked for the "Final Solution," that is, violent death, as it had been decided in the
notorious Gross-Wansee conference on January 8, 1942.
When Germany was overrun by the Allied armies in the
spring of 1945, they found only scattered remnants, mostly
living skeletons, of the 10,000,000 Jews.

It is difficult to make an accurate breakdown of how many
people were shot by SS firing squads, how many died in gas
chambers, and how many perished from exhaustion, disease,
and undernourishment. There is little doubt, however, that
more than half of the 10,000,000 Jews died in the gas chambers, together with a few million other nationals. Approximately 2,000,000 died in the indescribable massacres of the
SS Einsatzkommandos (Special Task Forces), in Gestapo cellars, and through the ill-famed "medical experiments." The
rest succumbed in labor camps and on transports. The foregoing figures may still be an understatement. A German study
group gave the staggering figure of 35,000,000 noncombatants
who perished under the impact of war and occupation in Eastern Europe alone.

Germany started the aggressive war with the aim of making the Germanic race masters of the globe. What Hitler
envisioned in *Mein Kampf* as *Germanische Weltherrschaft*
was a declaration of war against all other races. At the top of
Hitler's list of inferior races were the Jews. Yet it is too
often forgotten in the West that the extermination of the
Jews in Europe was only to be a prelude for much more
drastic action, a contemplated crime many times greater than
that committed against the Jews. Hitler's long-range aim
was the total destruction of the almost 300,000,000 people
belonging to the Slavic race. The Fuehrer's fantastic plan

was the creation of a world empire, grouped around a pure Germanic Lebensraum stretching from the Atlantic coast to far beyond the Ural Mountains. In order to achieve this goal, the Hitler-Himmler scheme called for a merciless race war against the Slavic peoples of the East. The German high command had hoped to crush the Soviet armies in a three-month blitzkrieg, and then, in Hitler's own words, they would be able "to cut up the giant cake according to our own needs."

Had the Germans succeeded with their plans they would have carried out a diabolical scheme of "resettlement" and of "special treatment" which would have caused the death of a couple of hundred million Poles, Czechs, Ukrainians, and Russians. The German conquerors intended to strip the East, as in fact they did, of all industry, and they would have sterilized the remaining peasant population and forced it into slave labor for the German overlords. A few weeks before the impending attack on the U.S.S.R., the experts on Goering's staff decided that "many tens of millions of people in this area will become redundant and will either die or have to emigrate to Siberia." [7]

The conservative diplomat Baron Konstantin von Neurath suggested to Hitler that "half of the Czech population be deprived of its power, eliminated and shipped out of the country . . . the other half used as forced labor" and gradually "Germanized." [8]

Even after the defeat of Stalingrad, Himmler still expressed the hope that the Nazis could develop a Germanic Lebensraum populated with "a total of 600 to 700 millions, and with an outpost area stretching in a hundred years beyond the Urals." [9]

The task of destroying the vanquished and building up the biological strength of the master race was given to the SS. To achieve both goals SS chief Himmler created a labyrinth of organizations, each serving a special purpose. There

were SS departments entrusted with the methodical destruction of "inferior" races, and there were medical SS groups experimenting with the most effective means for mass sterilization of millions in order to curtail the propagation of non-German races. On the other hand, there were such SS enterprises as Lebensborn, Ahnenerbe, and Heu-Aktion, whose aim was to facilitate the build-up of a tough German soldier elite, tightly controlled by the SS. The Lebensborn ran a chain of state-subsidized breeding establishments, where Hitler Youth leaders and SS men had to function as stallions. Girls in the female Hitler Youth (BDM) were encouraged to bear as many children as possible out of wedlock to contribute "to a German biological victory on the baby front." *
The children born under the Lebensborn program had to be reared and educated by the state.

Ahnenerbe was a gigantic scheme to curtail other races and to "Germanize" the conquered territories by building a vast network of large soldier homesteads where millions of slave laborers were kept under strictist control. Under the code word "Heu-Aktion," a large-scale kidnapping expedition was launched in 1944, during which tens of thousands of children, preferably blonds, were taken away from their parents by force and distributed among German peasants who were ordered to rear them as "German" children. The idea was to make up quickly the severe losses of man power which the German armies had suffered on the Eastern plains.

The record of the SS has been presented by the Oxford scholar Gerald Reitlinger in his expertly documented book dealing with the SS.[10] He shows how out of the original Schutzstaffeln (a small bouncer squad to protect the Nazi rallies during the twenties) a huge party army grew within a

---

* The neo-Nazi monthly *Nation Europa* in its issue for July 1959 praises the Lebensborn breeding farms as one of the "outstanding biological institutions" of the SS which became "a victim of the destructive hatred of the Morgenthau victors in 1945."

few years, in which each man was pledged by "blood oath" to stand loyally behind the Fuehrer.

On the domestic scene, the terroristic Gestapo ruled supreme and forced the opposing political groups to support the Nazi regime. Special formations of the SS operated the concentration camps and death factories, others organized large-scale man hunts to get a steady supply for Germany's always hungry slave labor camps. Finally, there were the ruthless Einsatzgruppen, which shot Jews, prisoners of war, and Polish and Russian peasants by the millions.

To carry out international espionage and conspiracy the SS had its own intelligence organization, the Sicherheitsdienst (SD), which also ran a highly efficient department for mass forgery of foreign bank notes and passports. In addition, the SS had its own economic branch, which ran a vast chain of factories, trade corporations, night clubs (in Germany and abroad)—for corruption and espionage—and a string of high-class and mediocre brothels.

For the looting of Europe the SS had a special organization, designed to strip foreign countries of industry and raw materials. There were expert detachments which swarmed like locusts over the Continent in order to seize every piece of art and jewelry and ship it to Germany. It is estimated that the SS, by stealing the property of the Jews and by plundering Europe, acquired billions of dollars' worth of valuables, of which a large part was brought to neutral countries for safekeeping.

The gigantic structure of the Nazi regime had its backbone in the thirty-six divisions of the Waffen SS which, excellently armed, was the nightmare of all occupied Europe. The Waffen SS is credited with the mass shooting of hostages in all subjugated nations and with such brutal massacres as that of Lidice, which was obliterated, and Oradour in France, where the SS shot and burned 645 women and children in a church. The destruction of the Warsaw ghetto and the

Malmédy mass murder of American G.I.s during the Battle of the Bulge are also on the Waffen SS "honor" list.

Although not part of the Wehrmacht, the Waffen SS frequently did front-line duty, especially in the years when the fortunes of war had turned against the Axis. But the chief task of the Waffen SS was to serve as a party watchdog in case some of the Generals played with the idea of an insurrection. It was the SS at home and in the occupied countries that quickly suppressed the anti-Hitler putsch of July 20, 1944.

What was the make-up of the SS, and what type of people flocked to this criminal organization? There was at the top the so-called "Honor SS," composed of thousands of members of the aristocratic and industrial upper crust, of high diplomats, party bigwigs, and the intellectual elite, such as university professors, judges, a few Protestant pastors, Catholic priests,* artists, writers, and leading men of the medical and scientific professions. Some respected figures of medical science played a particularly obnoxious role in the vast crime network of the SS. This came to light during the 139 trial days of the Nuremberg "Doctors' Trial" in 1947. Only twenty-three out of hundreds of such criminals were charged with "murders, tortures, and other atrocities committed in the name of medical science [during which] hundreds of thousands were slaughtered outright or died in the course of the tortures to which they were subjected." Seven of the defendants were sentenced to death and hanged, others received long prison terms.[11]

The rank and file of the SS were filled with middle-class businessmen, students, teachers, ex-officers, police, and civil service officials. A large number of enthusiastic Hitler Youths volunteered for the SS, eager to serve the Fuehrer and the

---

* During the Nuremberg Trials the defense counsel for the SS established the fact that the Roman Catholic Archbishop Groeber of Freiburg, a highly respected member of the hierarchy, had joined the SS (Bernstein, *Final Judgment,* p. 47).

glorious future of the Fatherland. There were misguided idealists, sadists, convicted criminals, and normal small-town burghers. The bulk was made up of the riffraff recruited from every corner of Germany and Europe.

One million members of this criminal organization are today scattered throughout Germany, many of them in public offices as administrators, judges, police officials, and burgher-masters; others are busy as doctors, dentists, resort directors, hotel managers, and headwaiters. These men do not look like monsters. You will find them as pleasant travel companions in trains and airplanes, and you will meet them as solid businessmen in the offices of industrial firms and in banking institutions.

The important fact is that the Bonn authorities have done nothing to prevent the SS from becoming active again. To-day every German city and town has a local SS group that has weekly meetings and larger regional rallies every few months. The SS organization calls itself HIAG, the German abbrevia-tion for "mutual assistance." Foreign correspondents have re-ported that at all HIAG meetings Nazi propaganda is car-ried on under pretense of giving assistance to veterans and their families.

Of all the neo-Nazi movements none has remotely ap-proached the vigor, drive, and fanaticism of the old SS, hid-ing today behind the HIAG label. In 1950, when Washing-ton showed its eagerness to create a new German army of 500,000 men, the SS, together with the old Wehrmacht of-ficers, started an all-out campaign for the immediate release of all war criminals. It was a superbly organized blackmail action, enjoying wide support from the public, from all parties, and carried toward success by Dr. Adenauer's astute maneuverings.

The Chancellor suggested an inconspicuous way to solve the whole problem with "parole," "sick leave," and other roundabout methods. The more the U. S. High Commission in Germany showed leniency, however, the stronger the pressure became: either "all so-called war criminals are released or there will be no German army." American diplomats followed Dr. Adenauer's plan to feed the nationalistic monster piecemeal. Every few days we quietly released one or two more from prison—the Krupps, the I. G. Farben directors, and dozens of former Wehrmacht Generals. On friendly advice from Washington, the British and French, extremely reluctant, had to follow suit. When the supply dried up, there remained behind bars only the SS, the mass murderers from Dachau, Belsen, and Buchenwald, and the toughs from the Waffen SS who had massacred American, British, and Canadian prisoners of war. This put High Commissioner John McCloy in a most embarrassing position. He had carefully checked the records of the SS mass murders, and he had also observed the reaction of the German public which turned "squalid butchers into patriots and martyrs." [12]

In the spring of 1952 the president of the German Soldiers' Federation, ex-General Hans Friesner, praised the "comrades from the Waffen SS" and demanded that "all of those still in prison must be released." The New York *Times* of January 5, 1952, reported from Bonn that the federal government found it "impossible to recruit desirable officers for the West German military contingents unless a substantial number of war criminals are released from Allied jails." On August 16, 1952, the *Frankfurter Allgemeine Zeitung* noted that "the discussion about the war criminals gains more and more momentum." Large sections of the German press, stirred by the propaganda in the SS paper, *Wiking-Ruf*, and the *Deutsche Soldaten Zeitung*, launched an attack against the Allies. Roosevelt and Churchill were almost daily branded as the real war criminals. Bundestag member Dr. Erich Mende, an influential politician in the Adenauer coalition, demanded the ultimate "release of all war criminals . . . whose acts were in no way different from those committed by the U.N. troops in Korea." The *Deutsche Soldaten Zeitung* heaped abuse on the Allies and emphatically denied that the victors had any right to pass judgment on the vanquished. On August 14, 1952, the *Soldaten Zeitung* stated: "Only we Germans possess the highest moral right to argue these matters, without any interference from the outside."

The meaning of the drive to "restore the German honor" was clear: the reputation of the Nazi criminals had to be restored by proclaiming loudly what an idealistic and high-spirited organization the SS was, dedicated "to defend Europe and the world against Bolshevism" and to "take care of the scum of the earth," the Jews, Communists, and other "undesirable elements." Why the constant criticism of the SS, the finest fighting force the world had ever seen? Never mind what happened during the war—any war is rough and ugly. Look at the British, "who invented the concentration camps during the Boer war," the French in Indochina and North Africa, and the "atrocities committed by Americans in Korea."

The propaganda offensive aimed first at brain-washing its people into believing that no war crime had ever been committed and that the Nuremberg Trials had been a hoax. The second objective was to force the Allies to ignore their own judicial position created at Nuremberg. Once this was accomplished the Germans would gain an important base from which they could launch a broad offensive against the "real" war criminals.

The story in brief is that the Western powers yielded on every point, that a shameful mockery was made of justice, and that the record of history was turned upside down. The *Deutsche Soldaten Zeitung* of August 28, 1952, pointed to the logic of the case: "If the Allied authorities during the last few years have been constantly freeing prisoners or reducing the sentences against former German soldiers, it is but their clear admission that they regard the former sentences as untenable." In other words, if the Allies felt that they had to show clemency, it proved that the trials and consequent sentences had only been evidences of revenge.

When Dr. Adenauer first visited the United States in the spring of 1953, he insisted on a speedy re-examination of all sentences and pointed to "the strong pressure at home." It was a few weeks later that he visited the war criminals at Werl and made his plea for "the poor devils of war criminals." Here again the Chancellor proved his genius for statecraft. In order to ease the embarrassment of the U. S. High Commissioner and the State Department, Dr. Adenauer suggested the formation of a review board, with three German members sitting in and having equal voice in making recommendations. The whole procedure was to be shrouded in secrecy, and it was decided that the names of those released should not be revealed to the public. In this way the last few hundred "poor devils," those SS mass killers and sadists, were quietly set free within two or three years.

One of the esteemed Nazi alumni is General Curt Meyer, "Panzer" Meyer, who once had commanded the Hitler Youth division of the SS. During the Normandy fighting his SS troops had savagely executed Canadian prisoners of war. On the basis of ample evidence, Panzer Meyer was sentenced to death by a Canadian military court. His sentence later commuted to life imprisonment, he was released in 1954 and welcomed as a hero in Germany. Soon thereafter Meyer was installed as chief of HIAG. Since his release from prison, Panzer Meyer has worked hard to keep the old SS spirit alive. His speeches are undisguised Nazi propaganda in which he exhorts his audiences to work for the resurrection of "our holy German Reich." He misses no opportunity to lambaste the Allies for their "brutal policy, which stands without parallel among civilized nations." [13]

Another illuminating case is that of Sepp Dietrich, the organizer of the Fuehrer's bodyguard. Dietrich carried out

Hitler's personal murder assignments, such as the assassination of Roehm in 1934, for which Hitler promoted him to the rank of SS General.* Sepp Dietrich was in charge of the liquidation of the Jewish population in the city of Kharkov. During the Battle of the Bulge his troops committed the Malmédy massacre, killing more than 600 military and civilian prisoners, among them 115 American G.I.s. He was sentenced to death, and the sentence was later commuted to life imprisonment. In 1955 he was one of the last "poor devils" quietly released from prison and greeted by the Bonn government with the homecoming pay of 6,000 marks. When his release became known in the United States, the New York *Post* of October 28, 1955, remarked sarcastically: "We are in the process of trying to liquidate all German memories of that international unpleasantness known as World War II."

Belatedly it was recognized that Washington's policy of leniency was a bad mistake. Angry protests came from U.S. veterans' organizations, from large Jewish groups, and from papers in France and Britain. The *New Statesman and Nation* of April 3, 1954, stated the essence of the case when it emphasized that it was Bonn's policy to bring the Western powers to the point where they must "cease to treat the leaders of the Wehrmacht as war criminals." The editorial described Bonn's strategy: "The concept of German war crimes must be expunged from the historical records. . . . To Germans, and particularly Army officers and civil servants, this issue of German honor is all-important."

There is no doubt that by restoring the German honor we have also restored the honor of the SS. By giving in to the

---

* Ernst Roehm was chief of Hitler's Brown-Shirt army (SA), whose noisy street brawls terrorized the Weimar Republic and finally brought Hitler to power. The assassination of Roehm and a few hundred other Brown-Shirt leaders broke the back of the SA and opened the way for Himmler and the SS to become the Praetorian Guard of the Nazi party.

German demand that we release all war criminals, we have expunged, at least in German eyes, all war crimes, including those committed by the SS. The implications of this policy are far-reaching. The German people today feel free of any guilt. What remains to be discussed, they believe, are only the real war crimes, those committed by the Allies.*

What is really disturbing is the attitude of the German people. The public has completely swallowed the propaganda slogans of the SS. In a dispatch from Bonn, the New York *Times* reported on November 26, 1954: "A large proportion, and possibly a majority of the German people, and members of the Bundestag, do not accept the doctrine of German war guilt."

It is a long way from the Nuremberg War Crime Trials to the "restoration of the German honor." In 1946, under the impact of the evidence, at least one of the leading Nazi criminals repented in open court. It was Hans Frank, the oppressor of Poland, who answered the question "Have you ever participated in the destruction of Jewry?" with the following significant words:

We have fought against Jewry . . . and we have allowed ourselves to make utterances—and my own diary has become a witness against me—utterances which are terrible. It is my duty— my only duty—therefore to answer your question with "Yes." A thousand years will pass and this guilt of Germany will still not be erased.

Postwar events have proved Hans Frank grossly in error. Only five years were required to erase the guilt and to pervert the truth. "There never was a German war crime," shout the neo-Nazi propagandists. The forty-two volumes of trial records, the testimony, and the tons of incriminating Ger-

---

* Several books and thousands of articles have been published in Germany about "Allied war crimes," about the "Nuremberg crime," and about Roosevelt as a war criminal.

man documents simply do not exist. Today the SS is marching again. Ten years of skillful propaganda have created a
new legend: The SS was not the terror of Europe but the
"heroic defender of Western civilization."

9 *Old Soldiers Never Die . . .*

A few years ago the following story was reported in the German press. An ex-Wehrmacht General, sentenced by the Soviets as a war criminal, was released after twelve years of captivity. When he arrived in the West German reception camp of Friedland, he was met by a Colonel who had once served on his staff. After an exuberant reunion they settled down in a quiet corner to reminisce. The General wanted to know how some of the other senior officers had fared after the great collapse.

"How did Admiral Doenitz make out?" was his first question.

The Colonel stared in amazement. "Doenitz? He is serving in Spandau!"

"In Spandau? What is the Admiral doing in Spandau?"

"Don't you know that Doenitz is doing time in the Spandau prison? He got ten years as a so-called war criminal!"

"Oh yes! Of course, of course. They sent him to prison. But what happened to Rommel's Chief of Staff, that brainy General Hans Speidel?"

"Speidel is sitting in Paris." *

"So he is doing time in Paris! How many years did he get?"

"No! He is not in prison! Speidel is serving as the top commander of the ground forces of NATO!"

"Oh, he is with NATO—hmm, with NATO! But what happened to that daredevil of the SS, that young General—what was his name—Meyer? Panzer Meyer?"

"Panzer Meyer came back from Canada last year."

"Serving with the NATO forces there?"

"No! Not with NATO! He was doing time in a Canadian prison."

"Oh, doing time in prison! Poor chap! But what happened to our last Chief of Operation, General Heusinger?"

"Er sitzt in Bonn—he is sitting in Bonn."

"You mean doing time in prison?"

"No, no! He is the top General in the Ministry of Defense."

There was a moment of puzzled silence. Then the General slowly rose and began to walk away.

"Where are you going?" shouted the Colonel.

"Looking for an insane asylum," answered the thoroughly bewildered General. He added: "If this makes sense, then either the world is crazy or I am."

The story of the return of the General illustrates the mood of utter confusion prevalent among the great majority of Wehrmacht officers in the postwar years. Some Generals were behind bars, denounced as war criminals. Others had been placed in commanding positions and were honored as defenders of Western civilization. Had not every one of them participated in the same crime, first under the Kaiser, then under Hitler? Twice in a lifetime they had tried to conquer the world. Armed with the world's mightiest steamroller,

---

* The German colloquialism *er sitzt* has a double meaning: "he is doing time" and "he is sitting pretty."

they won great battles, and each time early victories made them heady. Yet in the end they suffered humiliating defeat.

In 1945 they knew they were doomed. They had all been accessories to a gigantic crime of unprovoked aggression, wholesale looting, and unbelievable mass murder. They had shaped the Wehrmacht as an instrument to conquer countries and continents, with but one objective: to create German Lebensraum. They were the brains behind Prussia's military machine, molded by a century-old tradition. Their gods were Frederick the Great, Scharnhorst, Clausewitz, and Bismarck. They had been steeped in the religion of "Might is Right" and "Deutschland ueber Alles." Long before Hitler came on the scene they had worshipped General Count von Haeseler, who declared in a speech in 1893: "It is necessary that our civilization build its temple on mountains of corpses, on an ocean of tears and on the death cries of men without number."

A few years later the Pan-German paper *Grenzbote* (No. 48, 1896) stated in an editorial: "We teach that if the welfare of our Fatherland should require conquest, subjugation, dispossession, extermination of foreign nations, we must not be deterred by Christian or humanitarian qualms."

In July 1900 Emperor William II told his troops assigned to fight the Boxer Rebellion in China that they should behave like Huns: "I shall take vengeance, the like of which the history of the world has never recorded. . . . I command you not to give quarter, not to take prisoners, and to kill every enemy. . . . Following the example of Attila and his Huns, I shall spread terror in East Asia that will be remembered even after a thousand years."

Hitler brought nothing new to the Germans. When Otto Richard Tannenberg published his famous book *Gross Deutschland* in 1911, he proclaimed: "War must leave nothing to the vanquished but their eyes to weep with. Modesty on our part would be pure madness."

In 1914 the Kaiser wrote Emperor Franz Joseph: ". . . everything must be put to fire and blood. The throats of men and women, children, and the aged must be cut and not a tree nor house left standing."

Respected German professors, politicians, pastors, and Generals wrote scores of books and articles proclaiming that "the name 'barbarian' is a badge of honor for the German Soldier."* The official organ of the General Staff, *Deutsche Wehr,* predicted on June 13, 1935, that the coming war would be "full of indescribable atrocities":

In such a war there will no longer be any victors or vanquished, but only survivors and those whose names are stricken from the list of nations. . . . The elite lie torn to pieces and poisoned on the battlefields. The survivors, a mob without a leader, demoralized, broken in body and mind by unspeakable horror and suffering, by terror without end, are at the complete mercy of the victor.

Only a few years later the German General Staff executed this program to the letter. Millions of Jews were exterminated, and the Poles, Czechs, and even the Russians, although by far not yet conquered, were "stricken from the list of nations." † For tactical reasons, other European countries were treated a little differently, but they were also at the "complete mercy of the victor."

After the war a number of German Field Marshals and hundreds of high-ranking Wehrmacht officers were found implicated in countless war crimes. Their signed orders

---

* The foregoing were selected from hundreds of similar quotations published by the author in the booklet *Know Your Enemy* (New York, 1944).

† The militarists were assisted in their schemes by the diplomats and legal experts. The Ribbentrop-controlled *Monatshefte fuer Auswaertige Politik* of September 1941 proclaimed prematurely the dissolution of the Soviet Union as a state and nation, "whereby all positive norms of international law have become void and inapplicable." The author of the article was Ribbentrop's legal expert, Dr. Wilhelm Grewe, a member of the Nazi party and later Bonn's ambassador to Washington.

proved that they were responsible for the mass shooting of civilians and prisoners of war, the burning of villages and towns, wholesale looting, and the deportation of millions to slave labor camps.

Among the prominent military figures whose cases won the most attention in Germany were Field Marshals Erich von Manstein and Albert Kesselring. Both had fair trials before British courts. Kesselring was sentenced to death (his sentence was later commuted) for having ordered the shooting of 335 hostages in the Ardeatina Grotta, near Rome, on March 24, 1944. Von Manstein was sentenced to eighteen years in prison for having ordered war crimes committed in Poland and Russia. Manstein's army command worked closely with SS Colonel Otto Ohlendorf, who was hung for the mass shooting of 90,000 Jews and Russians. One of von Manstein's corps commanders, General von Salmuth, dispatched 300 Wehrmacht soldiers with special instructions to assist Ohlendorf in the mass killing of thousands.[1]

There were some officers and soldiers whose consciences were aroused by the indescribable scenes of marauding and slaughter. To keep these men in line, von Manstein, on November 24, 1941, issued the following order to his troops:

The Jewish-Bolshevist system must be destroyed once and for all. It must never again infiltrate our European Lebensraum. Therefore, the German soldier is not only charged with destroying the military might of this system. He also acts as an agent of the idea of racial supremacy. . . . The soldier must show understanding for the necessity of severe revenge on Judaism, the spiritual carrier of the Bolshevist terror. This understanding is also essential in order to nip in the bud all uprisings, which are mainly instigated by Jews.

Similar orders were given by the other army commanders, such as Field Marshals Gerd von Rundstedt and Walter von Reichenau. The latter told his troops on October 10, 1941:

The soldier in the Eastern Territories is not merely a fighter according to the rules of the art of war but also the bearer of a ruthless national ideology . . . therefore the soldier must have understanding of the necessity of a severe but just revenge on subhuman Jewry.[2]

Thus the German army commanders indoctrinated their soldiers with the idea that the systematic extermination of "subhuman Jewry" was essential to achieve racial supremacy and to secure German Lebensraum. Yet it is indicative of the spirit prevailing in present-day Germany that the overwhelming majority of the people believe that officers like von Manstein, Reichenau, and Kesselring kept the German honor intact. *Times* correspondent Arthur J. Olsen reported from Germany that von Manstein is held in the highest esteem in the new Bundeswehr, where he is regarded as "the most prestigious German soldier who survived the war [and who] emerged in the soldier's view with honor intact." [3]

During the war the Allies had solemnly stipulated that it was their "inflexible purpose to destroy German militarism and Nazism and to insure that Germany will never again be able to disturb the peace of the world." At Potsdam in August 1945 they decided that "all war veterans' organizations and all other military and quasi-military organizations, together with all clubs and associations which serve to keep alive the military tradition in Germany, shall be completely and finally abolished in such a manner as permanently to prevent the revival of reorganization of German militarism and Nazism." In spite of this Allied resolution, some high SS and Wehrmacht officers in the POW camps soon began to form a closely knit secret organization, the so-called Bruderschaft (Brotherhood). This organization flourished even during the American occupation, laying the plans for a German comeback. The Bruderschaft became the focal point for a vast network of pro-Nazi activities in and outside of the

POW camps. Behind it was a well-financed underground, stretching all over Germany, with contacts in Italy, Spain, and Argentina. The Bruderschaft worked closely with another organization, the Kameraden Hilfswerk, especially designed for the legal defense and care of the war criminals.

During the first two years of the occupation, the Bruderschaft had to operate secretly. The inner circle, the Bruderrat, was made up of some top SS functionaries and important officers from the General Staff. Among the leaders were the former commander of the Panzer Gross Deutschland division, Lieutenant General Kurt von Manteuffel; a high SS officer, Alfred Franke-Grieksch, who had once served in Himmler's Reich's Security Office; the former leader of the Hitler Youth, Gottfried Griessmayer; the ex-Gauleiter Lauterbach, stationed in Italy and directing the external affairs of the Bruderschaft; and finally, the former Gauleiter Karl Kaufmann, a close link to Dr. Naumann and Dr. Achenbach.*

The question of German remilitarization came up as early as 1946, when Dr. Adenauer and the CDU politician Dr. Karl Spieker first made their suggestions for a European union based on an integrated European army. In the summer of 1948, Dr. Adenauer submitted to U.S. authorities a secret memorandum proposing the implementation for rearming twenty-five divisions. On July 30, 1948, the *U. S. News and World Report* carried the item: "U.S. military officials in Germany are talking in terms of a re-building of the German army as an offset to Russian strength in Europe." Yet there were great difficulties in the way of German rearmament. The French, the British, and the smaller European

* The detailed story of the background and the activities of the Bruderschaft was given in lengthy articles which appeared in the *National Zeitung* in Basle, February 22, 1950; *Wochen Zeitung* of Zurich, March 2, 1950; and *Stuttgarter Nachrichten*, March 1, 1950. In the U.S. an informative article, "What Is Behind the Bruderschaft of German Officers," was published in the magazine *Prevent World War III*, No. 35 (1950).

countries were in deadly fear of a revived militaristic Germany.* The outbreak of the Korean War (June 1950) brought a total change. The provisions which banned all military and veterans' organizations lost all their meaning and were no longer enforced. Western Germany was allowed by the Allies to set up its own General Staff, camouflaged under the name Blank Office. Supported by Bonn and tolerated by the United States, a nation-wide network was created to reactivate the experienced officers and the man power of the old Wehrmacht. The short period of 1950-51 must be marked as the time when Hitler's old officers, SS leaders, and party functionaries returned to positions of power and influence. With the eyes of the world directed toward the hectic events of the Korean conflict, and with cold war tensions mounting, the SS and Wehrmacht officers had an ideal smoke screen behind which to mobilize their forces. The political objective was a repeat performance of the alliance formed in 1930 between the Nazi party, the ultranationalists, and the Stahlhelm veterans, which two years later brought the downfall of the Weimar Republic.

The figure behind this plan was Dr. Werner Naumann, who in 1950 found the situation sufficiently safe to allow him to emerge from his hiding place. Commanding a vast pool of old party connections from the Propaganda Ministry, the SS, the bureaucracy, and the Wehrmacht, Naumann was in an excellent position to make things move and to give advice on strategy and tactics. Through his close association with the corporation lawyer Dr. Achenbach, he was able to mobilize the financial resources of the industrial royalists on Rhine and Ruhr. Naumann was the directing spirit behind almost every organization and neo-Nazi publication that sprang up between 1950 and 1951. When the British

---

* *U. S. News* of September 16, 1949: "Question of a German Army of 25 divisions, as privately urged by influential Germans, is to be postponed. It's too hot to handle now."

handed over the evidence on the Naumann plot to the Bonn authorities in 1953, the Minister of Justice, Dr. Lehr, declared that "Dr. Naumann had pulled the strings from behind and used every opportunity to exert his political influence over all veterans' organizations." [4]

In July 1951, thirty former Generals and Admirals gathered in Bonn for a two-day conference, at which the "question of German rearmament was discussed." [5] At that time, in addition to the SS HIAG, two other veterans' organizations had been founded. One was the Stahlhelm, an extreme nationalistic group; the other called itself the Deutscher Soldatenbund (Federation of German Soldiers), and immediately after its inception claimed a membership of 85,000. The spirit of both organizations was expressed in their selection of two convicted war criminals as honorary presidents. The Stahlhelm's choice was Field Marshal Kesselring, and the soldiers' federation selected former Admiral Erich Raeder, who at that time was serving his sentence in the Spandau prison.

More significant was the founding of numerous *Traditionsverbaende* representing former Wehrmacht divisions and special army groups, such as the Afrika Korps, the Navy League, and the paratroopers (known as the "Green Devils"). The ex-soldier organizations started off with noisy nationalistic rallies. A few months later the U. S. High Commissioner noted the emergence of an "increased number of extreme Rightist and ultranationalist organizations." He admitted that the highest-ranking officers of the Wehrmacht were back in politics, organizing the veterans and "stocking the merchandise of nationalism." The High Commissioner noted with deep concern that "even some federal Ministers appear as nationalistic as the extremists." [6]

Among the many neo-Nazi and militaristic periodicals which came to life with the revival of the Wehrmacht tradition, the *Deutsche Soldaten Zeitung* may be singled out for closer scrutiny. Founded in 1951 by men who had once served the Nazi party chiefly in the Propaganda Ministry, the *Soldaten Zeitung* soon became the leading mouthpiece for the most aggressive elements within the Rightist movement.* The *Deutsche Soldaten Zeitung* (hereafter referred to as *DSZ*) has constantly featured and supported the views of such blatant Nazi propagandists as the ex-Generals Remer and Ramcke, and Hitler's much-decorated air ace, Colonel Rudel.

The story of the *DSZ* provides an excellent illustration of the mind of the German militarist. On the basis of hundreds of *DSZ* editorials and articles, the following may be summarized: Although professing support for Europe and NATO defense, every article reveals that the *DSZ* envisions a Europe more like that once blueprinted by the Waffen SS. The columns of the paper do not contain a single repudiation of Hitler's regime, the Nazi doctrines, or the wanton aggressions against Germany's neighbors; nor is there an outright condemnation of the crimes committed by the SS and the Wehrmacht. Almost every issue is filled with articles defending the Nazi past, glorifying "Prussia's great soldierly tradition," and praising the "honor of the SS." The *DSZ* has relentlessly attacked the Nuremberg Trials as "revenge of the victors"; it appeared as the loudest voice in the chorus demanding the release of all war criminals; and it has branded Democrats and Social Democrats as "licensed 1945ers," "traitors," and "fellow travelers." As its political objective the *DSZ* has peddled the old cliché of a powerful

* Among the editors of the *Deutsche Soldaten Zeitung* during the past years were A. W. Uhlig and Dr. Hans Hagen, both former high officials in the Propaganda Ministry, and Dr. Wilhelm Spenler and Werner Strecker, both former SS officers. The present editor-in-chief is Erich Kernmeyer (alias Kern), the author of several best-selling books glorifying the Nazi past. Under Hitler, Kernmeyer was the leading press official in the Saar district. According to the *Frankfurter Rundschau* of April 10, 1953, these men all had close connections with Dr. Werner Naumann.

Reich, the return of the lost territories in the East, and even the *Anschluss* of the Sudetenland.[7]

In 1957 a court action instituted by the *DSZ* revealed that from the time the paper had been founded in 1951 it had been subsidized by regular monthly payments from the Bonn Press Office. When the federal officials tried to enforce changes in the editorial staff, an open rift occurred which resulted in the withdrawal of financial support. The legal wrangle confirmed what had long been known among German journalists, namely, "that a number of newspapers and periodicals in the Bonn Republic enjoyed the financial support of the Federal Press Office." [8] Subsequently it became known that not only the Press Office but the Defense Ministry as well had subsidized the *DSZ*.

The millions of marks spent secretly by the Bonn Press Office every year explain why in 1951 a large number of nationalistic and militaristic periodicals mushroomed into existence. The evidence shows that the same system of financing applied to the *DSZ* was used to keep dozens of other Rightist papers and organizations going.* Moreover, the close ties between the Defense Ministry and such papers as the *DSZ* included more than financial arrangements. Editor-in-chief Erich Kernmeyer once boasted: "There is no secret in the Defense Ministry of which we are not informed through our friends in the Ministry in less than twenty-four hours." [9] Today the ex-soldier organizations hold a place similar to that which the powerful Stahlhelm occupied in the Weimar Republic.

A foreigner visiting the larger German cities like Hamburg, Cologne, Duesseldorf, Frankfurt, or Munich would see no huge veterans' rallies or the type of neo-Nazi activities

---

* *Die Freiheit,* Mainz, December 20, 1952. The *Frankfurter Allgemeine* reported on January 15, 1954: "It has been established that West German veterans' organizations get their financial support from Bonn and from U.S. agencies."

described in this book. The larger urban areas usually have Social Democratic majorities among whom such nationalistic manifestations could easily provoke political incidents. But there are hundreds of smaller towns in West Germany where the Rightist elements rule with full sway. This is the reason that for ten years now the soldier associations have held both their national and weekend rallies in towns with a population between 20,000 and 80,000 people. The national rallies—*Traditionstreffen*—at which often 10,000, occasionally up to 30,000, veterans gather, are arranged many months in advance. The ex-soldiers arrive in cars, buses, and chartered trains (at reduced fares), and occupy the whole town. Quarters are secured in private homes, schools, and public buildings. On the basis of several hundred reports of such rallies, printed in the *DSZ* and other papers, let us see what goes on. There is the ritual of marching, singing, heel-clicking, and *"Sieg Heil!"* shouting. Bands of the Bundeswehr and Border Patrol provide the stirring martial tunes of old, happy days. Ex-Generals, wearing all their medals, deliver fiery speeches which usually run along the same endless groove: the "defamation of German soldiers has to be stopped"; the real war criminals are the Allies—remember the Morgenthau shame of 1945, remember our destroyed towns, remember Roosevelt and Yalta. There are other formulas: it is high time to reawaken "Prussia's great tradition"; Germany is the only reliable bulwark of Christian civilization; the lost territories must be returned to the Fatherland; we are behind a United Europe, for which "the German soldier has fought so heroically in World War II." The last is the cliché to which each General or Admiral adds a poetic touch of his own. Admiral Doenitz addressed 3,000 U-boat raiders and declared to frantic applause: "We must hand down the brave, self-sacrificing U-boat spirit to our children and grandchildren." [10] General Kurt Student, commander of the airborne invasion of Crete in 1941, drew prolonged cheers from his paratroopers when he claimed in 1959: "The German soldier has regained his nimbus; today we have again become a factor in world politics." [11]

Every weekend in several provincial German towns so-called *Grosstreffen* are staged—reunions of one or another Panzer division, SS formation, the Marine Bund, or the Afrika Korps. Such a reunion is usually greeted by a cabinet member of the Bund or the Laender, by a General of the Defense Ministry, by the mayor of the town, and other officials. As an example let us take the Afrika Korps rally in September 1958 in Karlsruhe, which was addressed by the Adenauer cabinet member Dr. Lindrath, where 15,000 cheering members "vowed to uphold the immortal values of the German soldier, and to keep this tradition alive in the Bundeswehr." [12] A reunion of the paratroopers in Wuerzburg received particular attention when 5,000 of the "Green Devils" greeted war criminal Field Marshal Kesselring with a thunderous ovation, carried him on their shoulders to the platform.[13]

Ten years of SS and ex-soldier meetings have left their mark on West Germany. Observers have frequently stated that neo-Nazism has taken firm hold of the small towns and of the countryside. This is exactly what happened during the twenties. Hitler had his headquarters in Munich (where he was ridiculed), while his storm troopers and the Stahlhelm conquered the smaller towns and villages. In 1933 the large anti-Nazi cities, with the bulk of liberals and workers, fell like ripe apples. There is danger that this strategy may work again.

As early as September 11, 1952, the *DSZ* printed a front-page banner headline: "Period of defamation a thing of the past." The subheading declared that the "Soldaten *Treffen* are festive hours for population and ex-soldiers." The article proudly boasted that the meetings of SS divisions such as the Herman Goering, Das Reich, and others had become completely successful, because it was no longer necessary for SS men to meet secretly or for the people to hide their true feelings. "In every town," wrote the *DSZ*, "the people provide quarters, participate in the celebration and give us fullest recognition."

For those in the small towns who were opposed to Nazism and militarism it was wiser to keep silent. Why risk martyrdom against the concerted strength of the Herr Landrat (administrative chief of the district), the mayor of the town, the owners of the plant, the banker, the judge, the police chief, often the pastor, the teacher, and all others of status and influence? Behind them, on the local level, were the militarists, the Stahlhelm, the storm troopers, and the Gestapo. It is this array of forces, this formidable power in the provinces which will decide the future of democracy in the Bonn Republic.

In the early fifties, after the Ramckes, Remers, and Rudels had done their work, the *Kalte Machtergreifung*—seizure of power—had become an accomplished fact, at least in the small towns and in the countryside. It was not a new revolution that had occurred, but in many places the local authority had simply slipped into the hands of old Nazis. At that time, labor leaders and democrats lamented that the "brown rats had come out of their holes everywhere." Let us take as an illustration the "Battle of Goslar," where the cause of democracy suffered a severe defeat.

In 1955 the Stahlhelm selected the historic town of Goslar (population 28,000) for a *Treffen,* at which Field Marshal Kesselring was scheduled as the main speaker. The announcement aroused unpleasant memories among the democratic elements of the town. Some townspeople protested. They asked the government of the State of Lower Saxony, and Dr. Adenauer in Bonn, not to allow the scheduled rally. Their petition was supported by the local and regional labor unions. Apart from the fact that Kesselring had been sentenced to death as a war criminal (the sentence was later commuted to eighteen years' imprisonment), the argument was put forth that a noisy, nationalistic rally near the border of the East German Zone could easily be regarded as a provocation. Neither Dr. Adenauer nor his Interior Minister (head of the police), ex-Nazi Dr. Schaefer, thought it necessary to answer the protests of the uneasy democrats.

When the authorities refused to act, the labor leaders called up 6,000 union members for a protest demonstration in the nearby town of Bad Harzburg. Thereupon, on the "highest orders," 1,100 men of a heavily armed police formation were dispatched to Goslar for the protection of Kesselring and his Stahlhelm.[14]

Dozens of newspaper accounts described the Goslar meeting. Special police squads clubbed down a number of democratic hecklers who dared to shout "Kesselring go!" The onlookers and hecklers were brutally driven off, and the town was practically under martial law. Many demonstrators were beaten and more than a hundred were arrested. Photos showed that the Stahlhelm had its own uniformed goon squad, adorned with swastikas and armed with sticks. The *Stuttgarter Nachrichten* reported that a press photographer who tried to take Kesselring's picture was almost manhandled by a Stahlhelm officer: "Take your hat off when you approach our Bundesleader! And don't give us that stupid look, or you'll get your face slapped left and right."

There was indignation throughout the democratic press. A Munich newspaperman wrote the following comment:

In recent days, I viewed several dozen photographs taken at that Stahlhelm rally staged a week ago at Goslar. It is really horrifying what went on there. We have seen these pictures once before: Soon after the First World War when the nationalistic Right went all-out to attack the Weimar Republic. Today, as it was then, this spirit is again organized by officers who receive high pensions from the state.

They marched in Goslar and showed off their medals with the swastika. They wore field-gray uniforms and high riding boots. A few even appeared in steel helmets. . . . The pictures show the police standing around in droves. Wearing shakos with chin-straps down, the police were alerted to protect the Stahlhelm. Rough and tough as always, they surged forward to attack the protesting crowd. Many hecklers were beaten and many were arrested. It was said that, on the highest orders, the police had to clear a platform for Bundesleader Kesselring. Thus we have come a long way: The swastika is protected by the police and the resistors are put behind bars! Clear enough? [15]

Indeed, Goslar brought home its lesson to many a German democrat: The battle for freedom was almost lost. Today a large part of rural Germany is *vom Feinde besetzt*—occupied by the (fascist) enemy. Ever since the Goslar incident the Social Democrats and unions have seldom dared to challenge another ex-soldier meeting. In recent years the soldier associations have had huge reunions in larger cities like Karlsruhe and Wuerzburg. How soon will they appear in Frankfurt, Hamburg, and Munich? Dr. James Bryant Conant has told us that the Nazis are "dead and buried." There is a voice in Goslar asking, *"Who* is dead and buried?"

10 *Ten Million Expellees and the Old Homeland*

Among the thousands of Germans who come to the United States each year, either as exchange students or as invited guests of our State Department, there is one visitor who has scored a unique success in this country. His name, strangely enough, has remained absolutely unknown to the average American. He is Dr. Walter Becher, a local politician from southern Germany, a member of the Bavarian Landtag, and a leader of the refugees from the Eastern territories. It should also be said that this German politician is an "old Nazi fighter."*

Dr. Becher's success story in the United States is truly amazing. During the early fifties, when he first came to Washington, he began to build for himself a formidable political machine. His scheme was very simple. If he could obtain the support of leading politicians in the United States, his

* According to information from the U. S. Document Center in Berlin, published in *Die Zeit,* Hamburg, August 8, 1957, Dr. Becher became a member of the Nazi party on December 12, 1931 (membership card 896-129). He later dropped out and re-entered the party on November 1, 1938. He was also a member of the Nazi Brown-Shirts, and he belonged to the National Socialist Student Bund.

prestige and stature would grow enormously at home and he could reap huge dividends not only in his own political bailiwick in Bavaria but in West Germany at large. With a little cleverness, and the help of the McCarthy faction in the United States, he could establish a nation-wide reputation as the foremost leader in the anti-Communist crusade. With this objective Dr. Becher approached those senators and congressmen from both sides of the aisle who were interested in the fight against the "Communist conspiracy," a realm in which the ex-Nazi introduced himself as an expert. His early contacts were with William Jenner and Joseph McCarthy in the Senate, and with such men as Francis E. Walter, B. Carroll Reece, Albert H. Bosch and Walter H. Judd in the House. Dr. Becher soon set up an effective lobby in Washington; he also made considerable headway on the political stage of West Germany.

At the same time, Dr. Becher's burning ambition and his ferocious attacks against political opponents have made him one of the most controversial figures in German public life. "Who is Dr. W. B.?" asked the headline of a four-column article in the news magazine *Der Spiegel*.[1] According to this source, Dr. Becher as a young man joined Konrad Henlein's Nazi-type party in the Sudetenland, which at that time was plotting with Hitler to topple Czechoslovakia's republic. In 1937, Dr. Becher became editor of the Nazi paper *Die Zeit* (no connection with *Die Zeit* of Hamburg), whose pages he filled with anti-Semitic attacks comparable to Julius Streicher's disreputable antics in the *Stuermer*. As editor, responsible for the section "Culture and Science," Dr. Becher demanded the ousting of all Jews from the state-controlled radio in Prague. In signed articles ("Dr. W. B.") he called the Jewish actors "Ghetto hams," spoke contemptuously of "Jewish intellectual bedbugs," and ridiculed "fat Jewish dowagers."

During the Second World War Dr. Becher served the

Propaganda Ministry and the Wehrmacht as a war correspondent. The German collapse found him stranded in Bavaria,
where he joined the neo-Nazi Deutsche Gemeinschaft party
and was elected to the Bavarian Landtag. In the early fifties
he switched to the All-German Bloc, whose political make-
up differs not too much from the neo-Nazis'. The All-German
Bloc draws its support chiefly from the millions of refugees
who fled from the Sudetenland and the detached territories
east of the Oder-Neisse River.

With inflammatory speeches in the Landtag, Dr. Becher
kept his name constantly in the headlines. He has waged a
running battle against the state-owned Bavarian radio network and some of the largest newspapers, which he has
accused of being manipulated by "pro-Moscow conspirators."
In sweeping attacks he has called the Bavarian radio a "res-
ervoir of U. S.-licensed re-educators" and has asked for the
dismissal of its leading officials.[2] In his first "reform bill" introduced in the Landtag, Dr. Becher showed his old anti-
Semitic bias when he suggested that the seat held by the
Jewish congregation should be eliminated from the thirty-six-
man Advisory Council.

For many years now Dr. Becher has played a prominent
role in the affairs of the refugees and expellees. Besides
being the chairman of the All-German Bloc in the Bavarian
Landtag, he serves as the general secretary of the Sudetendeutsche Association. His influence rests chiefly on the fact
that he has solicited strong political support for the refugee
cause from both major parties in Washington. There is
wide belief in Germany that without Dr. Becher's close
contacts in America, especially those in the State Department and Congress, chances for a return to the old homelands might soon diminish.

Among the 53,000,000 people in West Germany, 10,000,000
are refugees who either fled from the Sudetenland or were
expelled after the war from the territories taken over by

Poland and other Eastern countries. These refugees, although for several years now completely integrated into West Germany's bustling economic life, have never reconciled themselves to the territorial decisions made by the victors at Yalta and Potsdam.*

In countless statements before the Bundestag and on other occasions, the Adenauer government has made it sufficiently clear that Germany "cannot accept the Oder-Neisse line as the present or future German frontier." [3] Spokesmen for the Bonn government have frequently demanded that the German Reich must be restored to its borders of 1937. Some cabinet members, such as Refugee Minister Oberlaender and Transport Minister Seebohm, have even asked for the annexation of the Sudetenland, just as Hitler did in 1938. Each year Dr. Adenauer's ministers speak before huge rallies of refugees, assuring them that sooner or later they will return to their homelands. They kindle hopes that the "lost provinces" will some day again become part of a German Reich.

The decisions of Yalta and Potsdam have been branded by the refugee leaders and their press as the "greatest crime in history." However, these Nazis and nationalists keep silent about the crimes committed by large groups of the *Volksdeutsche,* the ethnic Germans who, as citizens of Poland and Czechoslovakia, acted disloyally toward their countries and conspired with Hitler in favor of a Gross Deutschland. Take as an example the events in Czechoslovakia during the

---

* In the Potsdam Agreement of August 1945 the Allies stipulated that the territories east of the Oder-Neisse line be put "under the administration of the Polish state," pending "final demarcation" in a peace treaty, and that the "transfer to Germany of German populations or elements thereof, remaining in Poland, Czechoslovakia and Hungary, will have to be undertaken." Earlier, after the Yalta conference, President Roosevelt and Prime Minister Churchill stated that Poland "will be compensated with a large slice of German territory," pointing clearly to an irrevocable cession of Germany's Eastern provinces.

thirties. The 3,000,000 Sudeten Germans lived in a truly advanced democratic country and enjoyed the same political, cultural, and social freedoms as all the other citizens of Czechoslovakia. Yet 92 percent of them rallied behind Hitler, embarked on a policy of treason, and voted *"Ein Volk, ein Reich, ein Fuehrer."* According to captured German documents, in 1937 Hitler decided that Czechoslovakia "must be wiped off the map." A year later, at the height of the crisis, the Sudeten Germans revolted, helping to undermine the republic, and on March 15, 1939, Hitler occupied Prague and made the tiny remainder a German "protectorate." Subsequently the Sudeten Germans participated in the "Germanization" of the country by driving the Czechs (their neighbors for centuries) from their homes and by killing the Slavic intelligentsia by the thousands. Only recently a conservative Catholic paper in Austria printed the number of death sentences handed down in Prague and Bruenn alone from June 8 to June 21, 1942. Altogether 340 teachers, lawyers, officials, and Catholic priests were executed in the short span of two weeks, not counting the hundreds who found violent death in the Gestapo torture chambers and in the concentration camps. From 1939 to 1945 several hundred thousand Czechs were murdered by the SS.[4] It was for these crimes that the Sudeten Germans, the chief perpetrators of the terror regime, were expelled from the soil of Czechoslovakia.[5]

Another example is the Free City of Danzig, which Hitler used as a pretext to start World War II. Originally a Slavic settlement, Danzig was given to Prussia during the second partition of Poland in 1793. After 1918 the huge port on the Baltic sea became an independent "Free City" state, administered by the League of Nations. Germans and Poles lived side by side under democratic rule. In 1939 Hitler demanded another *Anschluss.* According to the *Frankfurter Allgemeine Zeitung* of August 29, 1959, everything was fixed for that

long-expected *Tag*. Here are a few facts given by the German
paper. The German cruiser *Schleswig-Holstein,* sent by
Hitler on a "visit of friendship" to participate in the city's
flower festival, was anchored in the Danzig harbor. Early
on the morning of September 1, 1939, tens of thousands of
Hitlerite Danzigers crowded the roofs to watch the harbor
with field glasses for a special kind of "flower festival." At
precisely 4:45 A.M., without a declaration of war, the *Schleswig-Holstein* opened up with a barrage from her heavy 28-
centimeter guns, pounding the nearby fortifications of the
Polish peninsula Westerplatte. At the same time, everywhere in the city the Germans arrested their Polish neighbors. The victims—men, women, and children—were taken
out of their beds, beaten mercilessly in the streets, and
rounded up by a quickly organized "emergency SS." The
entire police force in Danzig "changed into two Panzer
Grenadier regiments overnight" and started to attack every
official Polish building with its tanks. Nazi Gauleiter Albert Forster proclaimed the *Anschluss* to the Reich, and the
High Commissioner of the League of Nations, the Swiss
Jakob Burckhardt, had to leave the city forthwith. All Polish
schools and institutions were closed and the Polish population was driven out or shipped to a hastily set up concentration camp.

The "flower festival" was the opening of World War II.
A few days later Adolf Hitler, the liberator, had a jubilant
reception in Danzig such as "no King or Kaiser ever had
before him."

During World War II the Polish Government in Exile
(non-Communist) published a great deal of information
about the terror and the atrocities committed by the Wehrmacht and the SS in close coöperation with the *Volksdeutsche.*
The latter, of course, had the most intimate knowledge of
the Polish country and people and had been engaged long
before the war in considerable fifth-column activities for the

Reich. Like the Germans in Danzig, the huge majority of the *Volksdeutsche* had been fanatical followers of Hitler. They could hardly wait for the day when they received orders to make the Polish land *Polenrein*—free of Poles. A few days before the war, Hitler had given the green light for ruthless mass murder. He told his commanding Generals:

I have given orders to my Totenkopf formations [Death's-Head SS], for the time being applicable only in the East, to bring unmerciful and pitiless death to every man, woman and child of the Polish race.*

Thus Poland was "stricken from the list of nations," and the Polish inhabitants were exterminated by the millions. Gauleiter Forster announced on November 26, 1939: "I have received orders to Germanize these provinces in the shortest possible time. . . . In a few years everything that can in any way be reminiscent of Poland will have disappeared."

According to a report by the Polish Government in Exile, the Germans, "with the usual brutal vulgarity showed their mad hatred for everything Polish." [6] As in Czechoslovakia, the Polish intelligentsia—the teachers, officials, officers, aristocrats, and priests—were slaughtered by the tens of thousands. The *Volksdeutsche,* knowing every district and locality, furnished the lists of victims and assisted the Gestapo in carrying out the initial purge. During the first few months, 12,000,000 Poles were driven from their homes and farms. All property was confiscated and passed into the hands of the German settlers. Millions of able-bodied men and women were shipped to slave labor camps either in Germany or in the conquered territories. Thousands of healthy young Polish girls were rounded up and sent to houses of prostitution in Germany or to military brothels behind the front.

* The order, quoted in the *Frankfurter Rundschau* of August 25, 1959, said in German: ". . . *unbarmherzig und mitleidlos in den Tod zu schicken.*"

The rest of "those unfortunate people were loaded into cattle cars and transported to the badly overcrowded General Government of Poland [the occupied rump state] where they were decimated by starvation and disease." [7]

Motivated by race hatred and the obsession for Lebensraum, the Germans killed not only Jews but Poles, Ukrainians, and Russians by the millions. According to official German figures, of the 55,000,000 victims of World War II, 35,000,000 noncombatants were killed in Eastern Europe alone as a "result of the effects of war and occupation." [8]

Large groups of Sudeten Germans and *Volksdeutsche* in Poland played a vital role in the Hitler holocaust. They filled the ranks of the SS and they fought fanatically to Germanize the Slavic lands. It was in the light of this record that the Allies decided at Yalta and Potsdam to set the Oder-Neisse line as a final stop to Germany's century-old *Drang nach Osten*—push to the East. Most Nazis had fled, and the rest of the plotters were sent home in order to end all further conspiracies. What else could the Allies have done? Had not the cry *"Heim ins Reich!"* vibrated throughout Europe in the heyday of National Socialism? When in 1945 fate caught up with the Sudeten Germans and the *Volksdeutsche,* they were simply sent "home to Germany."

Soon after the end of World War II, the Germans started to use the expellee question as a lever for a revision of the Yalta and Potsdam decision. Under the Allied occupation statute the refugees were not permitted to organize. Nevertheless they appeared in public as early as 1949 with a highly effective apparatus for mass propaganda: the refugee newspapers, among them the *Volksbote* in Munich and *Die Stimme der Vertriebenen* in Hamburg, began to agitate openly. There is little doubt that the expellees played an important part in the calculations of Dr. Naumann and his associates in Madrid. A secret circular letter issued in 1950 by the Nazi headquarters in Madrid stated:

The millions of expellees must be regarded as a valuable trump card in our policy toward the restoration of German power. . . . The expulsion of 10 million German racial comrades was a blessing for the Reich. The expellees strengthened the biological substance of our race, and from the beginning they became a valuable asset to our propaganda. The expellees, discontented with their fate, infused a strong political dynamism in our demands. Very soon we were able to drown out the noisy propaganda about German "crimes" with our counteraccusation about the heinous misdeeds committed against 10 million German racial comrades. . . . The distress of the refugees has created a common political ground among all Germans, regardless of political affiliation. The demand for the restitution of the stolen German territories keeps our political agitation alive. The militant elements among the refugees are working according to the best traditions of National Socialism, whereas the broad masses among the expellees are kept close together in well-disciplined homeland organizations. . . . The expulsion of millions of our racial comrades provides us with a heaven-sent opportunity to exacerbate the problem of the bleeding border and to hammer constantly for its revision.[9]

For years there has been a tremendous propaganda drive to bring the more than 10,000,000 refugees "back to their homelands." This campaign has been carried on with the full support of the Adenauer government. Bonn has nourished the hope among the Germans that through a "policy of strength" the lost territories in the East can be recovered. It was precisely this view which motivated the Adenauer government to pursue a policy of diplomatic non-recognition toward all East-European states. In 1952 and 1953, Dr. Adenauer and his assistants openly advocated a program of liberation. The day after his election victory in 1953, the Chancellor, in a fiery speech in Bonn, demanded the *Befreiung* of the territories in the East: "But instead of reunification, let us talk rather of liberation [*Befreiung*]— the liberation of our brethren in slavery in the East. That is our aim, and that we shall achieve, but only with outside help." [10]

A year before that, at a press interview in Washington, the Chancellor's principal diplomatic assistant, State Secretary Walter Hallstein, defined the area to be liberated as reaching "up to the Ural Mountains." At that time the Germans dreamed of a third power bloc (between America and the Soviet bloc) of 550,000,000 people, including a Slavic population of more than 200,000,000 now living within the Soviet bloc. The liberation concept had been freely and frequently discussed at that time in the *Rheinischer Merkur*. One of the Chancellor's stanchest supporters, Dr. Robert Ingrim, admonished the German politicians to discard the sterile concept of reunification and substitute for it a dynamic program of liberation. "The task is not reunification but the liberation of all that has been lost," stated Dr. Ingrim in a lead article.[11] There remained little doubt that Bonn's liberation program envisioned the use of all possible means. It was Hitler's *Drang nach Osten* all over again. Among the cities pinpointed for liberation by Dr. Ingrim were Warsaw, Prague, and Vienna.[12]

The unrestrained liberation propaganda of the early fifties created such unease in diplomatic quarters at Paris and London that Dr. Adenauer was soon compelled to renounce military force as a means to recover the lost territories. Since then the new formula in the Chancellor's statements concerning reunification and revision of the Oder-Neisse line has become "in peace and freedom." However, apart from the Chancellor's official position, there is a very different cast to the speeches by other cabinet members before the huge refugee rallies. These revisionist overtones have not contributed toward dispelling the fears in the Eastern capitals of a revengeful Pan-Germanism.

Being aware of the deep distrust in Warsaw and Prague, the expellee leaders now speak quite diplomatically of the peoples' "right to a homeland." They also claim the "right to self-determination" as advocated by Woodrow Wilson in 1917.* This, however, is viewed in the Eastern capitals as a legalistic veil to cover up the old aggressive plans.

Each year in the spring or early summer, the Sudeten Germans and the expellees from Silesia, East Prussia, and Pomerania come together in rallies 200,000 to 500,000 strong, organized in the best Hitler tradition. "It has become customary," wrote the New York *Herald Tribune* correspondent Gaston Coblentz, "that a minister of the Adenauer government addresses each of the larger meetings and gives assurances that the cause is never being forgotten." [13] According to the *Tribune* report, Dr. Adenauer, at a meeting of 250,000 refugees from Silesia, "praised the Silesians for keeping alive the memory of their homeland." At another meeting, before 500,000 Sudeten Germans at Munich, Transport Minister Hans-Christian Seebohm suggested that "not only the Sudeten but also Bohemia and Moravia, which form a large part of Czechoslovakia, should be linked to Germany in the future." Cabinet Minister Theodor Oberlaender once declared that the reconquest of the European East is a "German and European task." [14]

The leaders of the various Landsmannschaften show even less restraint in stating their revisionist viewpoints. Dr. Rudolf Lodgman von Auen, the spokesman for the 3,000,000 Sudeten Germans, said in a speech in 1957 that "the Allies should be prepared to use force to get these [Eastern] territories restored to Germany." [15] The refugee leaders have stated quite openly that the ill-reputed Munich pact, which led to the downfall of Czechoslovakia, "still has international validity," that the borders of the Reich are those of 1939 (including Austria, Danzig, and Memel), that the Reich has a mission in the future, and that the geographic map of

* The expellee "charter" of 1950 is based on the "right of self-determination," but its true aim is the re-establishment of a "Greater German Reich."

Eastern Europe will be changed as soon as West Germany is again established as a military factor in world affairs. It does not require great imagination to recognize that this type of irredentist propaganda, supported by millions of expellees, militarists, and ex-Nazis, does not dispel the profound distrust of future German plans which prevails today in Warsaw, Prague, Vienna, Budapest, Belgrade, Sofia, and Bucharest.

When, in May 1959, 300,000 Sudeten Germans gathered outside the German borders for the first time for a huge open-air rally in Vienna, bitter denunciations were heard from Prague, Warsaw, and Pankow. Even politicians in Vienna saw provocation in the meeting. According to the New York *Times* of May 16, 1959, the politicians voiced their "dismay and worry over possible political repercussions." A similar meeting of Germans expelled from the Danube basin, gathering in Salzburg, Austria, was sharply criticized in Belgrade. Deputy Prime Minister Colakovic, in a speech, condemned the "rekindling of fascist and reactionary activities in Austria and in the Bonn Republic." [16]

In June 1959 a four-day rally of 300,000 refugees from Silesia was held in Cologne. Dr. Adenauer again praised the expellees for keeping their homeland spirit alive. A resolution was adopted which branded the expulsion from the Eastern provinces "a crime," demanded the "right of the homeland," and put in a "claim for future reparations." [17] The newspaper *Die Welt* reported that there was an angry reaction in Warsaw to the new *Drang nach Osten*.

What makes the expellee activities more dangerous is the fact that the Bonn government has supported the refugee leaders in arousing the hopes of millions of expellees for a return to their homeland. Any politician who dares to come forward with a realistic view in regard to the *status quo* is immediately branded a traitor.

The core of the expellee leadership consists of former

Nazis and extreme nationalists, who have their headquarters in exclusive Rightist clubs such as the Deutsche Kreis 58 (founded by Dr. Walter Becher), the Abendlaendische Akademie, the Rettet die Freiheit committee, and similar organizations. The expellee leaders have included cabinet members of the Bund and Laender, such as Dr. Seebohm, Dr. Oberlaender, Dr. Waldemar Kraft, Frank Seiboth, and Walter Stain. Other influential leaders, besides Dr. Becher and Rudolf Lodgman von Auen were revealed not long ago by the *Sueddeutsche Zeitung:* Hans Schuetz, Adolf Asbach, Professor H. Raschhofer, Baron Manteufel-Scoegge, Dr. Alfred Gille, Hans Krueger, Baron Bolko von Richthofen, and dozens of former high Nazi officials.[18]

Serving as a respectable façade for the expellees are a few Social Democrats, the most prominent among whom is Bundestag member Wenzel Jaksch, whose extreme nationalist views often differ from those of his party, but very seldom from the Pan-German gospel.

The expellee organizations, frequently influenced by Nazi concepts, have used every opportunity to defend the worst war criminals. When the former SS leader Hermann Krumey, known as the "butcher of 400,000 Hungarian Jews," was arrested in 1957, the Sudetendeutsche Association publicly supported him. It was revealed that Krumey had been chairman of an expellee association for several years and that he had obtained a government loan which enabled him to build up a prosperous business.

The still prevailing Nazi ideas among the refugees, their often expressed contempt for democratic concepts, and their hopes for a territorial change in the East constitute a long-range danger to the political stability of Germany, and Europe as well. It is this situation that in recent years has caused serious concern in Western capitals. At the beginning of 1959 an article in the London *Times* urged Bonn to reappraise its Eastern policies.[19] The article took the

Adenauer government to task for "keeping alive the sentiments and hatreds" so frequently expressed by the expellees.
The paper suggested that Bonn should adopt a realistic
attitude and recognize the Oder-Neisse line. The Federal
Republic, it said, "hesitates to pay the price of defeat" for
World War II, but the balance of power has changed and
"a new colossus has risen in the East."

This criticism by the London paper which often reflects
the views of the British Foreign Office was resented in Germany. The advice to accept the *status quo* was called by the
refugee paper *Volksbote* "unfair" and "criminal." A peace
"built on gangster methods will not last," said the *Volksbote,*
and no German government would ever dare to give up Germany's "rightful claims." [20]

Two months later, in March 1959, General de Gaulle
stated at a press conference that the Oder-Neisse line is
Germany's definite Eastern border and should not be
changed. To which the Bonn government replied that "the
German borders are still those of December 30, 1937." [21]

The *Christian Science Monitor* has published a series of
articles giving a realistic appraisal of the Oder-Neisse question.[22] The *Monitor*'s expert on Eastern and Central European problems, Ernest S. Pisko, recalls the "ruthless policy
of Germanization, dating back to the Bismarck era, and
reaching its tragic climax under Hitler." Recognizing the
"steadily growing revisionist propaganda campaign [as a]
disturbing symptom," Mr. Pisko blames Ministers Oberlaender, Seebohm, Waldemar Kraft, and Linious Kather,
president of the League of Expelled Germans, as the chief
advocates of the idea "that the German frontiers of 1939
should be re-established." Evaluating the expellee propaganda circulating in the United States, Mr. Pisko exposes its
methods of "falsification of statistics," "biased quotations,"
and misrepresentation of facts. "The Poles," concludes Mr.
Pisko, "may have confidence in Dr. Adenauer, but they can-

not be sure of the turn West German foreign policy may take under his successors."

Under Western pressure, the Bonn Foreign Office, in the spring of 1959, decided to offer Poland and Czechoslovakia nonaggression pacts. This would have amounted to a tacit recognition of the present borders. Dr. Adenauer left it to Foreign Minister von Brentano to make public this unpopular diplomatic move. The announcement caused a storm of indignation among the refugees. The leaders of the expellee organizations registered vigorous protests with the Chancellor. Within the cabinet, Ministers Oberlaender, Seebohm, and Lemmer objected vehemently.[23] Dr. Adenauer was forced to yield, and the plan for the nonaggression pacts was dropped.

The Oder-Neisse question is generally regarded as a key issue in the East-West conflict. John Foster Dulles finally recognized that a settlement had to be made, and the Oder-Neisse line stabilized, to keep the world from stumbling into the atomic holocaust. Unfortunately, until now no official statement has come from Washington to clarify the U.S. position, and Washington is still the last hope of the expellee leadership.

In 1955, after Dr. Becher's initial successes in Washington, he decided to install a permanent expellee representative in Washington.[24] His choice was a former Nazi diplomat, Dr. Richard Sallet, who had once served Goebbels and Ribbentrop in the German Embassy there. Dr. Sallet was known as an "expert on American affairs." His expertness was verified by captured German documents which contained several hundred pages attesting that during the thirties he was instrumental in launching an anti-Semitic campaign. He was also involved in large-scale anti-American activities aimed at undermining the confidence of the American people in President Roosevelt.

In Washington, Dr. Sallet conducted an effective campaign of pity for the poor *Volksdeutsche* who would make peace in Europe and the world an impossibility if they were not brought back to their lost homelands. This was the old familiar threat of "chaos" that Hitler had used so effectively before the Munich pact.

Dr. Sallet concentrated his main efforts on establishing close ties with the State Department, Congress, and the American press. His public-relations work had excellent results. In 1957, Congressman Usher L. Burdick inserted in the *Congressional Record* one of Dr. Becher's articles advocating "a realistic policy of liberation," a "breaking off of all diplomatic and economic contacts with Communist regimes in the East," and an "economic blockade of the Soviet bloc." [25] On August 10, 1959, the *Volksbote* reported "more successes in the U. S. Congress." Within a few months, seven statements and articles by Dr. Becher, Rudolf Lodgman von Auen, and other expellee leaders had appeared in the *Congressional Record*.[26] Whenever Dr. Becher toured the United States, usually for several weeks at a time, conferences were arranged with high State Department officials, influential senators and congressmen, and journalists and radio commentators. Early in 1958 the *Volksbote* ran three successive articles about Dr. Becher's accomplishments in the United States. During that visit, the *Volksbote* stated, Dr. Becher had meetings with German-American leaders, "long talks with leading officials in the State Department," and many conferences with senators and representatives. He had also had his political views presented in "71 newspapers, and to 32,000,000 listeners over the Mutual Broadcasting Network." [27]

Each year dozens of senators and congressmen send messages to Dr. Becher, assuring him of their sympathy and support for the aims and aspirations of the Sudeten Germans. These messages are usually read to the crowds at the large rallies and are reprinted in the expellee press. The claim in the *Volksbote* that "our work is supported by more than 150 congressmen" might well be accurate. A cursory count of the signers of messages in less than a dozen *Volksbote* issues revealed the impressive number of more than ninety communications coming from 36 senators and 57 congressmen.* In addition, the *Volksbote* published letters and telegrams from former President Herbert Hoover, retired U. S. Generals such as del Valle, Willoughby, and Wedemeyer, and a number of politicians.

It is this backing that helps make the expellee associations, the leaders as well as the 3,000,000 members, absolutely unyielding to any proposed *modus vivendi*. At the beginning of the Geneva Conference (in the spring of 1959) the expellee leaders insisted that the Adenauer government stand firm in refusing to let the Western powers make any concessions to the Soviets. State Secretary Peter Nahm, Minister Oberlaender's representative, gave assurance to an expellee delegation that "in all future decisions the refugees will have the first and the last words." [28]

There is little doubt that State Department officials and U.S. legislators have entangled themselves quite deeply in the liberation scheme of a group of Nazi intriguers. It is very probable that the refugees would have settled down in their national environment long ago had they not received constant encouragement in their revisionist aspirations from

* The following senators sent messages to Dr. Becher: Homer E. Capehart, Karl E. Mundt, Olin D. Johnston, James Murray, William Proxmire, Warren G. Magnuson, Homer Ferguson, James Eastland, Prescott Bush, Arthur V. Watkins, Allen J. Ellender, Albert Gore, Leverett Saltonstall, W. Kerr Scott, Styles Bridges, Francis Case, Charles E. Potter, Pat McNamara, John M. Butler, Frank A. Barrett, William Knowland, George W. Malone, Andrew F. Schoeppel, William Langer, Strom Thurmond, Carl T. Curtis, Herman E. Talmadge, Robert C. Byrd, Thomas J. Dodd, Milton R. Young, Spessard L. Holland, Stuart Symington, Edward J. Thye, Wallace F. Bennett, Dennis Chavez, A. Willis Robertson. Among the representatives, the following names might be mentioned: Joseph R. Martin, Francis E. Walter, Albert H. Bosch, Speaker John McCormack, B. Carroll Reece, Usher L. Burdick, Walter H. Judd, John Taber, Harold H. Velde, Charles J. Kersten and Philip J. Philbin.

Washington. At a time when Europe is longing for stability, it would have been sound policy not to arouse ambitions which once before in our lifetime caused one of mankind's greatest tragedies.

11 *"Jews Should Be Exterminated Like Vermin"*

In May 1959 *Look* magazine published a story which—judging by the response of its readers—appalled thousands of Americans. The outspoken article, "Hitlerism in 1959," was written by *Look*'s European editor, Edward M. Korry.

What has become known as the "Koeppern case" is the story of a Jewish family who returned from Israel eager to begin a new life in a supposedly "New Germany." In 1958, Kurt Sumpf and his family moved into the small town of Koeppern, twenty miles outside of Frankfurt, where they invested in an established bakery and coffee shop. Their venture might have turned out quite successfully, except for one important factor. The *Look* story summed up the situation as follows: "Today the Sumpf family is ruined, their nerves shattered, their savings gone and their hopes crushed. Kurt has been shot at, his wife beaten and his son bullied. Their business is boycotted by Koeppern's 3,800 people. All this is traceable to one reason only: The Sumpfs are Jews."

Painstaking investigations by a German newspaperman and the *Look* editor uncovered the following picture. The ordeal of the Sumpf family started shortly after they had settled in Koeppern. The townspeople soon began to show their animosity and anti-Semitism. They called Sumpf a "Jewish pig" or a "dirty foreigner" whom the Nazis "had forgotten to put in the gas chambers." There was an obvious intent to drive the "undesirable Jew" out of town. When Sumpf declared that he would remain, some troublemakers resorted to physical violence. Kurt and his wife Margot were assaulted, and one day in early October, a bullet was sent through the window of the bakery, narrowly missing the proprietor. Instead of intervening, the local police contributed derisive comments which amused the hoodlums. The climax came in December, when a riot was staged and the state police had to be called to the scene. According to *Look,* the police again sympathized with the mob and a patrolman shouted to Sumpf: "Why don't you close this filthy joint?" Since he was unprotected by the authorities, Kurt Sumpf finally had to sell his business, and he eventually took a job as a taxi driver in Frankfurt.

The Koeppern story would have remained unrecorded had not a reporter of the *Frankfurter Rundschau* taken an interest in the case. Reporter Botho Kirsch at first tried to mediate in order to avoid "unfavorable publicity." It was only when he saw that the Sumpfs were refused protection by the mayor, the pastor, the school principal, and the local and state police that he proceeded with publication.[1] Then the Hessian Ministry of the Interior tried to hush up the case and to excuse the guilty policemen.

The publicity which the Koeppern case received inside Germany and abroad resulted in an investigation. Eleven persons were brought to trial, ranging in age from twenty-one to fifty-three, among them a policeman and a Bundeswehr soldier. The defendants were charged with having made anti-Semitic remarks, assaulting the Sumpfs, and having committed a breach of the peace. The Frankfurt court acquitted six of them "for lack of evidence," four received fines from seven to fifty dollars, and one was jailed for four months.

Anti-Semitic incidents like the Zind affair in Offenburg and the outburst in Koeppern cannot be dismissed as isolated cases. During 1958 the German papers reported numerous such flare-ups, some of them almost identical to the Koeppern case. The *Frankfurter Rundschau* of June 14, 1958, gave details about similar riots in Floersheim against the innkeeper Brauman, whose wife, a "half Jew," was called a "Jewish pig" and was threatened with death. The Braumans were regarded as "undesirable," and the police refused to give them protection.

Mr. Korry pointed out in *Look* that "for the past few months, it has been almost impossible to open a serious German newspaper without finding some reference to anti-Semitism." Local German law-enforcement officials, instead of making every effort to combat these occurrences of racial hatred with stern measures, were in most cases remiss in their duties and often were participants in the anti-Semitic persecution. Such involvement on the part of the authorities was true in the case of a Jewish writer and critic, Siegfried Einstein, who had made his home in Lampertheim, Hesse. Again, as in Offenburg and Koeppern, the "undesirable Jew" had to be driven out. Einstein was harassed and threatened every day, and at night the Nazis disturbed his sleep with the Horst Wessel song. The police and county authorities did nothing for his protection. On the contrary, old Nazis in official positions brought trumped-up charges against Einstein and he was sentenced in court for alleged libel.[2]

In February 1959 the New York *Times* reported from Bonn that another anti-Semitic incident had been instigated by a tax official and a former SS officer. Both men had used insulting remarks, and a criminal libel suit had been initiated by the respected Social Democratic Bundestag Deputy Jeanette Wolff (whose two daughters had been killed in a concentration camp and whose husband had been shot by the SS). According to the *Times* report, Frau Wolff stated in her complaint that "the tax official had said concentration camps were desirable and too few Jews had been killed in them. She also testified that the former SS leader had publicly threatened to use a riding whip in the same way as he said he had done before on naked Jewish women." [3]

In January 1959, four weeks before Dr. Adenauer announced that anti-Semitism had "disappeared," Germany was stirred by several other occurrences, each one as serious as the Koeppern case. In Frankfurt the State Prosecutor, Dr. Otto Schweinsberger, was suspended for anti-Semitic statements and discrimination against Jews.[4] In another case, several officials of a restitution court in Wiesbaden handling Jewish claims had made insulting remarks to the Jewish petitioners; they had deliberately sabotaged cases, and had amused themselves by staging office parties livened with anti-Semitic Nazi songs. The officials were dismissed under public pressure.[5]

On January 28, 1959, the New York *Daily News,* in a special dispatch from Berlin, reported one of the "worst anti-Semitic demonstrations since the war." Hoodlums, organized by a secret anti-Jewish underground, had staged disturbances during a play showing Nazi terrorism in the Warsaw ghetto. The demonstrators "threw stink bombs, shouted anti-Semitic slogans, and scuffled with the audience." The incident was not reported in the German press.

The official Press Department in Bonn, operating under Felix von Eckardt, has developed an elaborate system for stifling reports of such events. The Zind affair, the Koeppern case, and many other incidents were kept out of the press for months. How the system works was neatly shown by an editorial in the *Rheinischer Merkur,* which severely reprimanded the school authorities for having allowed the Zind case to become public. The paper stated "that the scandal and trial could have been avoided if the authorities had compelled Zind to make an apology and then would have given the teacher a job in another town." [6] This declaration would indicate that Bonn is not so much concerned with anti-Semitism as it is with the unfortunate exposures of its existence.

It has been reported that "the old Nazi teachers and professors have all returned to the schools and universities." [7] In January 1959 the Minister of Education in the State of Schleswig-Holstein suspended a junior college teacher, Otto Stielau, because he had made anti-Semitic remarks in connection with *The Diary of Anne Frank*.[8] In another case, the Jewish community in Berlin finally dropped charges against a high school teacher on the occasion of the Christian-Jewish brotherhood week. The teacher had lost his job because he had stated in a restaurant that "all Jews should have been gassed." [9]

Anti-Jewish outbursts had reached such proportions during 1958 that early in January 1959 the Central Jewish Council petitioned Chancellor Adenauer "to take immediate legal steps." Within a few days the Bonn government had hastily introduced a new law in the Bundestag which stipulated that expressions of hatred against racial or religious minorities would be punished with prison sentences of not less than three months. A week later the New York *Times* reported that the Adenauer government "was sharply attacked by Social Democrats in the Bundestag for its allegedly lax handling of Nazi and anti-Semitic offenses." [10]

An independent newspaper noted that "hardly a day goes by on which it is not possible to find dispatches about anti-Semitic incidents." [11] In March 1959 it was reported that "in Berlin alone, more than 20 criminal libel suits had been initiated, dealing with serious anti-Semitic outbursts." [12]

In Britain, America, and elsewhere dispatches from Bonn reported "an alarming increase in anti-Semitic incidents, from the desecration of synagogues to anti-Jewish writings, speeches and even songs." [13] The anti-Jewish outbursts had become so frequent that, in early 1959, dozens of articles appeared in respectable German papers warning against a resurgent anti-Semitism.[14] Significant was an article in *Die Welt* of February 21, 1959, posing the question: "Must We Emigrate Again?" The article stirred a lively debate and the New York *Times* reported that on this one article alone, *Die Welt* had received "letters in response which would fill a medium-sized book." According to the *Times* dispatch, there was almost unanimous agreement that "the situation is alarming." [15]

Bonn, already embarrassed by criticism abroad, faced a growing discussion in the responsible German press about the lenient attitude of the courts toward anti-Semitic offenses. The *Sueddeutsche Zeitung,* in an editorial of January 24, 1959, pointed out that there was some kind of "latent anti-Semitism" within the machinery of justice. Finally the Bonn government was compelled to take sterner measures. Instead of small fines or suspended sentences, the courts began to send anti-Jewish troublemakers to jail. Here are some cases recorded during the first two months of 1959:

A court in Herford gave Carl Krumsiek, a textile salesman, seven months for having said it was "a pity all Jews weren't gassed by the Nazis." [16]

A sanatorium attendant in Bavaria was given a three-month sentence for having said: "If there were still death camps in Germany I would volunteer to put the remaining Jews under gas." [17]

A metal dealer in Hersfeld got two months in prison for anti-Semitic insults and threats.[18]

A waiter, Paul Rabe, was sentenced to six months in prison by a Duesseldorf court for calling a businessman a "dirty Jew whom the Nazis forgot to gas." [19]

A court in Mulheim ordered a clerk jailed without bail for having publicly praised the Nazi atrocities. He had insulted a Jew by calling him a "kike whom Hitler had forgotten to gas." The defendant had hinted that he would escape as Zind had.[20]

It is not difficult to understand why—even with only a few thousand Jews left in Germany—these extreme anti-Semitic statements are so frequently heard. During Hitler's days millions yelled in chorus, *"Juda Verrecke!"*—the Jew must perish. Today many Germans throughout the social strata still resent the fact that their country is not *judenrein*.

A housewife in Passau was fined two hundred marks for having called a neighbor a "dirty Jewish pig." [21] An engineer was sentenced to four months for having regretted that Hitler was not around "to gas the last of the Jews." [22] A policeman in Augsburg was suspended after having told a bartender: "Wait until the Adenauer era is over, then you and the other Jewish pigs will all be gassed." [23]

Several hundred cases of desecration of Jewish cemeteries have occurred in recent years, but these were seldom reported in the press. The otherwise very efficient German police have been unable to track down the vandals. At times the authorities have given ridiculous explanations for their lack of success: the demolition of up to a hundred heavy tombstones was ascribed to eight-year-old children.[24] In another instance, the police callously stated that the destruction of Jewish graveyards was "caused by a storm." Frequent cases of defacement of synagogues—smearing of swastikas in red and white paint on the doors—have also remained unsolved. Chancellor Adenauer, answering a letter of protest from the American Jewish Committee, had this explanation: "Anti-Semitic acts are inspired by Communist agents." [25]

Another form of anti-Semitism, reminiscent of the Hitler days, finds its expression in vicious anti-Jewish publications. In recent years a few publishers of anti-Semitic pamphlets have been given prison terms. In September 1959 a court in Hannover sentenced Arthur Goetze to nine months in prison for publishing libelous brochures and leaflets against Jews.[26]

In January 1959 the prosecutor in Munich started an investigation of the anti-Jewish hate peddler, Guido Roeder, who had for many years published and circulated the notorious *Protocols of the Elders of Zion* and other anti-Semitic pamphlets. At the same time the Jewish Central Council launched a criminal libel action against a Nuremberg evening paper which had published a story about an alleged "Jewish ritual murder." [27]

In May 1959 a trial lasting several days was held before the highest Federal Court in Karlsruhe. The defendant was Hans Robert Kremer, publisher and editor of the neo-Nazi periodical *Die Anklage*. The editor was charged with activities endangering the security of the state and undermining the constitution. There was a long list of specific offenses, such as abusive criticism of the democratic order, insults against the Bonn government, and the branding of the resistance fighters as "traitors." Herr Kremer openly proposed the re-establishment of a Nazi party and stated that democrats would be taken care of with summary justice on X day. *Die Anklage* was full of anti-Semitic material, frequently contributed by one of the most fanatical hatemongers of the old Goebbels staff, Dr. Johannes von Leers. In letters to the editor—often signed with "Heil Hitler!"—old Nazis threatened revenge in such statements as "Let us keep the knives sharp for the day when we will hang the Jews by their legs and then split open their bellies." [28] Similar scurrilous matter was published without hindrance over a period of four years, until the court finally caught up with Kremer and sentenced him to a two-year prison term.

Nor are these sentiments confined to the obvious rabble-rousers. Cases of open anti-Semitic bias have been found in recent years in the Bundeswehr and among the highest officials in the Bonn Foreign Office. In a litigation before a

Bonn court, the issue of anti-Jewish bias played a central role. An export merchant, Joachim Hertslet, charged that the Secretary of State Walter Hallstein and Ambassador Wilhelm Melchers "had denounced him to Arab governments as a Jew [which he is not], and had thereby seriously harmed his business connections in the Near and Middle East." [29] In another court case, witnesses confirmed the fact that the German diplomat Hans von Saucken insulted the New York correspondent of the *Neue Zuercher Zeitung* by calling him a "dirty Jew." Under pressure from many sides, Herr von Sauken had to be dismissed.[30]

In 1957 a biased and unproved statement by Minister Schaeffer about the drain on German finances because of restitution payments gave welcome propaganda ammunition to the anti-Semites. The majority of German people feel no regret for the crimes committed against millions of Jews, but believe instead that "world Jewry" is engaged in a plot to swindle the innocent Germans out of billions of marks. Kurt R. Grossman, a writer on German affairs, reported after a lengthy survey that "a casual perusal of various German publications yields article after article hammering away at the same theme: The Jews have willfully exaggerated the figures of Jewish deaths in order to secure more restitution." [31]

On February 14, 1958, the Social Democrats in the Bundestag demanded an investigation of the CDU member Jakob Diel, who reportedly had written in a letter to Dr. Adenauer that "in the opinion of the German people it is regrettable that all Jews had not been gassed, for in that case Germany would not have to make restitution."

Requests for restitution to victims of Nazi persecution are depicted as a "racket played by a bunch of greedy Jewish lawyers." Discussing this subject, the Finance Minister Etzel "voiced his shock over the wave of intense anti-Semitism which he found expressed in the flood of letters protesting against the restitution arrangement." [32] The Minister of Education of Baden-Wuerttemberg, Gerhard Storz, demanded safeguards against the widespread "paranoid obsession" of anti-Semitism which often results in violence. He stated that "many anonymous letters containing vicious threats are received by editors, state prosecutors and in the ministries of the Bund and Laender." [33]

Outbursts involving the desecration of graveyards and houses of worship, insults against Jews, and swastika-daubings, even in communities entirely free of Jews, occurred in 1954, 1957, and 1958. On Christmas Eve, 1959, the newly rebuilt synagogue in Cologne was defaced with huge swastikas and the words "Out with the Jews!" It was the signal for an epidemic outburst of swastika-daubings and vandalism in Germany and many other countries throughout the world. Within a period of six weeks the Ministry of the Interior registered 850 cases of anti-Semitic vandalism in widely separated areas in West Germany. The whole gamut of Nazi hooliganism was exhibited—from the scrawling of "Death to the Jews" and "Germany Awake" to desecration of graveyards, threatening letters to Jews, and the smashing of shop windows. The directorate of the Central Council of Jews in Germany declared that the excesses "evoke pictures that bring to mind the November days of 1938." [34] This reference was to the infamous "Kristallnacht"—the night of the broken glass—when synagogues were burned and Jewish houses were smashed to bits.

Although the arrest of two perpetrators gave clear proof that the anti-Semitic outbursts had been initiated by members of the neo-Nazi German Reichs party, Dr. Adenauer's government again hastened to counteract foreign criticism by declaring that the incidents were Communist-inspired. This was immediately contradicted by the Social Democratic opposition and by experts in Dr. Adenauer's own party. Professor Franz Boehm, a leading Christian Democratic deputy in the Bundestag, declared it a "dangerous self-delusion to

assume that Communists were masterminding the incidents."
According to Professor Boehm, "the outbursts appeared to
be synchronized acts of fascist elements throughout West
Germany." [35] The *Rheinischer Merkur* published an entire
page of material taken from neo-Nazi publications, which
clearly showed the extreme Rightist politicians as the ideological arsonists behind the anti-Semitic campaign.[36]

The effort to shift the blame onto the Communists was
a clever attempt to find an acceptable scapegoat so that the
Germans might be absolved of any responsibility. Adenauer's
story was repudiated by the Social Democrats as "nonsense."
The editor of the party's English-language newsletter, Heinz
Putzrath, told an American correspondent that Adenauer
was afraid to acknowledge the facts because he "doesn't
want to offend the Right and lose it as a solid voting bloc." [37]
Although more than 500 incidents had been investigated by
the end of January, the Interior Ministry in Bonn was unable to present a single piece of evidence proving Communist
complicity. The Interior Minister of North Rhine-Westphalia, after investigating 154 incidents in his state, told reporters he had "no evidence that East German Communists
or Soviet groups had directly instigated any of the incidents
in West Germany." [38]

Most German and foreign observers agreed that the vandalistic acts were chiefly the work of well-organized groups.
The police chief of Frankfurt, Dr. Littmann, was firmly convinced that most of the incidents "were carried out according to a central plan." [39] No doubt there were a number of
pranksters and psychotics who participated as amateurs. Un-
questionably, however, most of the slogan-smearing and
swastika-daubing was done by paint-brush experts.

The swastika campaign was obviously activated by the belief that the time had come to show the masses that Nazism
was still alive. According to a report in the New York
Herald Tribune, large factions of the German public were in

open sympathy with the vandals. "News correspondents heard West Germans suggesting that the Jews 'must have done something' if their synagogues were being desecrated in various parts of the world." [40] The same report pointed out that "a large part of the West German people remain poisoned by anti-Semitism. This is part of the fabric of West German life, and it is evident, day in and day out, to foreign observers in this country. No change from this state of affairs is in sight."

With the adverse impact on public opinion abroad, the Bonn government was compelled to take measures to stop the anti-Semitic vandalism. After a few months it petered out. Yet the danger of a relapse is still present. A United Press report from Bonn quoted government officials and Jewish leaders as saying that "anti-Semitism is dormant but not dead." One Interior Ministry official stated: "One can never say such an outbreak will not occur again." [41]

How much of a danger is the anti-Jewish sentiment in Germany today? A public opinion poll made in 1958 (the latest at the moment of writing) showed that "39 percent of the Germans were definitely anti-Semitic," 29 percent were "conditionally anti-Semitic," 25 percent showed no anti-Semitic attitudes, and only 7 percent were described as "philo-Semitic." * The study confirmed what many observers had long suspected—that "the highest percentage of anti-Semitism exists in the rural areas, particularly in small towns." This is borne out by the solid anti-Semitism manifested in towns like Offenburg, Lampertheim, and Koeppern.

It has often been argued that not too much emphasis should be placed on incidents such as I have cited in this chapter— that other countries have their share of cranks, racists, and criminals, and that it would be unfair to burden Germany as

---

* When releasing this survey in 1958, the American Jewish Committee, "despite the democratic political structure in Germany," saw danger of a "revival of racially motivated nationalism and anti-Semitism."

a nation with the misdeeds of a "minority" or a few political maniacs.

First, anti-Semitism is not a minority belief in Germany, but is still part of a *Weltanshauung* cherished by the majority. Second, there is a great difference between the milder forms of social and political anti-Jewish sentiments found in other countries and the anti-Semitism in Germany. The conviction that the Jews must be exterminated and that the living "should have been gassed" is evidence that German anti-Semites identify themselves even today with the Nazi outlook.

With nearly 70 percent of the population overtly or covertly anti-Semitic, it might seem almost a miracle that the Adenauer administration has been able to keep these sentiments relatively under control. But politically the Germans are a well-trained people. They have demonstrated during the twenties and the fifties that they can "behave," or rather that they can deceive *das Ausland*—the (gullible) foreigners. At the moment, circumstances compel them to play the role of a democratic people. But we must guard against the false assumption that the masses of the Germans have undergone a profound change of heart. Kurt R. Grossmann, after his lengthy discussions on the anti-Semitic problem with officials in Bonn, reported that the then President Heuss "admitted that the old hatreds still prevail, and agreed that the educational processes to battle these evils must be greatly intensified." [42]

12 *The Other Germany*

Is there "another Germany," set apart from the millions of militarists, ex-Hitlerites, storm troopers, SS butchers, and Deutschland-ueber-Alles nationalists?

Yes, there is. Rather, there are "other Germans." There are many politically mature and humane Germans who feel a burning shame about the crimes committed by Germany as a nation. There are many courageous Germans who are trying again, as in the twenties, to stem a tide which some day might throw Germany and the world into another catastrophe.

The riddle of the "other Germany"—and the often quoted "two souls" in every Teutonic breast—has baffled and intrigued foreign observers and German thinkers alike for more than a century. Goethe, Heine, Hoelderlin, Schopenhauer, and Nietzsche were plagued by the uneasy feeling that Germany's irrational romanticism and militaristic barbarism would one day lead to a revolt against Western civilization. These cultural leaders had no great hope for the other Germany. It was the poet Heinrich Heine who, in 1834, predicted that the day would come when Germany "will run berserk" against the civilized world and that "the German thunder will crash as it has never yet crashed in the world's history." Heine feared that under the savagery of Teutonic barbarism "the Christian cross will come tumbling down in pieces." [1]

There were others who foresaw the coming explosion. Toward the end of the last century a young educator and moral philosopher, who soon became a towering figure and the leading voice among the other Germans, predicted the coming upheaval with amazing accuracy. It was Friedrich Wilhelm Foerster who bluntly denounced Prussia's militaristic "blood and iron" policy in his magazine, *Ethical Culture*. In 1895 he was imprisoned for lese majesty and "criticism of the state." But Foerster's voice could not be silenced. During the First World War this fearless fighter spoke to tightly packed audiences at the University of Munich, denouncing the spirit of aggression and admonishing his young students to "abandon national egotism and join in a new European cultural order." Such ideas were condemned by the Munich faculty as national heresy which should "make every German ashamed." Soon Foerster came under censorship and all his lectures were *verboten*.

After the First World War, Foerster warned the Allies that they would lose the peace if they let themselves be fooled by the clever policy of dissemblance of the Weimar Republic, which hid the fact that the German war lords were preparing a new assault against Europe. When the German militarists threatened Foerster's life in 1923, he was forced to leave the country as an early exile. In his paper, *Die Menschheit,* Foerster continued to expose Germany's secret rearmament. On July 8, 1927, he printed this truly prophetic statement: "This much should at least be clear to us: The masters of Germany today need peace and want peace, but only in order to be armed on a date which will be decided by the weakness of her neighbors. That date will fall anywhere between 1933 and 1938." *

When the European statesmen were captivated by the "peace" siren songs of Germany's Foreign Minister Stresemann, Foerster wrote this realistic warning in *Die Menschheit:* "The leading German circles, with their battle cry of 'Deutschland, Deutschland ueber Alles,' are consciously pursuing their aim of a new European catastrophe. . . . As a prairie fire spreads over the dry grass, so Teutonic madness, inflamed by Prussianism, spreads unrestrained over the nation."

Foerster knew that there were thousands of peaceable, unmilitaristic Germans, but he felt that they were only a helpless minority, unable to assert political influence or leadership among their countrymen. To him this other Germany was like "a small boat tossed around by the waves of a storm-swept ocean of political madness."

Another German writer who saw clearly what was happening in his own country is Wilhelm Roepke, a university professor, today a supporter of Dr. Adenauer's policies. Professor Roepke described the spread of Nazism around 1930, three years before Hitler came to power:

Among our sensible peasants of Lower Saxony the Nazi activities were having really alarming success. There were very few people left with whom it was still possible to talk rationally. . . . Against this Nazi plague nothing seemed to avail, neither the appeal to common sense nor the moral appeal. . . . All classes were dosed with the poison in the most effective quantity and strength in each case, and everywhere every class was brought down, clerks, and mechanics with their employers, peasants and aristocrats,

* In his more than two dozen books, Foerster not only appears as an important educator and politico-religious philosopher, but he has also given us the deepest insight into German thought and behavior. Familiarity with his main work, *Europe and the German Question* (New York, 1940), is essential for an understanding of the Pan-German mania and the policy of deception practiced by the "democratic" statesmen of the Weimar Republic.

professors, officers, industrialists, bankers, civil servants. The friend of yesterday turned overnight into one possessed, with whom it was no longer possible to argue, and the more the movement succeeded the more the nervous, the cynical, and the ambitious joined the genuinely convinced fanatics, the crazy, and the moral perverts. . . . It was from the universities that most of the other intellectuals drew the disintegrating poison that they then distributed, duly packed and processed, to the mass of the people.[2]

What is the strength of the other Germany today and how great is its influence on the political life of the nation? The other Germany is there, fighting a heroic battle, but almost abandoned and in bitter despair. Compared to the time before the First World War and again during the Weimar Republic, more Germans today are conscious of the dangers that lie ahead. There is more active resistance against a new outbreak of German nationalistic mania, especially among the academic youth. In recent years German newspapers have printed an unusual number of letters to the editor protesting against the creeping renazification of the country.

Certain newspapers have given admirable support to the democratic cause by being alert and pointing out the dangers. Outstanding in this respect are the independent democratic dailies *Sueddeutsche Zeitung* and *Frankfurter Rundschau.* Among the periodicals, the monthlies *Frankfurter Hefte* and *Der Monat* deserve special mention.

Some of the more conservative dailies, such as the *Frankfurter Allgemeine,* the *Deutsche Zeitung* and *Die Welt,* have taken a firm stand against neo-Nazi and anti-Semitic incidents, but they seem to ignore completely the resurgent forces within the Adenauer government and its supporting parties. The great mass of the provincial newspapers are usually extremely nationalistic and are often staffed with editors who once served the Nazi press. For example, the publisher of six large provincial newspapers in Bavaria is Max Willmy, a one-time Nazi publisher who, together with Julius Streicher, owned the anti-Semitic weekly *Der Stuermer*. After the war Willmy was convicted as a "minor offender" and punished by a fine of 30,000 marks.[3] In 1959 one of Willmy's papers, the *8-Uhr-Blatt* in Nuremberg, was in the news again for having published the fabricated story of a "Jewish ritual murder." [4]

The highest praise is in order for the often heroic efforts by which individuals and small groups have battled the neo-Nazi and militaristic trends. Frequently, principled people sacrificed their positions rather than betray their democratic ideals. There is the case of Dr. Gustav Heinemann, a Protestant leader, who resigned from the Adenauer cabinet in protest against the restorative tendencies, the rearmament, and the high-handed, autocratic methods used by the Chancellor. Corvett Captain Werner Dobberstein, a Navy officer, tried for a long time to get action from his superiors against the growing pro-Nazi attitudes, the "Doenitz spirit," among the Navy officers. When he found his efforts were in vain, Captain Dobberstein, in 1956, wrote a letter to Defense Minister Theodor Blank, complaining about the unhealthy situation. Instead of ordering an investigation and backing up an alert and democratic-minded officer, Bonn ordered Dobberstein's dismissal a few days later (*Die Zeit*, May 17, 1956).

Another incident concerns the State Commissioner for Youth Guidance in Schleswig-Holstein, Dr. Ernst Hessenauer. Dr. Hessenauer told a meeting of students that he regarded it as unwholesome to the democratic process to permit former Nazi officials to run for public office or be appointed to responsible positions. He had stirred up a hornet's nest; he was immediately reprimanded and silenced by the Minister-President of Schleswig-Holstein.

One of the few democratic actions which ended successfully was launched in 1955 against the Minister of Education in the State of Lower Saxony. The appointment of Herr Leonhard Schlueter—right-wing extremist and owner of a pro-Nazi publishing house—to a cabinet position stirred the academic profession throughout Germany. The Rector of the University of Goettingen and nearly two dozen senior professors resigned, and a few thousand students went on strike. They marched in protest and demanded the ouster of Minister Schlueter. Public pressure forced Herr Schlueter first to go on "leave" and then to resign his office. The press reported that Dr. Adenauer was displeased because "mob action" had forced the ouster of a cabinet member.

In past years a small group of writers, newspapersmen, and radio commentators have tried to confront the German public with some unpleasant truths. In an earlier chapter I mentioned the name of Michael Heinze-Mansfeld, a young journalist, who revealed that Dr. Adenauer's Foreign Ministry was staffed by dozens of former Nazis, some of them war criminals. On October 22, 1952, the Chancellor countered with an angry speech in the Bundestag stating that "such snooping in the Nazi records must be stopped." This demand from the leader of the nation had the effect of bringing the curtain down on the Nazi past.

As also mentioned earlier, a group of writers and journalists, the so-called Gruenwalder Circle, has done much to expose the activities of neo-Nazi publishers and writers. In 1959 an excellent series of articles was published by Thomas Gnilka in the *Frankfurter Rundschau* under the title "They Have Learned Nothing." [5] It documented the far-flung network of neo-Nazi organizations and their growing influence on Germany's youth. As usual such revelations were dismissed by German authorities as alarmist or were branded by the Rightists as "Moscow-inspired."

A few years ago the gifted writer and critic, Erich Kuby, depicted the arrogant General Ramcke in a radio play, using him to demonstrate the criminal nature of Hitler's Wehrmacht. The play had its aftermath in a libel suit against the author, tried before a court in Hamburg. In a rare turnabout, the State Prosecutor sided with the author, and asked for dismissal of the case.

In the spring of 1957, eighteen leading atomic scientists in West Germany published a manifesto warning against the use of atomic bombs and giving their solemn pledge not to take part in any research or production of nuclear weapons. It was an almost revolutionary act, challenging the German philosophy of the unquestioned supremacy of the state and obedience from its academic servants. Dr. Adenauer answered the academic protest with an angry statement that arming with atom bombs was "a political question which should be of no concern to scientists because they are not qualified to judge such matters."

There is a long honor roll of religious leaders who have fearlessly spoken up against the trend toward renazification and remilitarization. Dr. Eugen Kogon, the editor of the *Frankfurter Hefte,* has been mentioned before. There is the Catholic paper *Michael,* outspoken in its criticism of the Nazi past and its latter-day disciples. There are Protestant leaders like the Reverend Dr. Gruber and Pastor Niemoeller, who have often admonished the German people to reform. There are pacifists like Dr. Klara-Marie Fassbinder, Fritz Kuester, and Otto Lehmann-Russbueld, who have continuously raised their voices against the revival of German militarism. Praise must also go to those Protestants and Catholics who have made great strides in promoting Christian-Jewish relations. Admirable work has been done by Erich Lueth, Director of Press and Public Relations in Hamburg, who organized friendship trips to Israel and also arranged mass pilgrimages of thousands of German youth to honor the victims who died in the Bergen-Belsen concentration camp.

Yet, in spite of the many courageous men and women who are fighting for a better Germany, this minority has little effect. The reality of the situation was made impressively clear to me during extensive discussions I had with a highly respected German newspaperman. When I suggested that the student protests against the Minister of Education Schlueter and the manifesto of the eighteen atomic scientists had raised my hopes for a reconstructed and politically more mature Germany, this well-informed observer warned me emphatically against drawing the wrong conclusions from such isolated incidents. He pointed out that behind the democratic façade of the Bonn Republic the conservative-nationalistic Germany was reorganizing her forces. Here is how my informant analyzed the political trends in present-day Germany:

There are a variety of power factors and purposes at work in Germany's body politics. It would be oversimplification to judge things according to the party labels, such as "Christian Democrats" and "Social Democrats," or to differentiate between "Left" and "Right." There are only a few who deeply believe in a democratic constitution. Most Germans are still imbued with a nationalistic fanaticism, even if outwardly they appear politically indifferent. The majority are satisfied to be ruled by a "strong man," an undisguised autocrat. The Chancellor is backed by the industrial and financial oligarchy of Rhine and Ruhr and by the powerful Catholic Church. With a highly interlocked officialdom running the federal administration and the Christian Democratic Union, Dr. Adenauer has a first-class instrument for controlling the entire country, manipulating public opinion, and winning elections.

The Social Democrats have little chance of gaining a majority. In the nationalistic view of the voters, they are not *stubenrein*—not reliable; they are regarded as "un-German." *

---

* Under the Kaiser the Social Democrats were accused of being "traitors to the Fatherland"; in the Weimar Republic they were blamed for the "stab in the back" that allegedly brought Germany's defeat in World War I; at present they have been branded, even by Dr. Adenauer, as "unpatriotic" and "unreliable." Yet the fact is that the late Social Democratic leader, Kurt Schumacher, was extremely nationalistic, and so is a large Rightist faction of the party.

As long as the boom economy lasts, the Social Democrats will be supported by a third of the electorate, chiefly by
union-conscious workers. But the majority of the nation will
always back the conservative-Rightist coalition. Most observers believe that if there is a slump there will be a strong
pull to the radical Right.

A trend toward the Left in West Germany is highly im-
probable, because the neo-Nazis and nationalist-activists
make up at least 20 percent of the people. They set the pace
for the indifferent masses. In case of a crisis they will have
the backing of the industrialists, the government, the police,
and the army. They will pull the majority of the people with
them. The democratic-liberal Left is not strong enough to
prevent another dictatorship; it represents less than 5 percent
of the population. They write letters to the editor today, but
they will not die on the barricades. They are individuals without leadership, and without a hope for the future.

Kurt P. Tauber, writing in the New York *Times* Magazine
(December 27, 1959), stated that under Dr. Adenauer's leadership "has come the return to social, economic and political
power of precisely those commercial and industrial elites who
supported a megalomaniac imperialism under the Empire."
These groups kept their privileges under Hitler and they are
wielding power again today: "They do not much care whether
they hold it under a monarchy, share it with a petty bourgeois
dictatorship or wield it in a conservative republic." Mr. Tauber found that they remained "what they always were: fiercely
anti-socialist, largely anti-democratic, authoritarian in their
social views and habits of thought, opposed to what they call
the excesses of party democracy. . . . They tend to be anti-
Semitic in a generalized way and they are intensely patriotic."

The German bureaucrats, reported Mr. Tauber, "are today largely recruited from the same authoritarian-conservative
circles as in the past. . . . To pretend that they have a deep
commitment to the democratic state they are serving is egre-

gious nonsense. . . . The total absence of any inner relation-
ship to the Bonn Republic gives rise to cynicism and apathy,
and plays into the hands of those who wish to discredit the
entire democratic process."

In spite of the large majorities that Adenauer polled in
the elections, the Federal Republic enjoys no popularity
among the masses. This was confirmed in a front-page editorial in the *Frankfurter Allgemeine* of May 14, 1958: "Nobody loves this republic, nobody shows her a friendly interest,
and there are only a few who speak politely of her institutions
and symbols."

Here then is the tragic situation of the so-called "other
Germany": It is made up of a woefully small group of mature
individuals, who are isolated and often bitterly despised and
vilified by their own people. They are democrats without a
democratic party; they are without a political home. Their
potential contribution to the postwar German republic has
never been nurtured. In fact, they have been almost completely ignored by the Allies from the beginning of the occupation.

PART THREE

Moral Insanity

13 *Nazis in the Courts*

In 1956 the Hamburg lumber merchant Friedrich Nieland published an anti-Jewish brochure entitled *How Many World (Money) Wars Do Nations Have To Lose?* Nieland's tract spoke of "the enormous lie about the gassing and slaughter of six million Jews." Germans, declared Herr Nieland, "are by their very nature unable to commit such brutal crimes." He then charged that "the entire maneuver of destruction was initiated by secret representatives of international Jewry." * Having relieved the Germans of all guilt, Herr Nieland warned that international Jewry is "plotting the extermination of the white race in a third world war," and insisted that "no Jew should sit in any important position, be it in the government, political parties, banking or elsewhere."

Two thousand copies of the brochure were mailed to all deputies of the German Bundestag and the Laender parliaments, and to officials in the ministries. Almost a year went by before one of the recipients requested an investigation.

* This shifting of blame for the mass gassing of millions of people to the "secret representatives of international Jewry" has been echoed in the neo-Nazi and expellee press, as well as in the *Deutsche Soldaten Zeitung*.

The public prosecutor in Hamburg saw neither libel nor danger to the state and therefore refused to sustain an indictment. The court reasoned that Nieland's attack was directed only against international Jewry, not against the Jewish people. On January 6, 1959, the Hanseatic Supreme Court rejected the prosecutor's appeal, thereby granting Herr Nieland legal immunity to give his brochure mass circulation.* Within a few days the Nieland case caused an uproar in the press— both democratic and conservative—which centered the public interest on the whole judicial system.[1]

The presiding judge in the criminal court that had first decided in favor of author Nieland was Dr. Enno Budde, a jurist whose unsavory political record was soon revealed in several leading newspapers. Dr. Budde, as a young law student, had been a fierce fighter against the Weimar Republic. In his antidemocratic actions Budde had often overstepped the limits of what was permitted under the very lenient Weimar regime. Yet this enemy of democracy was later appointed a judge in the Weimar Republic.

The Nazi victory in 1933 brought fulfillment to Judge Budde's nationalistic longings. In several articles he had praised the racial laws against the Jews and hailed Hitler as the oustanding protector and purifier of the Teutonic people. It was this Dr. Enno Budde, enemy of the republic, anti-Semite, and admirer of Hitler, whom the Bonn administration appointed as the presiding judge over the Verfassungsschutzkammer—the Court for the Protection of the Constitution. Dr. Budde proved to be a strange guardian of the law. There were a number of cases in which he acquitted SS men accused of brutal crimes in concentration camps. On other occasions this Nazi judge openly demonstrated his sympathy for the Gestapo by showing them extraordinary leniency.†

* The circulation of the brochure was later stopped by another court action.
† "Enno Budde—Richter aus Blut und Boden," *Frankfurter Rundschau*, Jan-

One of Germany's leading journalists, Dr. Paul Sethe, wrote a long editorial in which he stated bluntly that the Nieland-Budde affair could not be regarded as unique. Bonn's judicial system, Sethe contended, was still dominated by the spirit of the twenties which had caused the downfall of the Weimar Republic and had paved the way for Hitler. "We believe," said the editorial, "that this miscarriage of justice [*eine schlimme Fehlentscheidung*] would never have occurred if the judges had had some of the stench of the Auschwitz crematoria in their nostrils." Dr. Sethe suggested a thorough investigation of the political past of all judges who had participated in the decision. The editorial ended despairingly: "We are outraged and sorrowful; we feel ashamed, deeply ashamed." [2]

The German judiciary has posed problems since the early postwar years when the victorious Allies tried to reorganize the courts.* In Bavaria, which supposedly was "denazified" under the American occupation, the courts have been staffed with the old Nazi law officers. It has been reported that "as many as 85 percent of the judges have Nazi records." [3]

Because of America's preoccupation with German rearmament, very little attention has been paid by the U.S. press to the conditions in the German judiciary. In Europe, however, leading papers have frequently sounded alarms. An experienced observer of the German scene, Brian Connell, former chief of the *Daily Mail* bureau in Germany and later foreign affairs correspondent of the *News Chronicle,* has told in his book *A Watcher on the Rhine* of "hair-raising cases" in which Gestapo and Waffen SS mass murderers were acquitted in

---

uary 19 and 20, 1959. Because of the strong criticism of the press, Budde was soon quietly transferred to a court dealing with rent control and real estate cases.

* This chapter on the German judiciary is based on several thousand press reports on German war crimes and court cases which I have collected over the last twelve years.

spite of overwhelming evidence, even in instances where the accused had "blithely admitted" their guilt. Mr. Connell traced the frequent acquittal of Nazi war criminals to the fact that there is "little ideological difference between a judiciary partly staffed by ex-Nazis and the accused." [4]

An editorial in *Die Welt* stated that the German judiciary is unable to deal with the Nazi past: "It can be said that the misdeeds committed in the concentration camps and death factories could have been prosecuted much earlier if the German judiciary and administration had not been staffed with judges and bureaucrats whose own shirts are not free from dark spots and who, therefore, secretly sympathize with the culprits of the Nazi regime." [5]

The Nieland-Budde affair turned the spotlight on many more judges and prosecutors who had been appointed to important positions in the Bonn judiciary. On January 22, 1959, the Bundestag had a debate on the subject. The Social Democratic opposition charged that the Adenauer administration had failed to screen high officials, had been too eager to close the files of the Nazi past, and had not presented a full documentation of the crimes committed in the concentration camps.

In numerous newspaper articles, political and legal experts agreed that conditions in the judiciary were lamentable, to say the least.[6] And it was a high law enforcement officer, Prosecutor General Max Guede, who had the courage to point to the most sensitive spot in the German judiciary— the Nazi past of thousands of German judges and prosecutors. In a lecture before the Evangelical Academy in Bad Boll, on October 19, 1958, Dr. Guede declared that judges should become conscious of the fact that they "were all guilty of having betrayed the idea of justice" and that, by serving the Nazis, they had become "tools of injustice and instruments of terror." *

---

* *Frankfurter Allgemeine,* October 29, 1958. Dr. Guede supported his state-

The German authorities had created special laws of terror in Czechoslovakia, Poland, and other conquered countries. Everywhere German judges sent innocent people by the tens of thousands to the gallows or before the firing squads. The court records, still available, show them not as guardians of the law, but as "a legal terror squad," helping to establish "German order" over the world. It was these judges who kept Hitler's hangmen and the firing squads busy until the end of the war. The German press showed that death sentences were often given for the slightest infractions of German occupation rules:

For a critical remark.

For slaughtering a pig without a permit.

For stealing some bread.

For violating a curfew law.

For singing a *verboten* song.

For giving a cigarette to a prisoner.

For sheltering a six-year-old Jewish child for a few hours.

To a Pole for allegedly "hurting a German police dog."

To a German bank director for having "expressed doubts about the ultimate victory."

To a Catholic priest for having made a political joke.

To a German for having relations with a Jewish woman.

To a Polish servant girl for having been "disobedient" to her German mistress.

These few examples, taken at random, could be multiplied by hundreds.* In cases where no witness or no evidence was

---

ment with a frightful statistic. During the four and one-half years of the First World War, the German courts, by stern application of severe laws, sentenced altogether 141 civilians to death. During the Second World War, Hitler's judges sent at least 16,000 civilians to the gallows in Germany alone. The ratio in the military courts was: First World War, 48 executions; Second World War, 6,000 executions.

* *Der Spiegel* of January 13 and February 17, 1960, reported that Socialist students from West Berlin and Karlsruhe had arranged an exhibition of court documents incriminating several hundred high law officials who once had served as Hitler's instruments of terror. After inspecting the material, Prose-

presented, the judges declared that the accused "was capable" of being antagonistic to German aims. *Der Spiegel* called these court procedures "remarkable cases of legal lynching."

In an article, "Nazis in the German Judiciary," the *Manchester Guardian Weekly* reported that "around 360,000 Czechs died during the Nazi occupation between 1939 and 1945; many of them were judicially murdered." With 2,000 German legal officials having served in Czechoslovakia, the paper believes that there is an urgent need "for a large-scale investigation of the entire West German judiciary." [7]

According to newspaper reports, 17 of Hitler's former judges hold office today in Germany's highest tribunal, the Federal Court at Karlsruhe; 27 others are presidents or directors of provincial courts.[8] A judge of the Federal Constitutional Court in Karlsruhe, Wilhelm Ellinghaus, recently declared: "The worst thing is, it seems to me, that hundreds of former military judges who condemned thirty thousand people to death mainly for trifles, are today back on the benches." [9]

Here are the profiles of a few judges and prosecutors whose records have been cited in *Der Spiegel* and elsewhere in the press.

Dr. Ernst Kanter: known as the "hanging judge" in occupied Denmark; sentenced several hundred persons to death. Earlier, in Germany, he had condemned dozens of "enemies of the state" to death or hard labor. In 1950 he was put in charge of a department in the Federal Ministry of Justice. In 1958 he was appointed Senate President at the Federal Court in Karlsruhe, the equivalent of a U. S. Supreme Court judge.

Dr. Konrad Roediger: former legal expert in the Foreign Office; was implicated by documents and linked with the

---

cutor General Guede said: "These photostats were made from original documents. I checked these sentences and I am shocked."

liquidation of millions of Jews. He serves today as a high judge at the Federal Constitutional Court in Karlsruhe.

Dr. Eisele: notorious Nazi terror judge in Prague; was returned by U.S. authorities to Czechoslovakia to stand trial as a war criminal. When released, after serving five years in prison, he was appointed director of the Upper Provincial Court in Stuttgart. Under mounting criticism he was finally suspended in 1959.

Dr. Otto Schweinsberger: served as military judge in the East; sentenced dozens of people to be executed for minor violations of occupation rules. He became Senior Prosecutor in Frankfurt despite his Nazi record. He was suspended from office December 1958, and later retired.

Dr. Werner Rhode: was known as a fanatical Nazi prosecutor before a special court in Prague; asked for dozens of death sentences for persons accused of being "enemies of the Reich." Today he serves as head of a department in the Ministry of Justice in Schleswig-Holstein. His name has been linked with several judicial scandals in that state.

Dr. Rehder-Knoespel: once Chief Prosecutor in Prague; was called "the hangman" for his ruthless persecution of Czech patriots. On February 8, 1944, he demanded the death sentence for seven Czechs for having given food to a Soviet prisoner. One of the executed was a pregnant woman. He functions today as Senior Public Prosecutor in Mannheim.

Dr. Muhs: was president of a special court in Poland (Radom); left his mark there with many death sentences. He once condemned a Pole for having sheltered a Jewish child. He is today presiding judge at the Upper Provincial Court in Hamm.

Dr. Bruchhaus: has a notorious record as Hitler's overeager prosecutor in Poland; asked for the death sentence for a Dr. Neubeck for "being capable of hatred against Germany." He is today a prosecutor at the Provincial Court in Wuppertal.

Dr. Hucklenbroich: was presiding judge at a special court in Poznan; according to *Der Spiegel,* he "chopped off heads at the order of his Fuehrer." For "hostility to Germany" or stealing a piece of luggage, he imposed the death sentence. He serves today as senior judge at the Provincial Court in Wuppertal.

Dr. Reimers: was once presiding judge of the Appeals Court in Czechoslovakia; practiced "legal lynching" on a large scale. He serves today as judge at the Provincial Court in Ravensburg.

Dr. Arthur Neumann: Nazi judge of a military court; wrote his wife during the war that he was "proud to have earned the name the 'bloody judge.'" He became Senate President of the Provincial Court in Berlin (*Die Zeit,* December 12, 1957).

Dr. Harry von Rosen-Hoewel: was professor of law; in 1942 advocated the conquest of Lebensraum in the East through "special treatment of Poles and Jews." Today he serves as Senior Federal Prosecutor at the Oberverwaltungsgericht—a high administrative court.

Dr. Franz Schlueter: was one of Hitler's judges in Czechoslovakia and later in Austria; on April 28, 1945, he dispatched seventeen people at once to the execution block. In his denazification procedure Dr. Schlueter denied any guilt, but the presiding judge fined him 50,000 marks and stated: "Never before has a defendant appeared before this court who has told so many lies." In 1950, Dr. Schlueter became a high official in the Federal Ministry of Justice. Later he was appointed to an important position at the Federal Patent Office in Munich (*Frankfurter Rundschau,* July 1, 1957).

The "honor role" of the German judiciary would make a lengthy list. To the embarrassment of the Bonn government, a committee in East Germany published the names and records of more than one thousand military judges and prosecutors who had staffed Hitler's legal terror squads in the East and who now dispense justice in the Federal Republic. The Bonn government has until now kept all official records of Nazi judges and bureaucrats under lock and key.

In fairness it must be stated that not all judges and prosecutors permitted themselves to serve the Nazi regime. It certainly was not easy to dispense justice under Hitler, but there were ways and means of remaining honorable, even if one had to risk the scorn of the big and little tyrants.[10] Some judges retired, others used a kind of legal guerrilla warfare against the system. Such judges often sent the accused to prison for three to five years in order to keep them from being caught by the Gestapo and sent to the death camps of the SS. But these judges remained a pitiful minority. Even today this minority does not have the power or influence to enforce a general reformation of their profession. A courageous jurist like Dr. Guede has met considerable criticism from his colleagues.

Attempts have been made to pin the blame exclusively on Hitler and the "Nazi laws." The truth is that many German law officials have always shown a proclivity toward a callous disregard for justice and decency. The roots of this attitude reach deep into the German past. The judges and prosecutors in imperial Germany were known to be arrogant; they posed blatantly as the protectors of the ruling groups and were far removed from democratic concepts. *Klassenjustiz* was the term often used to characterize the judiciary of that period.

With the collapse of the monarchy in 1918, the German judges were taken over by the republic and not one law official was dismissed. The overwhelming majority of judges and prosecutors felt a burning hatred and contempt for the Weimar Republic, its representatives, and its institutions. The law was used to harass and vilify the supporters of the democratic system, and to protect the monarchists, the political saboteurs, and the Nazi street fighters and murder gangs.[11]

Wilhelm Roepke has testified to the hostility of German

students toward labor groups. He himself was present when some students "kidnapped fifteen workmen from a neighboring village and murdered them while under transport." The reason: "shot while attempting to escape." The perpetrators of the crime "remained unpunished," and those who had testified in court earned "the hatred and anger of the dominant groups of professors and students in the university." According to Professor Roepke, the students and the professors of law were the worst of them all:

In Germany there were indeed few faculties of law that were not filled with the spirit of obdurate antiliberalism, antidemocratism, nationalism and anti-Semitism, and it was this spirit that was thus carried into the life of the country by those who later became judges, administrative officials, and lawyers.[12]

Hitler's coming to power was acclaimed by these nationalistic judges and prosecutors. According to the aforementioned Judge Ellinghaus, the great majority of law officials became Nazi party members in 1933. The most fanatical and ruthless volunteered for the honor of becoming instruments of terror. These judges were appointed to sit on People's Courts, military courts, or special courts, where they competed with the SS in destroying enemies of the state and in liquidating the Jews. They ruthlessly decimated the Slavic nations in order to conquer Lebensraum for the German master race.

The majority of German judges have always served "the law" and the powers-in-being. Judges, prosecutors, and administrators—the Globkes, Kanters, and Buddes—like to pose as legal experts and technicians. They prefer to serve autocrats and they are eager to seize power, but they refuse to assume responsibility for their conduct and action. In every system of government they are "indispensable." They were indispensable to the Kaiser, and after 1918 to the Weimar Republic. In 1933 they became indispensable to the Nazis, and after 1945 to the occupying powers. In 1949 they became indispensable to the Bonn Republic. They will again become indispensable on some future day when a new "strong man" has appeared on the German scene.

14 *"Bureaucracy of Murder"*

When Adolf Hitler committed suicide in the bunker of his bombed-out Chancellery in April 1945, he left behind him a fanatical leadership corps which, in numbers and training, was without precedent in recorded history. What has happened to the several hundred thousand men who represented the elite of the Nazi party?

Let us take a look at the German police. Frequent complaints have been made by the democratic opposition that key posts in the police hierarchy of the larger states, such as North Rhine-Westphalia, Schleswig-Holstein, and Bavaria, have been swamped with former SS officers and Gestapo officials.[1] It has been reported that many of them "had forged their records to conceal their Nazi past." [2] On October 16, 1959, the Social Democrats complained that twenty SS officers had wormed their way into top police positions in the State of North Rhine-Westphalia. They named specifically the chiefs of the Criminal Divisions in such cities as Cologne, Dortmund, and Essen. It was pointed out that these former Gestapo officials had conspired with the Nazis in the dying days of the Weimar Republic. The Socialists charged that the whole police organization is dominated by a clique of former Nazis who see to it that promotions and appointments are awarded to reliable SS men.

In March 1959 the government of Baden-Wuerttemberg reported to the Diet that 152 former Gestapo officials were in the service of the state police and that 215 others received state pensions.[3] The chief of the Criminal Department in the city of Stuttgart is the former Gestapo official Dobritz, who was sentenced to death in absentia by a French court for torture and manslaughter.[4]

During the last two years, a number of high police officials were arrested and charged with being implicated in Gestapo murder cases. The police captain Friedrich Simon, of Gelsenkirchen, was charged with the shooting of 20 concentration camp prisoners.[5] In April 1959 the State Prosecutor launched an investigation of 23 police officers in the city of Berlin, all suspected of having been involved in the mass murder of 97,000 Jews in Bialystok, Poland.[6] In July 1959 the chief of the Criminal Division of the Palatinate state police, Dr. Georg Heuser, was arrested and charged with the liquidation of thousands of Jews in the city of Minsk, Poland.[7]

An important official in the state government of Lower Saxony, Gerhard Schneider, once commander of an SS terror task force, was charged with having ordered mass executions in Poland and Russia.[8] The head of the Criminal Department in the city of Saarbruecken, the former Gestapo official Klemmer, was arrested in 1959. He admitted having ordered mass executions in the East.[9] In January 1960 the Interior Minister of Hesse announced the arrest of the chief of the State Criminal Division, Police Commissioner Georg Lothar Hoffmann. He was charged with having committed mass liquidations in the Maidanek concentration camp in Poland.[10] A top official in the Criminal Department of the state police in Hannover, Bodo Struck, was charged with having participated in the murder of 95,000 Jews in a district in the East.[11] A special dispatch in the New York *Times* reported the suspension of the chief of the Bonn Criminal Police Force, Dr. Hans Maly. He was charged with "having misapplied the law while a member of the Nazi Security Police."[12]

For many years police officers involved in mass executions had little to fear from the courts. Their standard explanation was that they had acted "on orders" and were "not conscious of wrongdoing." This was often sufficient to obtain an acquittal. Criminal Inspector Ewald Sudau of Minden, a former Gestapo official, was charged with the killing of 150 Jews. He was acquitted for "lack of evidence."[13] Charges were dropped against "250 German policemen accused of murdering 20,000 Jews in Lithuania and Russia in 1941." Their defense was that "they themselves would have been killed if they had refused to carry out the executions."[14]

The appointment of former SS officers to responsible positions in the Bonn Verfassungsschutz—the Office for the Protection of the Constitution—has been mentioned earlier. This policy has caused sharp comments in the democratic section of the German press.[15] The chief of the Internal Security Department in the Interior Ministry, the German FBI, is Dr. Rudolf Toyka; he was a member of the Nazi party from 1935 to 1945.[16]

Bonn's super-cloak-and-dagger service is headed by Hitler's former Intelligence chief, General Reinhard Gehlen. The Bureau Gehlen is staffed with 4,000 former SS officers and SD (security) agents.[17]

The filling of sensitive law-enforcement and security agencies with thousands of ex-Nazi officials is bound to create problems for a democratic society. Serious problems have already arisen. Dr. Werner Hofmeister, Minister of Justice in Lower Saxony, believes that "a Nazi underground is working in Germany with the aim of obstructing law enforcement."[18] It is obvious that the law-enforcement agencies are remiss in their duties when an estimated 100,000 persons can live undetected for many years under false identities in a country which has an otherwise efficient police system.

It has been suspected for a long time that a secret bond exists between the former top Nazis and certain legal experts who today control the German police and the judiciary. People who have had the opportunity to study the Bonn bureaucracy at close range have noticed a dismaying intimacy between the old Nazi hierarchy and their former legal aides and subordinates.

The deep involvement of a whole governing body in a barbaric crime is the strongest agent for cementing group loyalty. Government and party officials, as well as the SS men, were all accomplices in the Nazi mass murder. The sadistic guards in the torture camps and the "technicians" in the death factories worked only at the end of the assembly line which originated with the legal experts who wrote the text and the commentary for the Nuremberg racial laws. Without the help of these officials Hitler could not have managed the war, administered occupied Europe, and carried out the "Final Solution."

Participation in such past crimes often has far-reaching consequences today. A well-prepared dossier that threatens to reveal the Nazi record of a high official, a prosecutor, an industrialist, or editor, often serves as a weapon to bring an official or public figure into line. The neo-Nazi press has frequently used blackmail tactics against political leaders by threatening to expose their former collaboration with the Nazis.*

---

* The best-known case concerns President Theodor Heuss, who was "reminded" that he had once written articles for the Goebbels newspaper *Das Reich* (see *Nation Europa*, Nos. 6 and 10, 1958). A similar "reminder" was given to Bundestag President Eugen Gerstenmaier in *Nation Europa*, No. 7 (1958).

It has been said that a "bureaucracy of murder" was functioning in Hitler's days.* It would be a fatal illusion to believe that this awful secret fraternity is no longer in existence. The Naumann case demonstrated the close interdependence of the old Nazi faithfuls. Justice was obstructed with the full knowledge and coöperation of top officials in the government and the judiciary.

In several other cases it has come to light that prosecutors and high officeholders "neglected" their duties and thereby helped make possible the escape of convicted Nazis. Collusion has been proved in the escape of the Bonn diplomat Dr. Franz Rademacher, who was found guilty of having ordered the gassing of thousands of Jews in Yugoslavia. The same collaboration was true in the escape of Dr. Hans Eisele, a concentration camp physician guilty of murdering thousands of prisoners.

Dr. Hans Eisele had been sentenced to death by an American court for mass killing and medical experiments on Allied prisoners in Buchenwald. According to press reports, Dr. Eisele's sentence was later commuted and he became a privileged prisoner. Some time in 1952 he was released for good conduct on the basis of an agreement reached with the Bonn government. As a "late homecomer" (the euphemistic German term for war criminal), he got an immediate sum of 6,000 marks. Next came a loan of 25,000 marks to enable him to open a medical practice. With it went a number of identification papers and certificates informing all authorities that Dr. Eisele had an unimpeachable record. Thus outsiders did not know that he was a former "red-jacket" (as the in-

---

* "Many acts of mass murder and torture originated at administrative desks. Those gentlemen who issued orders, worked over files, and stamped the documents, are the ones who bear the full responsibility. Today they represent the bureaucracy of murder even if they did not personally participate in the killings" (*Suddeutsche Zeitung*, July 14, 1958).

mates of the death cells were called) from Landsberg. He was admitted for practice in the State Insurance Office.

In 1954 a former Buchenwald inmate discovered that Dr. Eisele was living comfortably in a suburb outside Munich. It was then that the first official complaint reached the Munich prosecutor, Dr. von Decker. A lengthy correspondence followed. The prosecutor asked for more evidence. He was given names of witnesses and other detailed information. However, no action followed until almost four years later, in May 1958, when new complaints about Dr. Eisele reached the prosecutor and the police. By that time the name of Dr. Eisele had appeared in the headlines. The doctor had talked a widow patient of his into an agreement under which his wife would inherit a large, fashionable villa in exchange for medical treatment for the widow during the remainder of her lifetime. A will was drawn up, and soon afterward the widow died. Relatives of the widow contested the will and the newspapers reported that there was suspicion about the manner of her death.

During the trial of the SS guard Martin Sommer, witnesses named Dr. Eisele as the real mass killer of Buchenwald. Thereupon things became uncomfortable for the doctor. A senator in Munich approached the Chief of Police, Anton Heigl, and asked the immediate arrest of Dr. Eisele. By this time all the police knew about the Buchenwald doctor. But there was no action, either by the police or by the prosecutor.[19]

When the pressure mounted and the case could no longer be ignored, Dr. Eisele was warned in time to disappear. With the usual help of the Nazi underground, Dr. Eisele fled to Egypt, but he had enough time to sell some of his belongings. After a thorough investigation the Justice Minister dismissed the prosecutor, Dr. von Decker, for having neglected his duties. It turned out that the prosecutor was an "old fighter" who had joined the Nazi party back in 1931. The Association of Judges and Prosecutors protested. They demanded and got Dr. Decker's immediate reinstatement.

If there was ever the slightest doubt that a kind of Nazi Mafia, a "bureaucracy of murder," is operating on the highest administrative level, such doubts were eliminated in late 1959, with the exposure of the official protection given to the long-wanted mass murderer Dr. Werner Heyde.

In 1949, Dr. Heyde, under an assumed name, resumed his medical career in the northern town of Flensburg in Schleswig-Holstein, where he soon acquired considerable social standing.

Numerous reports and articles in the German press have told in detail how this Nazi fugitive lived unmolested for twelve years under his alias, "Dr. Fritz Sawade," without being asked for his diploma or credentials. Elevated to top medical positions by the authorities, "Dr. Sawade" was protected from discovery by key officials in the government departments and the judiciary.

In order to understand the significance and implications of this case it is necessary to take a brief look at the historical setting in which this member of the medical profession committed his crimes. Dr. Werner Heyde was thirty-one years old when Hitler came to power in 1933. As a young psychiatrist, he was as deeply devoted to his studies in neurology as he was obsessed with the nationalistic aims of his Fuehrer. The dapper SS officer Dr. Heyde soon became an intimate confidant of Hitler's chief medical advisers. His contacts with the Nazi hierarchy helped to pave the way for a quick professional career. The young neurologist and Brigadier General of the SS was soon rewarded with a professorship at the University of Wuerzburg. In 1939 he was appointed director of the Department of Neurology at the university clinic. It was the year in which Hitler decided to make an all-out effort to conquer Lebensraum for the master race.

Along with the military build-up, secret preparations had been made long in advance to mobilize reliable members of the medical profession in order to carry out a plan of mass murder. In a secret letter of September 1, 1939, Hitler gave authority to his trusted physicians "to the end that patients considered incurable . . . may be granted a merciful death." Under the euphemistic term "euthanasia," elaborate plans were made to get rid of all incurables, all the feeble-minded, crippled children, and invalids, in order to eliminate all "useless eaters" during wartime and to have "full utilization of hospitals and nursing institutions."[20] But this was not all. Included in the program was a scheme for the liquidation of tens of thousands of political prisoners and Jews from the concentration camps.

The enormous mass murder project was carried out behind the façade of three "welfare" organizations.* The so-called "mercy death" in many cases became synonymous with indescribable torture and agony. The indictment in the Nuremberg "Doctors' Trial" stated that the "victims of these crimes numbered in the hundreds of thousands."

According to testimony in the "Doctors' Trial," Professor Heyde not only emptied the hospitals and asylums but he also went to Dachau and other concentration camps, where, on the basis of Gestapo files, he selected "enemies of the state" and Jews by the thousands and marked them for liquidation in the gas chambers.

By the end of 1940 the mass killing had reached such pro-

---

* In 1939 the Reich Association for Hospital and Nursing Establishments was founded. Its purpose was to register and "process" all patients marked for liquidation. A second organization, the Charitable Foundation for Institutional Care, was entrusted with the financial arrangements and the installation of a dozen gassing and extermination centers. The appointed head of both charitable fronts was Dr. Werner Heyde. A third group, the Nonprofit Patient-Transport Corporation, run by the SS, as were the other two, had the task of shipping thousands of patients from the hospitals and asylums to the extermination mills (Mitscherlich, *Doctors of Infamy*).

portions that the extermination practice became common knowledge to large sections of the German population.* On August 3, 1941, the Roman Catholic Bishop of Muenster, Count von Galen, made his famous protest from the pulpit. Thousands of copies were made and circulated secretly among the opponents of the Nazi regime. Unable to keep the mass extermination a secret, Hitler decided in 1941 to transfer the gassing installations to the conquered territories in the East. Here the extermination process, according to Hoess, the commander of Auschwitz, was "improved" so that millions of victims could be accommodated.

The transfer of Hitler's main charnel houses to the East left Dr. Heyde and his medical colleagues in no way unemployed. They continued "euthanasia" on a smaller scale. "Only" a few thousand each month were killed by deadly injections, but many had to submit to medical experiments. It was revealed in the "Doctors' Trial" that victims were kept for hours in icy cold water, others got injections of deadly bacilli, and some were subjected to slow starving under painstaking observation.

When the Allies occupied Germany in 1945, they found everything: the complete files of "euthanasia," the reports and pictures of the "tests," the laboratories, the torture chambers, and the mounds of corpses—but they didn't find Dr. Werner Heyde. It was two years before the honorable professor was arrested in Wuerzburg. Soon, however, he

* Thousands of families who heard of the sudden deaths of relatives due to "heart failure" became uneasy and tried to penetrate the mystery. Heinrich Himmler stated in December 1940: "I hear that there is great unrest in the Wuerttemberg Mountains on account of the Grafeneck Institution. The people know the gray SS bus and think they know what happens in the crematory with its ever-smoking chimney. What does happen there is a secret, and yet it is a secret no longer." Dr. Franz Schlegelberger of the Reich Ministry of Justice wrote in March 1941 that rumors were spreading throughout Germany in regard to "the elimination of a few hundred thousand mental patients."

escaped from Allied custody under mysterious circumstances, on a transport. Heyde then went underground and found refuge with wealthy friends as a gardener. In 1949 he felt safe enough to reappear as "Dr. Sawade." Although the professor's picture appeared regularly on the "wanted" list, the fugitive with an impressive criminal record felt absolutely safe in Flensburg. His real name and his past deeds were known to many of his colleagues, to high police and court officials, and to the upper strata of the town.[21]

Dr. Heyde's new professional career in the Bonn Republic was phenomenal. From the start "Dr. Sawade" had the help of influential circles in Flensburg and prominent officials in Schleswig-Holstein.[22] In 1949 the mayor of Flensburg appointed "Dr. Sawade" a physician for the municipal athletic school. Two years later "Dr. Sawade" began a medical practice as a psychiatrist. Soon he became official *Gutachter*—an expert who prepared medical reports for the State Insurance Office. Later he was appointed *Obergutachter*—a senior expert officially employed in court cases involving medical testimony. It has been reported that "Dr. Sawade's" income as a *Gutachter* for the State Insurance Office alone was more than 300,000 marks, earned over a period of six years. "Dr. Sawade" became a man of wealth and reputation. He owned a well-kept villa in an exclusive section of Flensburg, and his cream-colored, flashy sports car was known all over town. Thus the honorable doctor was respected and liked as the "charming widower" who played the lion among Flensburg's high society. Had not his wife declared in 1951 that Dr. Heyde was dead? Had she not requested a pension as the widow of a man on the "wanted" list? (It has been estimated that Dr. Heyde was responsible for the deaths of 60,000 in the asylums and 140,000 political prisoners from the concentration camps.)[23] The "widow" received a pension of 64,500 marks from 1952 to 1959. Yet, at the same time, Frau

Erika Heyde and her two sons, living in southern Germany, kept up a lively correspondence with a "Dr. Sawade" up in the north.

When the story appeared in early November 1959, leading court officials and police officers came under suspicion of having stalled the arrest proceedings in order to give Dr. Heyde sufficient time to escape. Every day the papers reported additional names of high officials who had known the Heyde-Sawade secret for a long time. There were strong efforts to hush up the affair. Even the *Frankfurter Allgemeine Zeitung*, a loyal Adenauer paper, stated in a front-page editorial (December 15, 1959) that the Heyde case had grown into a major political scandal. The editorial said: "Something must be wrong if a Dr. Sawade could carry on his profession in official splendor for many years. Not all the facts have been made public yet, and we don't know who is responsible for the mess, but those frantic efforts to avoid a 'scandal' will in turn become the true scandal."

The Prosecutor General of the State, Dr. Adolf Voss, and several cabinet members, were accused of having known the Heyde mystery. Even the Minister-President, Kai-Uwe von Hassel, came under suspicion, but he denied any knowledge of the case. After the Social Democrats demanded an investigation in the Landtag, the president of the Provincial Court, Dr. Ernst Buresch, was suspended for complicity in the case. It was established that in 1954 Dr. Buresch had received a formal complaint charging that his official *Obergutachter*, "Dr. Sawade," and the mass killer, Dr. Heyde, were one and the same. This complaint came from a leading member of the medical faculty at the University of Munich, Professor Otto Creutzfeldt. Instead of making an arrest, the "bureaucracy of murder" attempted to settle the case quietly. A "respected jurist" (not identified by name or position) was sent to Munich, where he obtained a "gentlemen's agreement" under which Professor Creutzfeldt withdrew his complaint.

A number of other officials were suspended in 1959, among them two judges from the Schleswig-Holstein Provincial Court and two top medical officials from the State Insurance Office. These honorable judges and administrators had made themselves a direct part of the farce of submitting the pension claims of victims of Hitler's concentration camps and asylums for the medical opinion of an *Obergutachter* who in reality was the chief perpetrator in the destruction of 200,000 human lives.

The Minister of Justice, Dr. Bernard Leverenz, admitted in the Landtag on December 1, 1959, that "many officials in the State of Schleswig-Holstein had known for years that Dr. Sawade was not the real name of the *Obergutachter.*" When the minister announced that six prosecutors had been appointed to investigate the maze of complicity, a Social Democratic deputy sarcastically questioned whether these men didn't belong to the implicated group, and whether there was anyone left to investigate the investigators.

The whole affair gained an extra touch of irony through the fact that "Dr. Sawade" had lectured before medical audiences on the theme of "euthanasia." He spoke in detail of the crimes committed by Dr. Heyde, of the mass gassings, and the various "experiments." There were some among his listeners who were privy to the Heyde-Sawade secret; one was a physician who in earlier years had studied under Professor Heyde at the University of Wuerzburg.[24]

The Heyde affair may be taken as a classic illustration of what is happening in present-day Germany. The Bonn correspondent of the New York *Herald Tribune,* Gaston Coblentz, stated that the favoritism and protection extended by state officials and law-enforcement agencies to ex-Nazi criminals has "assumed the proportions of a national scandal."[25] In addition to the Heyde affair, Mr. Coblentz refers to Dr. Herta Oberheuser and Professor Werner Catel, whose cases have been widely discussed in the German press. Dr. Oberheuser was sentenced by an American court to twenty years for medical experiments on Polish girls. Her sentence was soon commuted, she was readmitted to practice, and she received extensive help from the state and medical authorities in Schleswig-Holstein. Professor Catel served the Nazi regime as a "race-purifier," like his colleague Dr. Heyde. Although he had given the "euthanasia" death to dozens of young children, he was acquitted by a Hamburg court, which reasoned that the Herr Professor "believed in the legality of his action." Among the three judges who handed down the verdict were the Provincial Court director, Dr. Enno Budde, and Judge Halbauer, a member of Hitler's legal terror squad in Czechoslovakia. The Bonn bureau chief of the *Rheinischer Merkur,* Paul W. Wenger, interpreted the actions of the court in such cases as "a denial of guilt in every realm of public life; it amounts to a general exoneration of the Third Reich, from the euthanasia killing and the racial laws down to the aggressive war policy of Der Fuehrer." [26]

As in the case of Drs. Heyde and Oberheuser, the acquitted Professor Catel enjoyed the benevolent backing of the highest state authorities. In 1960 the Minister for Culture and Education, Dr. Osterloh, appointed Professor Catel to the office of Director of the Children's Clinic at the Kiel University. Only when a few West German papers put a spotlight on this case was Professor Catel forced to resign.

Many German doctors were involved with "euthanasia," unethical experiments, and mass gassings. Only a few were sentenced by Allied and German courts, but usually their sentences were soon commuted and they were readmitted to practice. The release of the ill-famed Nazi physician Dr. Hans-Bodo Gorgasz caused much criticism. This doctor had personally supervised the gassing of at least 10,000 human beings, among them many women and children. It was established at the trial that this model of the medical profession had a habit of observing the slow agony of his victims through a little window of the gas chamber. When Dr. Gorgasz' sentence was commuted, the *Sueddeutsche Zeitung* of February 8, 1958, quoted the Justice Minister of Hesse as defending his release with the following statement: "There are hundreds of doctors who did worse during the Nazi regime, but they were never brought to court."

The Nazi criminals are free because prosecutors, judges, and politicians have gone to great lengths to cover up crimes like those committed by Dr. Heyde and Professor Catel. Their actions were and still are mainly determined by a deep-rooted sense of camaraderie which they call *Korpsgeist*—one for all and all for one.

Their common Nazi past has engendered a secret tie of brotherhood between the Globkes, Buddes, Rademachers, Kanters, Oberlaenders, and Heydes, who are united by a single ideology, mutual dependence, entanglement in a gigantic crime, the feeling of fellowship known to outlaws who have escaped the gallows, and the iron will to stay in power.

15   *From the Rogues' Gallery*

The general laxity of the courts in handling Nazi war crime cases has done much to undermine the confidence of world public opinion in a truly reformed Germany. Because of the previous close involvement of Nazi criminals and German law officials, it is quite logical, and almost natural, that prosecutors frequently hesitate to initiate indictments. This has been true in cases where witnesses and ample evidence have been available for years.

The story of the Waffen SS General and high police official, Heinz Reinefarth, has been published in leading German newspapers.[1] General Reinefarth played a prominent role in the murderous suppression of the Warsaw uprising in August 1944. The insurgents had formed a poorly armed freedom corps of 40,000, who tried to drive the Germans out of the Polish capital. General Reinefarth's SS moved in with tanks and defeated the resistance.

The documented record shows that Reinefarth and his troops not only fought against the combatants, but they took their revenge on the civilian population. More than 200,000 people were killed within one month. All wounded Poles, including doctors, nuns, and nurses were slain. Thousands of women and children were driven into churches, locked up, and burned alive. The most heinous acts were committed by the SS Dirlewanger Brigade, an outfit composed of notorious criminals who had been released from prison so that they could "regain their honor" on the war front. Some weeks later, Reinefarth reported with great pride in the Nazi paper *Ostdeutscher Beobachter* (October 5, 1944) that his SS force had liquidated "more than a quarter of a million Poles during the Warsaw fighting." For his heroic deeds, Reinefarth was decorated by Hitler.

When the occupation authorities ordered democratic elections after the war, the people of the fashionable North Sea resort of Westerland voted the former SS General and war criminal into office as burghermaster. In 1958, Reinefarth ran on the Refugee party ticket as a candidate for the Schleswig-Holstein State Parliament. When the press cited Reinefarth's record as a major war criminal, the Senior Prosecutor of Flensburg, Erich Biermann (who had Herr Dr. Heyde-Sawade under his protective wing at that time), closed the case and refused to issue an indictment. A few days later Reinefarth was elected as deputy to the Landtag and accepted as an honorable colleague.

The next case concerns the Refugee Minister, Dr. Theodor Oberlaender, who joined the Adenauer cabinet in 1953. As briefly mentioned in a previous chapter, Minister Oberlaender is accused of having been involved in the so-called "Lemberg massacre," in which several thousand Poles and more than 5,000 Jews were slaughtered. Dr. Oberlaender does not deny *a*] that he was the commanding officer of a special SS task force, the Nightingale Battalion, made up of nationalist Ukrainians; and *b*] that this battalion was the first German unit to move into the Polish city of Lemberg on June 29, 1941, where it remained for six or seven days.

Dr. Oberlaender does deny that his troops committed any

atrocities in Lemberg. He has said that during his stay in that city "not a shot was fired." This is not even accepted by his CDU party colleagues; they believe only that Oberlaender himself took no part in the massacre. Although formal complaints were launched against the Refugee Minister, and although witnesses in West Germany, in Israel, and in Poland were willing to testify, the German authorities delayed as long as possible before considering official court action.[2] In the Bundestag debate of December 10, 1959, a government spokesman declared: "Dr. Oberlaender has the full confidence of the Adenauer cabinet."

There was no denying that Dr. Oberlaender had written articles advocating the extermination of Jews and Poles in the East, that he was closely affiliated with the racial warfare section of Hitler's SS, and that he was the appointed leader of the fanatical Nazi unit, German Alliance in the East.

A wide-spread feeling prevailed in Dr. Adenauer's own party that Hitler's former expert on the East had become a political liability. The pro-Adenauer paper *Rheinischer Merkur* stated that Dr. Oberlaender "as a racial expert has an intellectual co-responsibility for the anti-Polish and anti-Jewish outbursts in Lemberg."[3] The Christian Democratic paper *Der Tag* (February 9, 1960) called for Oberlaender's resignation and described him as "a drag on the German reputation."

The Social Democratic opposition and the independent press demanded Dr. Oberlaender's ouster. *Der Spiegel* stated editorially: "This man should never have been appointed a minister." Pointing to Oberlaender's long record as a Nazi propagandist and Lebensraum expert, the editorial asked sarcastically: "Is a man sufficiently qualified to become a cabinet member in Germany merely by having it established that he doesn't have a record as a murderer of innocent civilians?"[4]

Nevertheless, in the summer of 1959, Dr. Oberlaender was given the honor of representing the Chancellor at the moral rearmament conference in Caux.[5] It was only the combined pressure of Social Democrats and a large faction of Christian Democratic deputies that finally forced Dr. Oberlaender to resign in May 1960.*

Two other unprosecuted cases among many should be briefly mentioned to show the scope of the crimes committed. The first concerns the SS General Erich von dem Bach-Zelewski, who was in charge of a special task force for the liquidation of Jews in the East. As one of Hitler's top police officers, he is held responsible for the killing of hundreds of Jews long before the outbreak of the war. According to a DPA report in the New York *Staats Zeitung* of April 14, 1952, it was Bach-Zelewski who organized a pogrom against the Jews all over Silesia on the "Crystal Night" of 1938. He reported to Hitler that his storm troopers had set fire to eighty synagogues and that he had made Silesia *judenrein*. During 1941, Bach-Zelewski's SS brigade shot more than 100,000 Jews and Poles in the East.

Although the Bonn authorities had full knowledge of Bach-Zelewski's record, they left the SS General unmolested until December 1958. At that time he was arrested for being implicated in a "private" murder case involving another SS officer. He has since been sentenced to four and a half years in prison.

Another example concerns the SS officer Hermann Krumey who played a decisive role in the murder of 460,000 Hungarian Jews. As an aide to Adolf Eichmann, Krumey, in the spring and summer of 1944, rounded up all Jews in Hungary and shipped them to Auschwitz. According to *Die Welt* of

* In September 1960 it was reported that a prosecutor in Bonn refused to open the case against Dr. Oberlaender "for lack of evidence that he had participated or was responsible for the mass killing" (*Deutsche Zeitung*, September 28, 1960).

August 16, 1958, Krumey today owns a drugstore in Korbach, Hesse, where he has been active in politics for the Nazi-infested Refugee party. The former SS officer was temporarily arrested in 1957, but was soon released. He was arrested again in connection with the Eichmann case in May 1960.

Many new facts about unsolved war crimes have come to light during the last two years. The extent of unpunished Nazi crime was revealed in three major court cases which were not tried until 1958. One was a trial against ten SS and police officials, held before a court in Ulm, Wuerttemberg. After months of testimony the court found that the accused had slaughtered 5,502 Jews in the Tilsit district. This was part of a larger action in which 132,000 Jews were liquidated in order to provide a Lithuanian frontier region for German settlement. Evidence of indescribable atrocities was produced. Thanks to bureaucratic thoroughness, the court was able to use the meticulously kept lists in which the police had recorded their daily number of victims.[6] The ten Nazis were given sentences from three to fifteen years.*

The second court case revealed the story of the SS sergeant Martin Sommer, the "butcher of Buchenwald." As master of the punishment cell block, Sommer whipped hundreds of prisoners to death, killed many with hypodermic injections of air, hung others from trees by their wrists, and amused himself by transforming priests into "snowmen" by dousing them with buckets of water and letting them freeze to death. Sommer was sentenced to life imprisonment, the maximum penalty under German law, and one rarely imposed.

Late in 1958, two SS guards were put on trial for tortures and mass killings at the Sachsenhausen concentration camp.

---

* In his summation the defense lawyer, Herr Aschenauer, declared: "The defendants only carried out those orders which the bureaucrats had issued at their desks" (*Die Welt,* August 12, 1958).

Gustav Sorge, the "Iron Gustav," and Wilhelm Schubert ("Pistol" Schubert), were accused by 150 witnesses of having savagely kicked and beaten inmates to death and of having immersed the heads of Jews in latrines until they suffocated. The indictment charged that both sadists were responsible for the death of 11,000 prisoners. These men too were sentenced to life imprisonment. In view of the previous reluctance on the part of most authorities to call Nazi war criminals to account, the prosecution of these trials was an amazing step forward.

The court cases of 1958 dramatized the fact that the high officials who gave orders for the mass executions and the Nazi judges who legalized terror were still living comfortably as well-paid government officials, judges, burghermasters, and police officials. "The murderers are in our midst," stated the *Frankfurter Rundschau* in an editorial of December 13, 1957. "They are going around well dressed, and in the evenings they are to be found as jolly citizens crowding our *Bierstuben.*"

As an aftermath of the Sommer-Sorge-Schubert trials, the Justice Ministers of the Laender created, in December 1958, a Central Clearing House for Investigation of Nazi Crimes, located in Ludwigsburg. The German press reported that this center was investigating four hundred major Nazi war crimes. The head of the center, Senior Prosecutor Dr. Erwin Schuele, has done excellent work in ferreting out major war criminals. Some observers doubt, however, that the work of the center will ever materialize into actual court proceedings, because it would mean that many leading officials would have to stand trial. It is argued that under no circumstances would Dr. Globke and the men around him run such a risk.

Strong pressure is being exerted in the Bundestag, as well as in the press, to make a clean sweep and close the whole chapter of the "undigested past." What is suggested is a general amnesty for all crimes committed under the Nazi regime.[7] Such an act would bring the "bureaucracy of murder" out of the danger zone.

16   *The Heroes Come Home . . .*

During the early fifties, German towns and villages competed in spectacular receptions for their homecoming
"heroes"—the convicted Nazi war criminals who, under
mounting German pressure, had been released from Allied
custody. The Nazi Generals and SS officers were greeted with
flowers, brass bands, ringing church bells, and banners strung
across the streets. Huge crowds jubilantly joined in singing
"Deutschland, Deutschland, ueber Alles."

Many of the returning war criminals were given expen-
sive gifts, and some were even rewarded with new cars—a
Volkswagen, Porsche, or Mercedes-Benz. The noisy wel-
comes of these "late homecomers" were much more than
mere expressions of human sympathy. These manifestations
amounted to an open show of solidarity between the German
people and those who once represented the elite of the Nazi
regime.* Dr. Adenauer expressed the sentiment of the over-

* In 1952 the Bundestag voted unanimously to introduce a "Treue-Woche"—
Loyalty Week—in order to assure the last 800 war criminals, those most deeply
implicated, that they were "closely bound to and deeply revered by their com-
patriots." The *Deutsche Soldaten Zeitung* of October 16, 1952, hailed this step
as a "united act of the entire German nation."

whelming majority of his countrymen when he made his demonstrative visit to the prison in Werl, where he shook hands with Nazi war criminals who had once been condemned to death for their crimes. And when Field Marshal Albert Kesselring, who destroyed Warsaw, Rotterdam, and Coventry, was released from jail, he was honored by the Chancellor with a two-hour audience.[1]

Upon his release from the Spandau prison, Baron Konstantin von Neurath was warmly congratulated in long telegrams from President Heuss and Chancellor Adenauer for the final ending of his "martyrdom." The German press, with few exceptions, published glowing articles about him, and the people from his home district gave von Neurath a triumphant welcome.[2] A cheering crowd of thousands lined the streets for miles. The German people and their leaders were welcoming a man who had worked closely with Hitler in the preparation of aggressive war and who, as "protector" of Bohemia and Moravia, was the architect of an elaborate plan to enslave or kill half of the Czechs and Germanize the other half. The Baron had "reached the lowest rung on the ladder which led him from international diplomacy to international brigandage." [3]

The release of Baron von Neurath from the international prison in Spandau had long been suggested by Adenauer and was announced by the Soviets in November 1954. The Soviet step came as a complete surprise to the Western powers; it was the result of lengthy, secret negotiations that had been carried on between Bonn and Moscow since 1952. These secret talks were climaxed in 1955 by Dr. Adenauer's visit to Moscow.* The Chancellor's admitted aim was to

---

* The *Christian Science Monitor* reported on April 17, 1954, that "secret talks between Bonn and Moscow have been going on for about three years," and that "in August 1952 a group of Bonn diplomats and industrialists had a secret meeting with high Moscow officials in a hotel in Copenhagen."

work for the release of the Nazi war criminals, whom the Soviets had sentenced to long prison terms for their crimes against millions of Slavs. In 1955 the Soviets no longer held any regular prisoners of war, but had in their custody 9,626 convicted German nationals from Field Marshals down to SS concentration camp guards.

There have been conflicting reports about Adenauer's negotiations in Moscow. The officially inspired German explanation was that the Chancellor tried his utmost to persuade the Kremlin leaders to release all German prisoners still in their hands. A pact was made under which the Soviets agreed to set free the convicted war criminals, while Bonn promised to open diplomatic relations with Moscow. By way of an amnesty the Russians unconditionally released the great majority of the prisoners, except for 749 men whose crimes had been of such a nature that the Russians refused to take the responsibility for letting them go free. According to some reports the Soviets had asked Adenauer to keep these 749 war criminals in detention until the German authorities had made a careful check of the complete court records, which Moscow would hand over to the Germans.

When the returning war criminals were received at the German border, the Bonn authorities outdid themselves. Newspaper articles spoke of the "greatest event in German postwar history." [4] Thousands of cars converged on the reception camp in Friedland, where the celebration was held, and as usual the crowds sang "Deutschland ueber Alles." Welcome speeches were given by members of the Adenauer cabinet and other government officials. One transport of several hundred war criminals was addressed by Refugee Minister Oberlaender. In this particular gathering of SS men were the "euthanasia" killer Professor Clauberg of Auschwitz and the prison camp sadists Gustav Sorge and "Pistol" Schubert. They were greeted by Dr. Oberlaender with the following welcome: "Every one of you had to suffer for all of us. But now I invite you to serve as the yeast in our comradeship."

The transports from Russia were chiefly made up of Hitler's Waffen SS men, members of the Gestapo, the Sicherheitsdienst, and the Feldgendarmerie—a military police unit entrusted with mass extermination. The remainder were Nazi party officials and concentration camp guards. Most of them had been sentenced to twenty years of hard labor. When newspapermen asked for names and the wartime units, not many of the prisoners volunteered information. One of the returnees, shrugging his shoulders, said: "I don't think I care to discuss that. We all did a lot of killing. That's war." [5]

As stated earlier, not one of the war criminals remained in detention.* Each of the returnees received 6,000 marks and all became eligible for interest-free loans and pensions. The press reported that flowers and gifts arrived in Friedland by the carload. In praising the heroes who had "suffered for Germany," the newspapers revealed the identities of some of the returning prisoners. In that way the survivors of the concentration camps noted the names of such men as Clauberg, Sorge, and Schubert. Yet it was many months before the German authorities rearrested some of these criminals and brought them to court.

During the Sorge-Schubert trial it was revealed that a smooth Nazi underground had operated in the prisoner reception camp at Friedland. All returning war criminals had been given strict instructions not to admit to any former crimes and, in case of an investigation, to take counsel from

* An American correspondent reported from Bonn that the Soviets had asked for further imprisonment of those who had committed atrocities. This the Germans would not agree to. "Public opinion in this country would be violently opposed to any measures against the returned men. It would be almost out of the question politically to begin court proceedings against any sizable number of them" (New York *Herald Tribune,* January 15, 1956).

a list of selected lawyers who would defend them free of charge.*

Effective schemes had been developed by the Nazis and militarists to obstruct law and justice. After they had reached success, after thousands of Nazi criminals had fled to Spain and Egypt, after other thousands had been freed from Allied prisons, there appeared accounts in some Rightist newspapers, congratulating a group of Nazi ringleaders on accomplishing an almost impossible task. The *Deutsche Soldaten Zeitung* (June 1958) published a full-page account of a far-reaching secret organization which had been founded in 1948 in violation of Allied rules. The purpose of the organization was to free the war criminals in defiance of law and justice. The author of this remarkable report, Major General Hans Korte, describes how a kind of General Staff, or "steering committee," was set up in Munich to direct all the anti-war-guilt propaganda in occupied Germany and throughout the entire world. A group of Nazi jurists who had served in Nuremberg as counsels for major war criminals formed the nucleus of the directing body. Prominent among them were Dr. Rudolf Aschenauer of Munich and Ernst Achenbach (of the Naumann circle) of Essen, the latter having excellent financial connections on Rhine and Ruhr.

In order to conceal certain activities from the occupying powers, a number of fronts or subagencies were created to serve as special task forces. To furnish the press with propaganda on the war-guilt question, an "independent" monthly newsletter, *Die Andere Seite* (*The Other Side*), was issued, in which material about the "so-called war criminals" was

---

* *Frankfurter Rundschau,* January 12, 1959. Later it was discovered that the official in charge of records and identifications in the Friedland camp was a former SS officer, Garwinski, who, up to 1960, had lived under the false identity of "von Rosen." According to *Die Welt* (January 2, 1960), his case is under investigation.

cleverly introduced among other news items. This distorted and slanted news was reprinted not only in the provincial press but in such leading papers as the *Frankfurter Allgemeine,* the *Stuttgarter Nachrichten,* and *Die Welt.* In addition, a circular letter was mailed periodically to organizations and influential personalities in Germany and abroad in order to gain their support for the release of all war criminals.

To camouflage these activities well-known German church representatives were brought into the organization, so that both major denominations joined the common defense for the convicted Nazi war criminals. A Committee for Christian Aid to War Prisoners was formed in 1948; among its sponsors there were prominent Roman Catholics—Cardinal Josef Frings of Cologne and Bishop Johann Neuhaeussler of Munich—and leading Protestants—Bishop Theophil Wurm of Stuttgart and Bishop Meiser of Munich. These church leaders had already issued several strong protests against the Allied war crime trials. Now Cardinal Frings and others demanded a halt to the hanging of convicted Nazis. In May 1946, Washington had ordered a stop to all executions in Landsberg. But there were still 230 Nazis sentenced to death for having committed mass murder. In 1948, Cardinal Frings again asked President Truman for clemency for the last two dozen convicted Nazis, whose executions were pending.[6]

Under the sponsorship and prestige of Cardinal Frings and Bishop Wurm, a wide network of organizations coördinated their efforts to save the convicted criminals from the gallows. The church leaders were supported by two powerful religious organizations—the Roman Catholic Caritas and the Protestant Evangelisches Hilfswerk. The latter had given jobs and shelter to dozens of Nazi officials, especially former Ribbentrop diplomats. This group issued a weekly newspaper, *Christ und Welt,* in which the campaign for the war criminals had top priority.

Cardinal Frings and Bishop Wurm headed another organization under the slightly confusing name, Committee for Justice and Trade, which served as a rallying point for the former Nazi elite. According to General Korte's account, this group consisted of ex-officers, high government officials, jurists, educators, industrialists, and church leaders. Its purpose was to raise money to assist all war criminals financially and legally and to create a climate of public opinion conducive to the release of all convicted Nazis. The organization had a mysterious bank account ("Konto Gustav"), to which more than sixty unnamed industrial and financial tycoons regularly contributed large sums. According to the report in the *Deutsche Soldaten Zeitung,* this group was closely affiliated with a propaganda center in Switzerland, the Centro Europa, which carried on a world-wide campaign to bring quick freedom to Hitler's professional mass murderers. Two other organizations were working toward the same goal, but they extended their activities into the exclusive circles of high society and among aristocrats in Germany and abroad. One was the Stille Hilfe (Silent Help), headed by Princess Helene von Isenburg, and the other was called Helfende Haende (Helping Hands), and was directed by Princess Stephany zu Schaumberg-Lippe.

The common characteristic of all these groups was their dual activity; first, they solicited financial aid for Nazi prisoners, and second, they stirred propaganda against the "war-guilt lie," climaxing it with a demand for speedy release of all war criminals. Working in coöperation with the Christian Aid center in Munich were such notorious Nazi organizations as the SS HIAG, the Society of Late Homecomers, the Stahlhelm, the Federation of German Soldiers, and the various expellee groups. Among the organizations abroad we find the Kameraden Hilfe in Spain, headed by the SS Colonel Otto Skorzeny, a similar group working in Latin America under the leadership of the Luftwaffe ace Colonel Hans Ulrich Rudel,* and various German "relief" and propaganda organizations in the United States under the political guidance of the Steuben Society.

In his article General Korte gave due credit to the German press which, "despite Allied censorship, courageously published demands for a clean sweep of the whole war criminal problem and, by doing so, made its readers aware that German soldiers were still in Allied custody, thus stirring the conscience of the nation." Among the papers praised for their courage in protesting the occupation law were the *Frankfurter Allgemeine* and such neo-Nazi periodicals as *Der Heimkehrer,* the *Deutsche Soldaten Zeitung,* the *Notweg,* and *Der Stahlhelm.* Also of great propaganda value were "a number of foreign newspapers and periodicals" which General Korte did not identify.

From the Christian Aid headquarters in Munich a stream of often repeated propaganda was channeled through all media of communication. The war crime trials were branded as a "victor's justice of revenge"; all prisoners were declared "innocent"; and the worst Nazi mass murderers were glorified as "martyrs." †

Long before Dr. Adenauer had been made Chancellor,

---

* Skorzeny and Rudel, assisted by the SS Colonel Eugen Dollmann, ran a smooth underground for the escape of war criminals to Spain, Egypt, and Argentina. According to the New York *Times* of March 21, 1953, the Rudel group had even hatched a plan to raid the prison at Werl and free all war criminals in British custody. Rudel was discouraged by the Bundestag member Dr. Erich Mende, who knew that the Western powers had promised gradual release of all prisoners. Rudel's act would only have spoiled Germany's chances for regaining her sovereignty.

† An editorial in the *Frankfurter Allgemeine* of October 26, 1954, used the German term *Rachejustiz*—justice of vengeance—and the weekly *Christ und Welt* of May 12, 1955, spoke of the Malmédy killers as "unfortunates who were thrown into prison although they were all innocent."

the anti-war-guilt campaign and free-the-war-criminals propaganda had reached a high pitch. It was psychological warfare in grand style and the impact on the Pentagon was quite noticeable. The Generals in Washington knew that they could not have the desired German army of 500,000 men without letting all war criminals free. It was bargaining in which the Germans clearly had the Pentagon brass at a disadvantage. During 1948 and 1949 the sentences of hundreds of war criminals were commuted by General Clay. When Ilse Koch, known as the "bitch of Buchenwald," was released after serving only three years of a life sentence, protests came in from all over the world.

After Dr. Adenauer became Chancellor in 1949, the German demand for freeing the war criminals became an undisguised policy of political blackmail. Many politicians stated the case quite bluntly in the press and in the Bundestag: They would not ratify the treaties (creating a common Western defense) without a "clean sweep on the war crimes question." Although the politicians were well aware that Washington had tacitly yielded to German demands, they relentlessly increased the pressure. The State Department had to grapple with the delicate problem of how the Western Allies could gradually release a few thousand war criminals without arousing indignant protests in their own countries.* Yet the German pressure groups approached the newly appointed High Commissioner, John McCloy, with strong demands. As a result McCloy had to set free those Nazis whom he himself had termed "the worst war criminals still alive in Landsberg." [7] More than two hundred of these, originally sentenced to death by U.S. courts, had had their

---

* According to official figures, in April 1950 there were still 3,600 convicted war criminals in Allied custody in Germany. In additon, there were more than 2,000 Nazi war criminals held in other non-Communist countries. In August 1952 there were only 800 war criminals left in U.S. and British custody in Germany.

sentences commuted to life imprisonment or even shorter terms.

At the end of 1950 there still remained more than two dozen men in the death cells waiting for a decision on their fate. They consisted chiefly of two groups: members of the SS unit which had committed the notorious Malmédy massacre, and commanding officers of the various SS special task forces who had carried out the brutal mass executions of several hundred thousand Jews, Gypsies, and Poles in the occupied East during 1940 and 1941. Some of these men were responsible for the deaths of 60,000 and 100,000 human beings. These "red-jackets" became the focus of a campaign for mercy which mobilized the whole German nation.

In January 1951 the Christian Aid committee in Munich, with its leading churchmen and politicians, and dozens of organizations again flooded High Commissioner McCloy with telegrams and petitions demanding that he immediately commute the sentences of the few "red-jackets" still in the Landsberg prison. At the same time, Mr. McCloy's "mail became heavy with threats against his life and that of his family." What he had to face, according to his own words, was "a well-organized conspiracy to intimidate me." [8] In brief, the Germans had started one of their famous blitzkriegs (this time only psychological) in order to demonstrate their close solidarity with the convicted Nazi war criminals and to rescue all of them from the gallows.

The following facts are taken from Arthur Krock's illuminating account in the New York *Times*. On January 9, 1951, the U. S. High Commissioner received a delegation of German parliamentary leaders in his office. The group urgently requested that he "commute the death sentences of those in the Landsberg prison convicted as war criminals." The delegation was made up of Dr. Hermann Ehlers, president of the Bundestag, Heinrich Hoefler, Carlos Schmid, Jakob Altmaier, Hans von Merkatz, and Franz Josef Strauss, each

representing one of the various political parties. The Bundestag leaders told Mr. McCloy that West Germany had
abolished the death sentence and "they wanted no more
blood spilling in Germany." The Social Democratic leader,
Carlos Schmid, said: "We want to create a new moral climate
in Germany." And he added: "If the United States would
carry out the executions, it would shock the German conscience." Franz Josef Strauss argued that "the long delay in
carrying out the death sentences called for a commutation."
Should the prisoners be executed, "the blow to German
morale would be great and the effect on German-American
relations would be devastating."

According to the *Times* report, Mr. McCloy "expressed
surprise and distress that none of the pleaders had mentioned the horror and enormity of the crimes of Nazi authorities which evoked, among others, the trials of those for
whom . . . blanket clemency was sought." And he called attention to the fact that "there are no prisoners in the world
whose cases have received the same painstaking review." The
High Commissioner remarked that it was "a bad thing for
the German soul to put these things under the carpet." He
pointed out that the "bishops, lawyers and the man on the
street . . . don't know, and they don't want to know, what
happened to the other people." He concluded: "If our relations depend on these individual cases, then our friendship hangs on a thin thread indeed."

Even stronger personal efforts were made by Princess
Helene von Isenburg, who had earned the honor of being
named the "mother of the red-jackets." The Princess sent
urgent telegrams to President Truman, Secretary of State
Acheson, and Mrs. McCloy, with a plea for commutation.
A few days later the Princess was invited to dinner by the
McCloys. According to a long report in *Der Spiegel,* the
Princess pleaded for two and a half hours that the High Com-
missioner spare the twenty-eight "red-jackets" who "had suf-

fered horrible torment in fear of death and are almost insane." Just how deeply the Princess impressed the High Commissioner has not been reported, but Mrs. McCloy sent her a check to aid the prisoners and wrote: "I too feel that we have to bridge our mutual problems, and I assure you, it was for Mr. McCloy and myself not only an honor but also a great joy to have had you as our guest." [9]

Needless to say, the U. S. High Commissioner was walking a tightrope. There was no one with a friendlier attitude toward the beaten enemy; *Der Spiegel* once described McCloy as having an "almost pathological love for Germany." His attitude was exploited by the Germans to the utmost. The newspapers stated the case very bluntly: either the war criminals would be freed or there would be no German army. Delegation after delegation filed through John McCloy's office—high church dignitaries, women's organizations, professors, politicians, an *ad hoc* committee, "Rescue the Red-Jackets," the representatives of the ex-soldier organizations, and many others. Through the mail came tens of thousands of pleading letters and telegrams from Germans and sympathizers all over the world. There were a few telegrams of protest from veterans and Jewish organizations in America, which made the decision for Commissioner McCloy no easier. "For days," reports the former U. S. diplomat Charles W. Thayer, Mr. McCloy "locked himself in his home, reading and rereading the testimony. His nerves got tauter and tauter, his temper shorter and shorter." On the evening before the High Commissioner had to make his fateful decision, Dr. Adenauer's military advisers, Generals Adolf Heusinger and Hans Speidel, called Mr. Thayer, a U.S. liaison diplomat, to an urgent conference. They asked him to convey one last plea to Mr. McCloy before it was too late. "If the prisoners at Landsberg were hanged, Germany as an armed ally against the East was an illusion." [10]

The campaign was largely successful. By the end of January 1951, Commissioner McCloy and U. S. General Thomas Handy had commuted the sentences of twenty-one of the twenty-eight "red-jackets" and had left the fate of the other seven undecided.* The American lawyer for the remaining seven made an appeal for a habeas corpus before the Supreme Court in Washington. In addition, the Germans rushed 610,280 signatures by air mail to the White House in a plea for mercy. When the last appeal was rejected, the seven "red-jackets" were hung on the night of June 6-7, 1951, in the courtyard of the Landsberg prison.

The balance sheet of Germany's Christian Aid crusade is quite impressive. Hundreds of Nazi mass murderers, once condemned to death, had their sentences commuted to life imprisonment, and soon were released from Allied prisons. Toward the end of 1952, a mixed review board of three Germans, one American, one Britisher, and one Frenchman was burdened with the task of gradually and quietly releasing the last "poor devils" who once had lived in the death rows of Landsberg and Werl. Within a few years, all but a few German war criminals in the Western countries had been set free. The Soviet Union followed suit by releasing her 9,626 war criminals late in 1955.

Thus the heroes came home. Ten years after the most horrible crime in recorded history, the sun of mercy was shining down on all. Today, up to 20,000 unreconstructed criminals are free to go about their business in Germany. A few thousands more are scattered through Spain, Egypt, and Argentina. Tens of thousands more still live under false papers, and other untold thousands have not even been touched by an investigation. There has never been a clearer and more convincing identification between a nation and its "heroes."

---

* The seven "red-jackets" were the SS special task officers Oswald Pohl, Otto Ohlendorf, Erich Naumann, Werner Braune, Paul Blobel, and the Dachau SS guards Georg Schallermair and Hans-Theodor Schmidt.

17 *Villains and Victims*

On March 14, 1960, a historic encounter took place at the Waldorf-Astoria Hotel in New York. In the living room of the presidential suite, Chancellor Konrad Adenauer met the Prime Minister of Israel, David Ben-Gurion, for the first time. During a two-hour private talk the two leaders discussed the implications of the recent world-wide epidemic of anti-Semitic outbursts and the future of German-Israeli relations. At the close of the meeting, the two statesmen were photographed shaking hands, and the press officers read their statements into the microphones.

Dr. Adenauer said: "I am deeply moved by my meeting today with Prime Minister David Ben-Gurion. . . . The German people draw deep satisfaction from the fact that, through their restitution to victims of Nazism, a contribution was made toward the process of rehabilitation in Israel."

Prime Minister Ben-Gurion stated: "I was glad to meet Chancellor Adenauer. I belong to a people which cannot forget its past. . . . I said last summer that 'the Germany of today is not the Germany of yesterday.' After having met the Chancellor, I am sure that judgment is correct."

There is little doubt that the actions of both leaders

were motivated by political expediency as well as by mutual good will and respect. Their meeting was possible only after they had overcome strong political opposition in their respective countries.

Dr. Adenauer had risked his personal prestige and the stability of his coalition government when he told the Bundestag on September 27, 1951, that the German people must be "conscious of the immeasurable suffering brought upon the Jews in Germany and the occupied territories during the National Socialist period." The Chancellor stated plainly that "unspeakable crimes were committed in the name of the German people which call for moral and material restitution."

According to the Chancellor's biographer, Paul Weymar, the suggestion of paying reparations to Israel was met with "serious disapproval" by members of Dr. Adenauer's own party and by the politicians making up his government coalition. There were many who had not the slightest recognition of the need for reparations, not the faintest feeling that the past had to be redressed, if only in the form of financial indemnity.* The Finance Minister, Dr. Schaeffer, was opposed to making reparation payments to Israel. The Adenauer press and German commerce and manufacturing circles feared that compensation to Israel would alienate Germany's friends in the Middle East. "The Arabs had always been pro-German, they had been the only asset German diplomacy had possessed after the collapse, and now this traditional friendship was being jeopardized." [1]

---

* On March 18, 1951, Israel transmitted a note to the three Western powers and to the Soviet Union, calling attention to the fact that the unending stream of hundreds of thousands of homeless and destitute Jewish refugees from Germany and German-occupied Europe which it had been compelled to receive had placed an unbearable burden on the young Jewish state. The Nazis had confiscated Jewish assets in the amount of eight billion dollars in Germany alone. It was expected that Germany would make amends to alleviate the burden placed upon Israel.

Apart from the moral principle involved, there were important political and psychological considerations which compelled Dr. Adenauer to reach an agreement on the Jewish claims.* Despite boycott threats from the Arabs, Dr. Adenauer pressed for a settlement which called for payments in goods and materials to Israel amounting to $715,000,000, extending over a period of twelve years. When the bill reached the Bundestag for final approval on March 18, 1953, the Chancellor found himself deserted by a large faction of his own party and by most members of his coalition. Out of 402 members of Parliament, only 238 voted in favor of the bill; the remaining abstained or voted against it. Without the support of 125 Social Democrats, Dr. Adenauer would have lost the day. Of his own 143 party members, only 83 voted for the bill. More than 50 percent of the Adenauer coalition members refused to support the settlement with Israel. Among those who abstained were cabinet members Dr. Schaeffer and Dr. Seebohm. Some critics declared that the Adenauer coalition had exposed itself in a "shameful act of moral depravity" by disregarding the bare essentials of justice and human decency." [2]

Thus the Chancellor's statement that the Germans "draw deep satisfaction [from making] restitution to victims of Nazism" has little validity. There is almost nothing more unpopular in Germany than the reparations payments to Israel and the indemnification to the victims of Nazism. Nevertheless Dr. Adenauer has insisted that the Israeli agreement be carried out to the letter, a stand for which he has earned ample praise in Israel. From the beginning the

---

* It is often forgotten that the Israeli agreement was closely tied to the London Debt Conference in 1952, at which the U.S. canceled more than two billion dollars of German postwar debts in order to enable the Bonn government to make indemnification to the Jewish state. The U.S. was pushing for a settlement. The Minister of Justice, Dr. Dehler, declared: "The settlement with Israel is a business for which the Americans will compensate us quite handsomely" (*Frankfurter Rundschau*, February 24, 1953).

Chancellor saw certain advantages in a settlement with Israel. Not only was the United States willing to cancel two billion dollars of Germany's postwar debts, but such a gesture on Germany's part would enable her to recover, to some extent, the trust and prestige she had lost so completely during the Nazi regime.

In sharp contrast to the execution of the Israeli agreement is the implementation of the Indemnity Law, which was designed to compensate individual victims of Nazi persecution. Such compensation has often been systematically hampered and delayed by German authorities.* Hundreds of complaints from lawyers and Nazi victims have been published.

Although the Bonn Republic has pampered the Nazis and war criminals with high pensions, interest-free loans and other privileges, more than a million survivors (50 percent) of Nazi persecution—inmates of concentration camps, those whose property was stolen, whose livelihood was destroyed—have not received a penny up to the moment of this writing. (The multibillion-dollar aid from the United States was used primarily for the benefit of those who had brought untold misery to Europe and the world.†) Tens of thousands, scattered all over the world, have died in the meantime. Some lost all hope and committed suicide. German newspapers reported the story of a seventy-three-year-old Jew who had come to Germany from Israel to inquire about

* Outrageous cases of outright sabotage by bureaucrats and courts have been reported in the Bundestag. The American Jewish Congress charged "actual malice," and pointed out that a general antagonistic attitude "emboldened indemnification officials and certain courts to vent their bias." There is "a consistent decline in the percentage of cases decided favorably to claimants. From a high of 71.7% of claims favorably decided . . . in 1957, the percentage steadily and sharply dropped to a figure of just slightly more than half, 51.0% as of June 30, 1959" (*The German Dilemma,* issued by the American Jewish Congress, New York, 1959).

† The *U. S. News* reported on December 14, 1951, that the United States had poured nine billion dollars into Germany and that "the Germans took it for granted."

the progress of his restitution case. After a while, having been sent from one bureaucrat to the other, the old man committed suicide in despair.[3]

In a recent review about the shortcomings of the indemnification procedure, the American Jewish Congress stated that the slow implementation has caused "bitter complaints and shattering disappointments among those who have suffered persecution." The claims for indemnification "are lost in the snarled administrative machinery." The statistical record demonstrates the gravity of the situation: "Only 36.8 percent of all indemnification claims were settled by the middle of 1959 . . . out of the total of 2,888,884 claims submitted, only 1,081,463 had been processed. . . . out of the 2.6 billion marks appropriated in 1958/1959 for indemnification payments, about 1 billion were not paid out. These figures translated into human suffering mean this: Since the average value of an indemnification claim is below 10,000 marks, over 100,000 claimants have had to defer their hopes even though the necessary funds were available." [4]

There have been reports of a few cases in which substantial sums were paid to people who either had close connections with officials in Bonn or who had been helpful in promoting favorable propaganda. In the majority of cases, however, the German authorities have built up barriers of difficulties by demanding clear proof and detailed documentary evidence of any loss or damage suffered twenty-five years ago. In countless cases indemnification is often refused on the basis of legal technicalities. A typical case of sabotage was reported in the *Sueddeutsche Zeitung* of February 23, 1960. A victim started legal proceedings in 1949, and twice had to go as far as the highest court of appeals. In October 1959, ten years after the start of this legal marathon, the highest court rendered a favorable verdict. This time the execution of the verdict was halted by an interdict on the part of the provincial governor. The victim is now over eighty years of age.

The *Christian Science Monitor* of February 1, 1960, reported that even by 1963 the individual claims of Nazi victims might not be settled. The New York *Times* of November 21, 1954, reported that "Bavarian officials are systematically withholding payments to victims of Nazi persecution but rewarding former Nazi officials and their heirs with jobs and pensions." The *Times* cited the case of a seventy-six-year-old widow of a man killed in the ghetto of Riga, whose claim for indemnification was rejected "because she could not produce witnesses who had seen her husband murdered. . . . The officials have taken this line despite documentary evidence that all 27,000 inmates of the Riga ghetto had been liquidated by the Nazis."

In 1952 the widow of the executed General Sack was refused a pension because her husband had been a member of the resistance. The German judges obviously still regarded resistance to Hitler as treason. In contrast, the widows of Himmler, Goering, and the SS butcher Reinhart Heydrich all receive handsome pensions.

In another case, reported by the *Aufbau,* a widow had made derogatory remarks about the Nazi regime during the war. A Nazi called her a "Jewish-indoctrinated whore" and brought her to court. Luckily she was given only a three-year prison sentence. After 1945 the widow sued this Nazi for damages. The case went to the highest court, which ruled that the widow had undermined German morale and that the denouncer was justified in bringing her before the People's Court. The result was that the widow received neither damages nor a pension. The denouncer, however, receives a monthly state pension of 960 marks. In addition, as a board member of an industrial firm, he earns a monthly salary of 4,000 marks. Thus the denouncer has a 60,000-mark income a year, whereas the woman gets a welfare dole of 120 marks ($30) a month.[5]

A clerk in a Catholic welfare organization, Frau Piendl,

had been imprisoned for several years by the Gestapo. The charge was that she had helped Jews to escape from the country. After considering her request for indemnification, the court ruled that the Gestapo was correct in punishing such "treasonable activities," and her plea was refused.[6]

The Bonn government has also refused to make any financial compensation to the victims of Nazi persecution in foreign countries. When a group of 57 Polish women who had been used as human guinea pigs for medical experiments in the Ravensbrueck concentration camp requested indemnification from Bonn, they received an "icy and cynical rejection" from the Federal Ministry of Finance. The excuse was that no diplomatic ties existed between Bonn and Warsaw and therefore no payments could be made.[7]

In 1958 a group of 2,294 Polish ex-prisoners, the survivors of slave labor for the I. G. Farben concern in Auschwitz, brought in a modest suit for 10,000 marks each for past sufferings. Far from suggesting a settlement, the court in Frankfurt rejected the suit on the basis that the "statute of limitations had expired."

In the same year, the Minister of Justice (once the Finance Minister), Dr. Fritz Schaeffer, complained that excessive expenditures for indemnification would endanger the stability of the German currency. Yet there are the secret bank accounts of Nazi leaders which have never been touched by the German authorities (twenty million marks were discovered in two Berlin banks in 1956). Other large accounts were hidden in various West German banks. And instead of using every available penny for the rehabilitation of the victims of persecution, tremendous sums were paid yearly to ex-Nazis.

In 1954 the *National Zeitung* of Basle, in an article, "The Bonn Rehabilitation Scandal," reported that "about 85 percent of the middle and upper dignitaries of the Nazi party, and SA and SS are today receiving their full pensions. In approximately half of their cases the pension amounts to 1,000 marks a month." [8] The same is true for the Generals of Hitler's Wehrmacht, whether or not they were sentenced as war criminals. At the beginning of 1960 the German press reported that more than 1,000 Generals and Admirals were receiving pensions averaging 2,636 marks each month. There were 668 widows or relatives of Generals who were getting 60 percent of the full pensions.[9] Similar high pensions are paid to 12 former Secretaries of State, to 59 directors of ministry departments, and to several dozen widows of such high officials. The former SS General Karl Wolff, who at one point was shipping 5,000 Jews daily to the Treblinka concentration camp, today lives comfortably on a General's pension in Kempfenhausen.[10] Dr. Franz Schlegelberger, Hitler's State Secretary in the Ministry of Justice and one of the chief architects of Nazi terror laws, was sentenced to life imprisonment in 1947. His sentence was commuted in 1950, and he receives a monthly pension of 2,890 marks.[11]

The pampering of war criminals is not of recent date. It started in 1949, when, in quick succession, with an overwhelming majority, the Bundestag approved several laws in behalf of former Nazis. First came the abolition of death sentences; then an amnesty for all Nazi crimes except manslaughter and murder; then the 131 Law, which directed all federal, state, and municipal administrators to rehire almost every ex-Nazi; and finally came the Lastenausgleich, a special law under which billions of marks are dispensed each year to Hitler's most devoted followers, the expellees, in the form of pensions, grants-in-aid, low-interest loans for homes and businesses, restitution for lost property, and so on. The amount spent for the Lastenausgleich during 1959 alone came to nearly five billion marks.

It is significant that the builders of the Bonn Republic did not make a new beginning with the rehabilitation of those who had survived the Nazi persecution. They could have made a law that would have demonstrated to the world that the nation was determined to purge itself completely of the Nazi past. They could have said: "Not a penny for Nazis and militarists before the last victim is rehabilitated." No such law was made, no such sign was given. The prevailing attitude in Bonn was bluntly expressed by a leading Adenauer cabinet member. The Minister of Justice, Thomas Dehler, stated in 1953 in Hamburg that "no compensation should be paid to victims of Nazis until justice is done to the whole German people." [12] Sympathy for ex-Nazis has become a dominant factor in German life, reported an American magazine. "If a German lawyer wants to get a light sentence for his client, he need only remark in passing that the defendant once suffered in an Allied prisoner-of-war camp." [13]

The so-called "New Germany" being rehabilitated with the multibillion-dollar aid from the United States became the grand benefactor of the Nazis and militarists.

According to the *Esscher Tagblatt* of June 17, 1952, the SS General Erich Reeder, the "bloody judge" of the military court in Brussels, convicted as a war criminal and set free under pressure of the Adenauer government, received "back pay" of 44,000 marks after his release, and was awarded a monthly pension of 1,400 marks. Similar high pensions were given to the SS General Walter Schroeder, once the Nazi Chief of Police of Lubeck, and to the SS General Judicke in Wiesbaden. The papers reported the granting of high pensions to Hitler's former Ministers Schacht, von Papen, and Ohnesorge, to the former Secretaries of the Chancellery Otto Meissner and Hans Lammers, to Goering's personal aide, Dr. Erich Gritzbach (1,300 marks), to Dr. Goebbels' aide, Herr von Zittwitz, and to the one-time aide to Alfred Rosenberg, Helmut Stallrecht.

On September 30, 1958, the *Frankfurter Allgemeine* published a report ("Into the Pockets of Former Nazis") which charged that year after year hundreds of millions of marks are paid to ex-Nazi officials. The long list contains the names of ex-Gauleiters, Nazi mayors, Gestapo officials, and concentration camp commanders. Among a dozen ex-Nazi mayors who receive high pensions is Dr. Friedrich Krebs of Frankfurt, under whom 35,000 Jews were hounded out of the city. The former Lord Mayor of Stuttgart, Dr. Karl Stroelin, receives a monthly pension of 2,000 marks. Dr. Stroelin was once head of the Nazi Ausland Institute and was the chief promoter of subversive propaganda of the Nazi Bund in the United States.

Two of the top jurists in Hitler's courts, State Secretary Kurt Rothenberger and the Senior Prosecutor of the People's Court, Dr. Ernst Lautz, have been awarded monthly pensions of 2,000 marks and 1,600 marks respectively.* Rudolf Diels, the first chief of Hitler's Gestapo, was also given a high pension.

There have been countless reports of cases in which former Nazi officials filed claims in the amount of 100,000 marks and more for belongings lost in war action. One Nazi, the ex-Reichstag member Dr. Helmut Stallrecht, claimed damages of 90,000 marks for a manuscript on Nazi race theories which he had written and which had been lost at the end of the war.[14] Very often the courts have given full recognition to such claims. In 1958 a member of the Bundestag, Jakob Altmaier, declared that each year almost two billion marks are paid to Hitler's Gauleiters, ministers, SS officers, and tens of thousands of "old fighters." [15] From the Nazi Gauleiters down to Hitler's valet, a former SS guard, every Nazi was eligible for a comfortable pension from the Bonn Republic. The most celebrated case is probably that of a swineherd, who, in recognition of his early allegiance to Hitler, was

---

* The case of Dr. Lautz, who had demanded the death sentence for 400 people, stirred much criticism. In 1958 his pension was cut in half (*Die Welt*, April 12, 1958).

elevated in 1943 to the status of a *Beamter,* a state official appointed for life and eligible for a pension. The "old fighter" received his salary up to 1955, when someone discovered his past and decided it was a disgrace for a swineherd to be classified as a *Beamter.* His salary was canceled, and this would have ended the case, had it not been for the highest Federal Court and the 131 Law which provides for ex-Nazis. The swineherd was reinstated as *Beamter,* and when he dies his relatives are eligible for a state pension.[16]

The I. G. Farbens, the Krupps, Flicks, and Mannesmanns have multiplied their fortunes. Sepp Dietrich and his colleagues are free and enjoy the financial blessings of the Bonn Republic. Men like Seebohm, Oberlaender, Schroeder, and Globke grace Dr. Adenauer's official family. But fifteen years after the end of the war, more than a million victims are still waiting to be compensated for their past sufferings.

18 *The Lost Generation*

Early in 1959 an enterprising television reporter, Juergen
Neven-DuMont, visited a dozen elementary and secondary
schools in various parts of Germany, where he interviewed
students between fourteen and seventeen years of age. In
the glaring light of his TV cameras, the reporter put a few
questions to hundreds of pupils in upper-grade classes:
"What do you know about Adolf Hitler and the concentration camps?" "How many people were murdered under the
Nazi regime?" The answers were startling. Nine out of ten
students either had heard nothing of Hitler or knew him
only as "the man with the funny black mustache" or
"the builder of the Autobahns"—Germany's superhighways.
Some youngsters knew Hitler as "the ruler from 1933 to
1945" who "had arrested the criminals and had revived
Germany." Those who recited a few facts about the concentration camps and the anti-Semitic persecution said they
had heard about this in their homes, not in the classrooms.
They estimated that a "few thousand" had died in the concentration camps.

The teachers, also interviewed, hesitantly admitted that

recent German history is a delicate problem. They traced their pupils' ignorance chiefly to a "cramped curriculum" which allowed for little history since 1918. They gave other reasons. Some said that not enough time had passed for an objective history of the Hitler period to be written; others blamed parents who indoctrinated their children with a glamorized version of the Nazi past.[1]

Fourteen years after the war, German students either professed ignorance of Hitler and his regime or thought Hitler had done "more good than harm." *Die Welt* of Hamburg commented: "There is something rotten in our schools." Careful surveys, however, established the fact that the majority of children knew more about Hitler and the Nazi past than they would admit publicly, and it was pointed out that they were merely imitating their parents, who prefer to keep silent when asked about the Hitler period.[2] Flora Lewis, in a penetrating analysis in the New York *Times,* reported that there is "an almost nation-wide need to pull the blinds on the past." [3]

German history textbooks which, under Allied occupation, contained fifty pages and more about the Nazi atrocities and concentration camps, are today completely revised and show great charity toward the Nazi record. The Hitler terror is mentioned in a few lines, but no facts and no figures are given. For example, a textbook for the upper grades of the elementary school deals with the mass extermination of Jews: "Jews fared worst under Hitler. They were expelled from the German people. They were shipped by the thousands into concentration camps. Because of hunger, diseases and maltreatment, many died."

There is a tendency not only to forget but to suppress the history of the Nazi past. In its 1949 edition, a widely used textbook, *Man in Changing Times,* had an eight-page description of the concentration camp terror; the 1958 edition makes no mention of this topic. The same 1949 edition strongly condemned the persecution of the Jews in more than three pages; the 1958 edition gives this subject fourteen lines. Most textbooks absolve the German people outright of any responsibility for the Nazi regime and even of knowledge of the atrocities in the concentration camps. Some textbooks minimize the Nazi crimes but glorify Hitler's military successes in World War II.* There are a few history books available which give a fuller account of the Nazi past, but these books are systematically ignored by the school authorities. The choice of textbooks is left entirely to the principals and teachers—a privilege much misused by the former Nazis.

As might be expected, many teachers in elementary and secondary schools often show Hitler and the Nazi system in a favorable light. Others simply skip the Nazi period entirely. A check of the top grades in 266 schools, made by the Ministry of Education in the State of Hesse, revealed that only 50 percent had devoted five hours or more to the history of the Nazi period and World War II. The rest had not gone beyond World War I, or had mentioned the Hitler regime only briefly.[4]

Teachers frequently excuse themselves by pointing out that it is difficult to correct the false historical image their pupils have as long as the majority of parents harbor old Nazi ideologies and resentments. A survey in "one of Frankfurt's finest high schools" indicated that "even among well-educated German youth there were many who were highly prejudiced against the Jews . . . the prejudice of their parents had infected them."[5] Anti-Semitism is sometimes expressed by students publicly in such statements as "Israel must vanish," or "Our fathers were Nazis and so are we."[6] Rabbi Zvi Asaria, of the Synagogue in Cologne, has stated that

* This is particularly true in the following three textbooks for high schools: *The Living Past* (1952), *Basic History* (1956), and *History from 1789 to the Present Day* (1959).

most Germans have not reformed but have instead poisoned the young generation with their bias. The rabbi declared that Jewish children in various schools in Cologne are frequently insulted by other pupils with the old cliché: "It's a pity that you and your parents weren't gassed by Hitler." [7] According to Dr. Hanna Vogt, educational adviser to the State of Hesse, the attitude of some youngsters seems to be that "if so many Jews were killed by the Nazis, the Jews must have given some cause for the persecution." [8]

An analysis presented by the *Frankfurter Allgemeine* comes to the conclusion that a large majority of Germans "are still smarting under the trauma of the Thousand-Year Reich," that there are "few teachers who can jump over the shadow of their National Socialist past," and that the Nazi ideology "still lingers in many circles."

Tests have shown that up to 70 percent of the German youth are indoctrinated with Nazi ideas and anti-Semitic concepts. Most of the youngsters have heard from their parents, relatives, or friends, that under Hitler the Jews and Slavs were killed by the millions. But they also know that it is not wise to admit openly that they have knowledge of these facts. The German masses are extremely conscious of the fact (and are often reminded by the press) that "the *Ausland*—the world abroad—is watching you," and the old bias is often suppressed, not because of moral scruples but rather because of expediency, since open Nazi manifestations "have unfavorable repercussions abroad." [9] Thus the people seem to take refuge behind the generally accepted defense that "no living German had been a Nazi and none had participated in or condoned the Nazi crimes." [10]

A survey made by the American Jewish Congress gave a pointed description of the German attitude:

Many Germans were glad to accept the contention that the Nazis had not committed any crimes of magnitude. There were, to be sure, concentration camps, but the accounts of bestial treatment were flagrantly exaggerated. The inmates of those camps were reasonably well fed and cared for. The films shown to the German people by the occupation powers were fake. The figure of six million Jews was a fabrication. . . . In any event, the crimes of the Allies balanced the Nazi crimes and the suffering of the Jews was offset by the suffering of the Germans who endured bombardment of their cities and starvation through blockade. This rationalization of the past achieved two major purposes: It not only relieved the German people of the obligation to atone for their crimes against humanity but prepared the ground for the rehabilitation and reinstatement of the Nazi criminals into German life. . . . Slowly but surely the German people—except for a small minority—allowed themselves to be persuaded by the apologetics.[11]

It is correct to say that the tremendous collective effort to repress the evil record of the Nazi past from the national conscience has created a nation of self-styled "historical illiterates." When a hundred students from a teachers' college in Bavaria were questioned about the Nazi past, 75 percent pretended complete ignorance, and the rest showed only superficial knowledge of the Hitler period.[12]

Again, when a group of fifty university students and young teachers were questioned about the number of Jews who perished under the Nazi terror, the majority said they had no knowledge of such killings. Only a few made estimates, with the highest figure given as 40,000.[13] It is likely that more than 80 percent of the youth of voting age have never acquired accurate information about the Nazi regime and the events that brought about the German defeat of 1945. Yet it is obvious that Nazi doctrines are very much alive. A report in *Die Welt* declared: "We must take it for granted that the virus of Nazi propaganda is still present. Everything that Hitler, Rosenberg, and Streicher's *Stuermer* once preached about the Jews is still alive." The report goes on to say:

In most schools, there is a lack of readiness to touch the hot iron. . . . There is a general reluctance (on the part of the teachers) to discuss such themes as National Socialism and the Jewish question. . . . The number of teachers who are willing to preach tolerance and convey a true understanding of the Nazi past to their students seems to be alarmingly small.[14]

Threats and intimidations are made against those who dare to explain the character of the Nazi regime and against newspapermen who publish stories about the way Nazism is taught in the schools. The *Frankfurter Allgemeine* published a report about a regional conference of educators, at which young teachers complained about intimidation by older colleagues, school directors, and government officials when they tried to deal critically with the Nazi period. It was charged that "senior teachers and school directors only pay lip service to the democratic institutions" and that the glorification of nationalistic ideals is prevalent.[15] In a letter to *Die Welt,* a young teacher reported that he was advised by the director of his school not to speak adversely about National Socialism. The significant hint was: "Why should such times not come again?" In his letter the teacher asked the editors not to publish his name or the town where his school is located.[16]

On March 28, 1959, the *Frankfurter Rundschau* printed a long story about a newspaperwoman in Bremen, Frau Lilo Weinsheimer, who had shown in several articles how the topic of Nazism was evaded in the schools and had warned against the growing neo-Nazi influence in youth organizations. Frau Weinsheimer received several threatening phone calls. One anonymous voice told her: "Either you stop your criticism or we will hang you." Similar threats were made against the director of a high school in Erlangan, Dr. Herbert Paulus, for having permitted a lecturer at the school to describe Hitler as a "dangerous psychopath." [17]

A large number of children of former Hitler followers

have been organized in Nazi-type youth organizations. At least 70,000 indoctrinated youngsters, many of them sporting Nazi-style uniforms, constitute the hard core of the Federation of Rightist Youth Organizations. These neo-Nazi youth groups are known under such names as Eagle, Viking, German Youth, Kyffhaeuser Youth, and German National Student Alliance. Little is done by the authorities to stem this trend. German officials have said that "the problem is complicated further by the glamorized versions of the Nazi era which young West Germans repeatedly encounter in mass-circulation illustrated magazines and in some motion pictures." [18]

German school authorities, by their own account, have not been capable of overcoming the resentment of teachers and parents against a factual evaluation of the Hitler era. Education from the elementary school to the universities is administered by the ten individual German states. Although the states have coördinated their efforts by setting up a Permanent Council of the West German Educational State Ministries, the implementation of the directives depends entirely on the good will of the school authorities. Unfortunately most officials on the supervisory level are old Nazis who are in no way eager to embark on an ideological crusade which condemns their own past.

The educational picture is complicated by the fact that other federal agencies are working in quite different directions. The Bundeszentrale fuer Heimatdienst (Federal Agency for Domestic Affairs) issues factual material about the Nazi past for the enlightenment of the German public. Very few teachers, however, are inclined to use this material in the classrooms. In an interview with the *Sueddeutsche Zeitung,* Dr. Schweitzer, the secretary of the agency, stated that the teachers "are flooded with books and brochures which extol the nationalistic spirit of the recent past." [19] This propaganda material is financed directly or indirectly by various federal ministries, such as the Bundeswehr and the Ministry for All-German Affairs, which exclusively advocate the fight against Communism and the liberation of the lost territories in the East. This of course is political fare much more appropriate to the nationalistic taste of the majority of the German teachers than dwelling on the sins of the Nazi regime.

When Westerners or representatives of Jewish organizations visit Bonn, they are shown the efforts made by the Bundeszentrale fuer Heimatdienst. There Western visitors see the brochures and posters which are aimed at instilling public officials, teachers, and students with an objective view of the Nazi past. However, foreigners are not told that this material is not accepted and not used by the overwhelming majority of teachers and students. In his interview with the *Sueddeutsche Zeitung,* Dr. Schweitzer went on to say:

The Heimatdienst has no illusions as to whether its material is really used in the classrooms. . . . The agency has issued documentary reports, testimony of eye witnesses and factual data about the persecution of Jews and the mass extermination in the gas chambers. Ten thousand copies of a book were distributed to all history teachers. Thus there is no lack of source material. If the pupils are not acquainted with the Nazi past, it is entirely the fault of the teachers.

What the student reads is often a distorted view of history. In the German schoolbooks one finds the old intoxication with the "invincibility" of Prussia and the imperial Reich; the glorification of munitions czar Alfried Krupp; the "encircling of Germany by greedy enemies"; the suffering under the Versailles Treaty; Hitler's rise to power and unification of all German-speaking peoples; France and Britain's "declaration of war on Germany" (but with no explanation of why); Hitler's blitzkrieg victories; Germany's "heroic fight against Bolshevism"; the "horror nights under Allied bombing"; and finally the "tragic downfall" of the Fatherland.

The immorality of the Nazi regime is often treated with complete silence. Rightist newspapers explain Germany's military debacle as due to the gigantic superiority of material wealth on the part of the Allied powers. Hitler's attack against the Soviet Union appears as justified, since Communism is certainly the greatest danger. Unfortunately the Allies were blind and Churchill and Roosevelt were led by a fanatical hatred against Germany. Today the Americans have belatedly seen the light and have made West Germany their closest ally. In an academic journal, high school teachers were told: "Many features in today's Western policy toward Bonn are based on the assumption that without a strong Germany the Soviet bloc cannot be contained. The recognition of this fact implies that the National Socialist measures of preventive war against the East were sound and justified." [20]

According to a statement by Dr. Kurt Frey, Executive Secretary of the Permanent Council of the Ministers of Education, "German textbooks have become constantly softer on recent [Nazi] history." Dr. Frey declared that teachers and parents refuse textbooks which give a realistic and factual presentation of the Nazi period. He expressed this gloomy view about the present German generation: "This nation is still mentally ill, more than is generally thought. . . . Ninety-nine percent of the people do not yet understand that we have to have really new ideas, that there is no more Reich and there never can be." [21]

There are of course small groups of young people, who, with the help of democratic parents or an able teacher, or through their own interests and efforts, have tried to build a new, tolerant, and broad-minded generation. There have been encouraging manifestations of a strong democratic spirit among youth groups in the larger cities like Hamburg and Berlin, where a liberal movement cannot be stifled too easily. Some youth groups have honored the memory of Anne Frank, others have organized annual pilgrimages to the mass graves at former concentration camp sites, and students at the University of Goettingen even staged successful demonstrations which led to the ouster of the Minister of Education, Leonhard Schlueter, a nationalistic demagogue. But unfortunately these democratic youth groups are not held up as praiseworthy examples. They have found neither the hearty support of the Bonn administration nor that of the Laender. For the purpose of window dressing, the existence of these democratic groups is loudly advertised in Bonn's propaganda abroad, but in Germany proper they are viewed with suspicion. They are regarded as "too re-educated." If they dare to criticize the presence of former Nazis in high cabinet positions, they are branded as "fellow travelers" and are harassed and even threatened by the police.

The attempts at educating a new democratic generation must contend with many problems. Most young Germans are attracted by the economic boom and are absorbed in their efforts to share in the prosperity. In addition, they are fed nationalist reading matter of all kinds. An AP dispatch from Bonn told of action taken by a censorship board against the book *Of War and Peace,* written by Colonel Hans Ulrich Rudel. The board, charged with banning publications regarded as "dangerous to the youth," classified Rudel's work as "a hate and propaganda book against the present democratic order." The AP dispatch went on to say that "hundreds of war-adventure booklets have been flooding the West German market lately." The booklets "usually portray the Germans as super-heroes" and "always deal with sex, sadism and brutality." They obviously suit the taste of a large majority of German youngsters, for the war stories are bought in such quantities that this trade has become very profitable. The report says that in the past "publishers have sold several million of the booklets each month for fifteen cents each." [22]

Perhaps it is not surprising that there are a number

of flourishing nationalistic youth organizations, thoroughly trained and indoctrinated. These Rightist groups are driven by a fanatical ideology, deeply rooted in the Nazi past. They enjoy the backing of influential circles in the Bundeswehr, in industry, and among reactionary government officials. No less a figure than the director of the Department of Political Science at Bonn University, Professor Bracher, warned that the existence of ultra-Rightist groups and their affiliated nationalistic youth organizations "constitute a latent danger which in a time of crisis could lead to fatal consequences." [23]

The 850 anti-Semitic outrages officially reported during the first six weeks of 1960, committed mainly by young people between the ages of fifteen and twenty-five, are a clear indication of the present danger. It does not speak well for the Western powers or for the Adenauer administration that another "lost generation" has grown up in Germany.

PART FOUR

Image and Reality

19   Behind the Adenauer Façade

Several years ago the able Washington bureau chief of the New York *Times,* James Reston, made this striking observation: "There has been a growing tendency in Washington since the war for the government to put out not what it knows to be true, but what it wants the people to believe to be true." [1]

What does the State Department want the people to believe to be true about Germany? First, that the decision to transform the defeated enemy into an ally was a wise one; second, that the Germans have changed profoundly and have formed a truly democratic society; third, that in Chancellor Konrad Adenauer the Germans have found a leader and statesman whose counsel is sought throughout the Western world.

It was mainly on the basis of this last point—the Adenauer image—that the State Department and the Pentagon succeeded in gaining the support of the American people for a close alliance with the Bonn Republic. During the early postwar years America's feeling about Germany was still affected by knowledge of her Nazi past. The very word "German" was in ill repute—it was generally equated with "Nazi." In a survey made as late as 1958 by the Gilbert Youth Research Organization, hundreds of young people between fourteen and nineteen years of age gave the following responses when the word "German" was mentioned: "Nazis . . . war . . . concentration camps . . . persecution . . . Hitler . . . falling bombs." [2] The report noted that the teen-agers were "influenced by old war movies [on TV] and by the still vivid recollections of parents and older friends who lived through those years of atrocities and propaganda."

Given our alliance, it was obvious that there was a need to obliterate the existing picture of Germany and supplant it with a new one. The American people were told that Adenauer had emerged as a forceful democratic leader untainted by the German past, an outstanding politician, and a statesman of historic significance.

The success story of the first Chancellor of the Federal Republic is indeed a remarkable one. When Adenauer entered German national politics in his early seventies, many of his younger colleagues were firmly convinced that the Lord Mayor of Cologne—well known as a conservative, nationalist, and stubborn egocentric—was no longer a man of much political significance. Even after Adenauer had reached some prominence as a politician in the Rhineland, there were few who believed his career could go further. Delbert Clark pictured him as "a bad-tempered but extremely astute reactionary." In his party he was regarded as "the great symbol of extreme political toryism," and a former admirer described him as "a malicious old man." [3]

"The Old Fox," as he was called by friend and foe, proved his superior political acumen by outsmarting dozens of younger but equally ambitious contenders in the field of party politics. In 1949 the Bundestag elected him with a one-vote majority—his own—as the first Federal Chancellor of the newly formed West German state. At that time the Bonn

Republic was still under the tutelage of the victors. The three Western High Commissioners had supreme authority and ruled on the basis of an occupation statute.

For Konrad Adenauer it was a difficult uphill struggle in every respect. He had to consolidate his position as leader of his party, he had to establish his authority as Chancellor and secure majorities in the Bundestag, and he had to whittle down the supreme power of the Allied High Commissioners in order to obtain full sovereignty for the Bonn Republic. Dr. Adenauer accomplished all three feats almost simultaneously—sometimes operating alone, but more often with support from Washington.

When Adenauer became Chancellor in 1949, his name was completely unknown to the American public. Most European and American newspapermen, however, were skeptical about the new German leader. They doubted his sincerity and trustworthiness and quoted his party friends who described him "as an old fox whose obstinacy is matched only by his capacity for intrigue." [4]

Despite these unfavorable press reports, Dr. Adenauer had made a strong impression on U.S. government officials. General Lucius Clay described the Chancellor as an "interesting personality" and a "capable politician" who has "the intelligence and character to act as a statesman." [5] With the growing East-West tension, the German military potential became important to Washington. Dr. Adenauer, who had proposed German remilitarization long before he was elected Chancellor, became a favorite of the Pentagon and the State Department. With the blessing of Washington, a publicity campaign was launched in America which presented Konrad Adenauer as an almost legendary statesman. The Bonn government retained a New York public-relations firm whose main task was to promote the Adenauer image.

When the German Chancellor made his first official visit to the United States in April 1953, he scored a great diplomatic success with the new Eisenhower administration. During his coast-to-coast tour American newspapermen pointed out that the Chancellor possessed a "most unusually sharp instinct for publicity." In San Francisco, Adenauer addressed a gathering of seven hundred prominent representatives of the political and economic world at the Commonwealth Club. He spoke before huge press conferences, meetings of the Foreign Policy Association, exclusive clubs, and universities. At Harvard, Chancellor Adenauer was introduced by Dr. Conant to a distinguished academic gathering. It was a success which, according to Adenauer's biographer, "no European statesman had yet been able to achieve in the United States." Here is the story in round figures:

Sixty million Americans, it was estimated, had seen the German Federal Chancellor on their television screens. Five hundred American radio stations had devoted a daily average of ten minutes to news broadcasts on the Chancellor's visit. More than five thousand newspaper articles had been written about him, and over one thousand different photographs were published in the papers. And some fifteen thousand movie theaters all over the United States had shown newsreels of his visit.[6]

Bonn left nothing to chance in its effort to build up Dr. Adenauer as the great crusader for democracy and Western ideals. According to a German press report, the cost of these public-relations activities amounted to the staggering sum of no less than twelve million dollars![7]

Adenauer had shown himself to be a master of publicity and timing. His tour through the United States was the opening move in the election campaign for the Bundestag. His biographer pointed out that the CDU focused their election campaign on Adenauer, and that his successful mission to the United States "was now redounding to his credit with the German public in general." Dr. Adenauer earned prestige and new votes by the millions in his homeland. When the

election returns came in on September 6, 1953, the votes for
the CDU had surged from 7,000,000 in 1949 to 12,500,000.

Adenauer, says Paul Weymar, was presented to Americans
as the wise reformer of the "New Germany," a stanch democrat and firm friend of the United States, a leader "to match
with the great Churchill himself," a statesman who had become the "passionate defender of Western civilization."

There is no doubt that publicity efforts in Adenauer's behalf were effective. It was difficult to sustain the memories of
tortures and mass atrocities, concentration camps and charnel
houses, and the rape and pillage of a dozen European nations
when confronted with the painstakingly created image of the
upright Chancellor. The German people, Adenauer assured
his listeners, have reformed and "they will never forget this
lesson." Declaring that the "democratic heritage of ideas is
alive and strong" in Germany, the Chancellor said: "There
can be no serious talk about the danger of neo-Nazism, or
right-wing radical influence on the federal government." [8]

Year after year, Dr. Adenauer returned to the United
States. And gradually the term "Adenauer's Germany" began
to establish in people's minds the concept of a "New Germany." When in early 1960 the wave of anti-Semitic outbursts aroused world-wide indignation, Adenauer made arrangements with his New York public-relations firm, Roy
Bernard, "for a new and much wider campaign to present a
favorable picture of Germany to the American public." [9]
Indeed, his visit to the United States in March 1960 had all
the characteristics of a high-powered publicity campaign.
According to the semi-official monthly *Aussenpolitik,* Dr.
Adenauer scored an extraordinary success:

Within nine days, Dr. Adenauer delivered 12 long addresses, 22
speeches and held four news conferences. He appeared as guest at
14 official banquets, and he had 20 individual conferences, each
lasting half an hour. He conferred with Eisenhower, Nixon, Her-
ter and other officials for several hours. The whole schedule

allows us to draw a significant conclusion: The fact cannot be overlooked that the information given to the public by the visiting statesman is equally important to his contacts with top officials in Washington.[10]

During his press interviews and speeches, the Chancellor assured his listeners again and again that there were no more Nazis in Germany and that the rash of swastika-daubings was the handiwork of nonpolitical teen-agers, drunks, cranks, and "a few Communists."

There is no doubt that for a great many people these are satisfactory answers and that the large-scale publicity offensive has had the desired effect. And there is more to come. In a full-page article, the *Deutsche Zeitung,* a voice of German heavy industry, recently described the long-planned establishment of a German propaganda center in New York. Its task will be to create "smooth relations with the press and other communications media," to establish "close contacts with academic circles and with leading representatives of business, and to court those personalities whose liaison activities are indispensable to the creation of good will and in presenting to the public the German point of view." [11]

The following organizations were named as leading agents in Bonn's propaganda efforts: the German-American societies, Goethe House in New York, the American Council on Germany, described as the "mouthpiece for German interests," and a "number of public-relations firms retained by Volkswagen, Mannesmann, and other large German companies."

In one way or another these organizations and agencies present an optimistic picture of modern Germany that often bears little relation to reality. Certainly it is a flat distortion of the truth when Dr. Adenauer assures British and American audiences on television that there are no Nazis in Germany. The German Chancellor must know from the reports of his Minister of the Interior that the Bonn Republic is studded with hundreds of Nazi-type organizations. It is interesting to note that in 1956 New York *Times* correspondent A. J. Olsen reported that Bonn officials keep 100 extreme Rightist groups under surveillance, "all rating the neo-Nazi label." Officials stated that "there are at least 35 youth groups among the Right radical organizations; most are fitted out with romantic names . . . with uniforms patterned after the Hitler Youth outfit." The Bonn officials told Olsen that "a number of Right radical leaders could be picked up any time on charges of subversive activity. The official policy is to ignore them as long as they pursue their present ineffectual rounds." [12] In May 1960 the Prosecutor General in the State of Hesse, Dr. Fritz Bauer, announced after a thorough investigation of the records of a former high Hitler Youth official, Karl-Heinz Priester, that this Nazi leader had kept contact with no less than "800 groups and organizations of neo-Nazi character." [13]

There is another aspect of the Adenauer portrait which, in the eyes of many observers, does not faithfully represent the original. Much has been said and written about Adenauer as the "stanch democratic leader," who has laid the foundations for constitutional freedom and democratic order under law in the traditionally autocratic Germany. The truth is, as most Germans know, that Dr. Adenauer throughout his life has ruled with the iron hand of an autocrat, first as Lord Mayor of Cologne, then as Chancellor of the Federal Republic. Dozens of German cartoons have depicted Konrad Adenauer as the strict disciplinarian, holding the whip hand over Parliament and his cabinet, presiding like a headmaster over an unruly class. "Der Alte" ("The Old Man") is actually feared by his closest aides, cabinet members, and his own party deputies in the Bundestag. Professor Theodor Eschenburg, a leading German authority on constitutional law, recently compared Adenauer's rule with that of a "medieval king" who held sway over his principality by absolute power. [14]

For Adenauer, the constitution exists only as a convenient democratic window display. There is no cabinet deliberation

such as that known in the West. The British newspaper correspondent Brian Connell reports about Adenauer: "There
is in him the tendency toward intolerance that seems a characteristic of almost every German politician. . . . When
asked, during his first government, whether he could get cabinet approval of a particular measure, he answered bluntly:
'Don't worry, I am at least 70 percent of that cabinet.' " [15]
Many German democrats believe that even this is an understatement, that Adenauer alone is the cabinet and his ministers are just orderlies. In 1950 the Minister of the Interior,
Dr. Gustav Heinemann, was forced to resign after having
rebelled against the Chancellor's rearmament policy. Adenauer had insisted on total agreement by his cabinet. [16]

Charles Thayer points to the Chancellor's "steamroller
tactics in Parliament and his tendency to make minor sacri-
fices of ethics to political expediency." Thayer also feels that
the majority of Germans vote for Adenauer as a popular political figure "because he fulfills the traditional German dream
of a strong man." [17]

Granted that grave psychological and political mistakes
were made by American and British military authorities during the first few years of the occupation. Granted further that,
with the stepped-up cold war, Allied denazification policies
became unpleasant and cumbersome burdens which the Western powers wanted to get rid of as quickly as possible. All this
does not free Dr. Adenauer from the responsibility for the
present situation. The Chancellor himself has contributed
enormously to the present mental and moral confusion by
stubbornly championing cabinet members, top advisers, and
other high officials whose unsavory Nazi records had been
publicly discussed throughout the nation. It was Adenauer
who demanded, in 1951, that the opposition should halt its
"snooping around in Nazi records." It was Adenauer who
steadfastly stood by his Secretary of the Chancellery, Dr.

Globke, and it was Adenauer who defended his cabinet member, Dr. Oberlaender, in spite of his Nazi past.

No one has ever suggested that Adenauer himself was a Nazi or a sympathizer of Nazism. Yet this refusal on the part of the Chancellor to take a principled stand on ousting those of his officials with dubious records has had a catastrophic effect on the moral climate of a sick nation.

The great majority of the Germans are quite satisfied with the way "The Old Man" is running the affairs of the state. Under him Germany has gone a long way toward regaining her position as a world power, and that is all that matters.

20 *A Dependable Ally?*

A few years after the second collapse the Germans were on their feet again. Energetically they went to work rebuilding their shattered cities and regaining their prewar production levels.

Today the Federal Republic is the strongest economic and military power in Europe. For the last ten years Germany has enjoyed an unprecedented boom, the so-called *Wirtschaftswunder*. With more than seven billion dollars in gold and foreign exchange in her coffers, Germany has become the strongest financial power next to the United States. The Federal Republic has even pushed Great Britain from second place as an industrial exporter.

The boom on Rhine and Ruhr surges on with unabated strength. Because West Germany is short of man power, tens of thousands of foreign workers have had to be imported from Spain, Italy, and other countries. By the middle of 1960 there were 550,000 jobs going begging. Only a little more than 100,000 persons are registered as unemployed; they are either sick or belong in the category of those considered unfit for work.

With regained vitality, Germany is back in circulation. From all corners of the world come reports telling of a stepped-up German trade offensive. During the war Germany attacked her neighbors with Stukas, tanks, and submarines; today she conquers with machines, cameras, and Volkswagens. In addition, the Bonn Republic is building a modern army, which they are pressing to have equipped with long-range missiles and nuclear weapons.

Although limited to a relatively small area in the heart of Europe, divided Germany is regarded in European capitals as the world's biggest problem nation. How will this dynamic country use its regained strength, in what direction will it move, and what will be its ultimate aims? Both East and West fear or distrust a Germany which has re-entered the stage of world politics with such unmistakable vigor.

The question of how to control Germany is answered differently in every capital. Washington wants a Germany closely allied to the United States via NATO. American policy planners fear that a freewheeling and uncontrolled Germany may soon become very troublesome. In 1958 the following exchange took place between the late Secretary of State, John Foster Dulles, and Senator George Aiken in a hearing on foreign policy in the U. S. Senate:

SENATOR AIKEN   "After the end of World War II, Germany was divided to make sure that that nation was not a threat to the peace of the world a third time. . . . Is it your opinion that if East and West Germany should be reunited, the country might again in the future be a threat to the peace of Europe and possibly the whole world? . . ."

SECRETARY DULLES   "I think it is very important, Senator, that a reunited Germany should be integrated into the West through its association with NATO. . . . I believe that a Germany which was left in a position of neutrality, or some people call it disengagement, in the center of Europe, would be under an almost irresistible temptation to play one side or the other, and that that would be a very dangerous situation, dangerous for the West, dangerous for the Soviet Union, and dangerous for the Germans themselves." [1]

Paris, quite understandably, has even stronger fears. France in the past has always been one of the first victims of German aggression. It is precisely for this reason that General de Gaulle wants West German economic and military power closely tied to a European federation which he thinks can be controlled by a revitalized France.

London would like to see a Germany economically linked to the West but limited in its military establishment and controlled by international treaty arrangements.

Moscow wants a demilitarized or a neutralized Germany, unattached to any power bloc, limited to conventional weapons, and controlled by a four-power agreement. The Soviets are convinced that a resurrected Germany, armed with missiles and nuclear weapons, would some day plunge the world into another disaster.

Out of this common fear a tacit understanding has grown in the East and West that it would serve no good purpose if the two German states were to be reunited. The nightmare of the Western powers is that the Soviet Union will some day play her "German card." As Walter Lippmann and others have pointed out, only Russia is in a position to reunify Germany. She can at any time begin negotiations with Bonn that would turn Germany against the West. Such a Russo-German rapprochement is a possibility that haunts statesmen and diplomats in all Western capitals.

Historians are well aware of the long record of close collaboration between Russia and Germany. From the time of Frederick the Great to Bismarck's "Reinsurance Treaty" to the Rapallo Treaty in the Weimar Republic, and to the Hitler-Stalin pact of 1939, expediency has always governed Russo-German relations. In an excellent study on this subject, Edward Hallett Carr has shown the effectiveness of the old seesaw policy which enabled the German government "to manoeuvre freely between East and West, playing off the two rivals against one another, disclaiming any firm or irrevocable commitment to either, extorting concessions from this one by threatening to fall into the arms of the other, and always keeping its own choice open." [2]

The same formula is dominant behind the Adenauer façade. During the postwar years, former Ribbentrop diplomats, geopolitical experts within Adenauer's own party, and leading industrialists from Rhine and Ruhr have openly advocated a policy of close collaboration with Moscow.[3] The fact that the Germans are vehement anti-Communists does not necessarily mean that they are not free to play a shrewd game of *Realpolitik*. Hitler's pact with Stalin is remembered in Germany to this day as the greatest diplomatic accomplishment of the Fuehrer's career. On the other hand, Hitler's attack on the Soviet Union is widely regarded as his gravest mistake. In 1955, when Dr. Adenauer visited Moscow, Alistair Horne, the *London Daily Telegraph* correspondent in Bonn, reported that Adenauer's trip caused "almost universal jubilation in the Federal Republic." [4]

The popular Western view of the Bonn Republic as a bulwark against Communism is a dangerous illusion, nourished by German propaganda. No German statesman or government would hesitate for a moment to strike a bargain with Moscow if the Kremlin were willing to make an attractive offer, such as the return of the lost provinces or a new partition of Poland.

When in 1949 the foreign press revealed that a group of ultraconservative businessmen and diplomats (among them Dr. Herman Puender, banker Hermann Abs, ex-Minister Dr. Andreas Hermes, Professor Ludwig Ehrhard, and ex-Ambassador Count Rudolf Nadolny) had discussed the possibilities of Russo-German collaboration, Dr. Adenauer admonished his party friends to be extremely careful: "We must move very cautiously. We ought not to give the impression, either in Germany or in the United States, that we shall collaborate in any way with the Russians." [5]

There have been frequent hints in the Adenauer press that the Chancellor was pursuing a "tremendously bold plan" of first consolidating a United Europe and then turning to the East to make a deal with Moscow: "The Chancellor is stubborn but he is a realist. . . . He follows the correct thesis of doing two things at the same time: namely, to increase our strength by coöperation with the West, and not neglecting the other, to come to an agreement with the East." [6]

In 1954, four former Chancellors of the Reich (Dr. Heinrich Bruening, Franz von Papen, Dr. Hans Luther, and Dr. Joseph Wirth) appeared before influential gatherings, such as the exclusive Rhine-Ruhr Club, advocating a new Rapallo policy and a friendly understanding with Moscow.

In 1955, Dr. Adenauer solicited his own invitation to Moscow, where he had long secret talks with Bulganin and Khrushchev which resulted in the establishment of diplomatic relations between the Federal Republic and the Soviet Union. In Moscow, Dr. Adenauer brought tumultuous applause in the packed Bolshoi Theatre when he embraced Bulganin in a well-staged gesture. Satisfied with his visit, the Chancellor praised the Soviet Union as "an immense world power that has to be accepted as a reality," and he stated that "Bulganin and Khrushchev are men whose words I fully trust."

Leaving Moscow, Dr. Adenauer vowed to the press:

I swear that we haven't signed any secret agreement and that furthermore the Soviet Union never has at any point in the negotiations asked us to abandon the Western alliance and the North Atlantic Treaty Organization . . . We believe that what we have done here will help the cause of peace in Europe and all the world. [7]

Adenauer's performance in Moscow was reminiscent of Germany's Rapallo policy of 1923 and the Hitler-Stalin pact of the fateful year of 1939. The New York *Times* printed this comment:

The whole concept of dealing with the Soviet Union from strength has collapsed overnight. . . . It is one of the ironies of public life that Dr. Adenauer, the archpriest of the policy of strength, the inspirer of Western intransigence against concessions, the man who cautioned Washington against weakness at the Big Four Geneva conference, should today be the author and defender of a policy he abhorred less than ten days ago.[8]

Under the leadership of Adenauer the Germans are today admired as the crusaders for a United Europe. However, the loudly demonstrated support given by most Germans for the idea of a United Europe should not be considered an indication that the cadres of Hitler's master race have been transformed overnight into a society of coöperative Europeans. For many years now, Switzerland, Austria, and other European countries have raised their warning voices: "They talk of Europe, but what they have in mind is a Gross Deutschland— a Greater Germany." [9]

The European commentator of the *Christian Science Monitor,* Ernest S. Pisko, reported not long ago that Nazis and nationalists are backing the United Europe idea and that a "vast amount of nationalist thought has crept almost unnoticed into the officially sponsored supranationalism of the postwar period." Mr. Pisko further states:

These hard-core Nazis . . . have for the past nine years made a determined effort to reach their goal by swimming with the current. They have, figuratively speaking, hitched their trailer, piled with all the impediments of radical nationalism, to the tractor of supranationalism. They ride waving a flag with the inscription "Onward to Nation Europe" and under this slogan, which seems to support and parallel the efforts of the truly sincere

Europeans, they hide their plans for establishment of a radically oriented, dictatorially ruled, and German-dominated "Third Force" strong enough to let them talk on even terms with both East and West.[10]

Thus German nationalism is still the critical mass that some day may cause another chain reaction engulfing Europe and the entire globe. Washington, which has backed a strong Germany and European integration, is hopeful that nothing unpleasant will happen during the next few years. There is widespread apprehension in Britain, however, that the rapidly growing economic and military power in Germany will some day result in the complete domination of the European continent. In a recent analysis, the Paris bureau chief of the *Christian Science Monitor* reported British fears that a resurgent Germany "may threaten to repeat its past aggression in trying to dominate all Europe." Germany's long-term strategy is to weaken France with the help of former collaborationists, and to transform Europe into a greater German Lebensraum. According to the *Monitor,* after General de Gaulle's exit there will be "no other leader in an otherwise politically soft France to prevent it from quickly yielding to a powerful Germany, particularly within the structure of the United Europe of the Common Market." The *Monitor* quoted British officials as saying: "Dr. Adenauer cannot be expected to stay in power very much longer and . . . there is no one to replace him and hold back the ambitious German forces." [11]

The question whether Germany can again become a threat to the world will be determined to a large extent by the domestic developments in a nation which has so often baffled her neighbors during past centuries. If conditions remain as they are now in the Federal Republic there is little danger of a Nazi or nationalist upheaval. But if there is a recession of the present prosperity or if a political crisis should arise, such an upheaval is entirely possible. Nothing radical, however, will ever happen without the express consent or even directive of the all-powerful bankers, industrialists, and military masters in Germany. The latter group has until now remained discreetly in the background. But the role and influence of the military is rapidly growing, and the day may come when a militant leader will again dominate the German scene.

21 *"A Policy of Calculated Risk"*

After the Second World War, Washington's policy planners in great haste transformed our former enemy into a close ally. The State Department called the approach toward the new Germany "a policy of calculated risk" based on realistic optimism. Once before we tried a similar experiment when America helped in rebuilding a strong Germany after the First World War, and almost overnight that "reformed" Germany of Weimar was replaced by the Third Reich of Adolf Hitler.

It should be noted that the picture of Germany presented here is far from complete. There are other important areas in German life which have been excluded from consideration in order to deal more fully with the central theme of this book—whether or not Nazism is still alive. There is no doubt that these other problems are closely related to the main issue. For example: the return of Nazi industrialists and bankers to their former positions of power—the Krupps and Flicks and Hitler's bankers, Hermann Abs and Robert Pferdmenges—symbolizes the restoration of the old aggressive Germany. Abs and Pferdmenges were on the Allied war criminal list, but both remained unprosecuted.* Minister-President Meyers of North Rhine-Westphalia has stated that more efficient controls over Germany's economic captains on Rhine and Ruhr are needed. They had wrecked the Weimar Republic and they are a potential danger to the Bonn Republic. "Only a single financial tycoon," says Herr Meyers, "is necessary for the support of another Hitler, and all security measures to uphold the democratic order would prove to be inadequate." [1]

The return of the rulers of Rhine and Ruhr constitutes a problem of such prime importance for the future safety of Europe and the world that it can only be treated appropriately in a separate study. The same is true in regard to the essential facts behind Germany's rapidly growing army, the Bundeswehr. Led by Hitler's younger General Staff officers, the Bonn military planners have recently demanded the most modern weapons for their new divisions—Polaris missiles and nuclear bombs.[2]

I have left a variety of subjects largely undiscussed: namely, German reunification; the political ineffectiveness of the German labor unions and the Social Democratic party; the United Europe plan, advocated so strongly by Dr. Adenauer; NATO's role as an umbrella for German rearmament; Bonn's far-reaching geopolitcial plans in the Middle East and Africa; and a great number of other important problems.

It will be argued that although a large segment of the German people still cling to Nazi ideas, there must be many, perhaps the majority, who have become reconciled to the present system of a "Chancellor democracy." The fact is that Dr. Adenauer's autocratic rule has had a blighting effect on the

---

* In *A Watcher on the Rhine*, Brian Connell names Abs and Pferdmenges as Dr. Adenauer's "closest advisers" and describes Pferdmenges, who is the head of the Oppenheim banking house in Cologne, as the Chancellor's "most intimate friend."

tender democratic roots that sprouted under a well-phrased constitution. Most Germans, understandably, have accepted the domineering regime of "Der Alte."

The democratic forces, as we have seen, are far too weak to serve as an effective bulwark against the return of militarism, jingoism, and Nazism, and there is justified fear that the trend is rapidly toward an authoritarian state.

The fact that today there is no large organized Nazi party, according to Charles Thayer, "does not dispose of the danger of another dictatorship." Thayer also points out that "many editors, politicians and commentators have grave doubts about Germany's ability to survive under a parliamentary system." [3]

Unfortunately the United States did not help create a climate for democracy when the country was occupied in 1945. The tragedy, as Delbert Clark has pointed out, is that from the beginning of the occupation the U. S. Military Government gave little or no encouragement to the few potential German leaders who had democratic or antimilitaristic sentiments. The democratic forces were simply "ignored or brushed aside in favor of the old-line Nazis who thrived during the Hitler regime." What Clark wrote in 1949 is still valid:

Today the "little men" of Germany are unchanged, awaiting only a new leader to tell them what to do. They believe in authority and are lost without it. Democracy to them means American folkways, American political forms, carbonated soft drinks, chewing gum, baseball and anti-Communism. The real spirit of democracy has never been made clear to them. [4]

The Germans have never experienced real democracy. To them democracy is a strange concept, entirely alien to their national heritage. This was strongly emphasized by the ideological interpreter and co-founder of Dr. Adenauer's party, Professor Friedrich von der Heydte. Stating that twice after the Germans were defeated, in 1918 and 1945, the "idea of democracy was brought by the victorious enemy together with the army of occupation," Professor von der Heydte pointed out that in the eyes of every German "democracy is linked with collapse, defeat, and foreign uniforms stalking German soil." In the *Rheinischer Merkur,* he goes on to say:

Today it is fashionable in Germany to be a democrat. Every German is a good democrat as a matter of course—if you want to "belong" you have to be. But basically the Germans do not cherish democracy. They submit to it as perhaps people submit to a fashion, although deep inside they resent their uncomfortable plight.[5]

This frank description of Germany's real feeling toward democracy was published in the leading ideological paper of the CDU while Dr. Adenauer was on his first visit to the United States. It did not hinder the Chancellor from assuring his audiences in America that "the democratic heritage of ideas is alive and strong in Germany."

A Bonn government official stated the case quite clearly to an American correspondent: "You know, we Germans will always be willing to obey the man who drops the coin into the slot machine." He said further that the German people "would discard their democratic vestments without hesitation the moment a new and more dictatorial leader elbowed his way to the slot machine dispensing offices, honors, and profits." [6] This means that a new Fuehrer could be backed by an authoritarian clique, entrenched in industry, bureaucracy and the army; he would not necessarily have to depend on the noisy support of marching storm troopers, mass rallies, flag waving, and all the other trappings of the Hitler period.

It is clear that we made two basic errors in our policy. First, we believed that if we gave the Germans prosperity—if they were well fed and well housed—and, in addition, if we gave them the opportunity to vote, they would be safe for democracy. The problem is not that simple.

Second, we were naïve enough to assume that if we integrated the Germans into NATO we could pacify and control them. We hoped, furthermore, that Germany's neighbors would soon forget the past. This has also turned out to be an illusion. We have indeed prodded the Europeans into acceptance of Germany as a military partner, but they do not trust the new ally.

We have spent billions of dollars to rehabilitate the defeated enemy—we have made Germany a going concern up to a point where she has become strong in the world market. We have made Germany the center of our cold-war policy against the Soviet bloc, and we have stationed 250,000 of our best troops between Rhine and Elbe.

Nevertheless, our efforts in Germany have achieved neither democracy nor military security. Despite his strength, Adenauer has been barely able to keep the Nazis and nationalists in line. Soon the old leadership will have to give way to the younger forces. They will not be bound by gratitude to the United States; they will work for German interests only.

Will the post-Adenauer politicians destroy the Bonn Republic as effectively as their fathers strangled the Weimar Republic thirty years ago?

At the beginning of 1960 the *Rheinischer Merkur* published several editorials and articles which pointed with alarm to the internal situation in present-day Germany. In brief, the paper contends that: *a*] the Nazi invasion of the federal government and the administration of the Laender is an established fact; *b*] the return of Nazi judges to the judiciary has created an intolerable situation; and *c*] the packing of schools and universities with ardent Nazi teachers and their promotion to key positions must be regarded as a public danger.[7] This appraisal by the *Merkur* indicates that the conservative (but anti-Nazi) wing in Dr. Adenauer's own party feels the country's security threatened by the growing power of the nationalistic, militaristic, and neo-Nazi elements. The failure to stop this growth is accepted by the paper as evidence that "the Hitler spirit, still harbored by the German people [*Hitler in uns*] has belatedly triumphed to an unbelievable degree." [8]

When a paper such as the *Merkur* appeals to the Bundestag and the Laender parliaments to apply stern measures and to "take control over the executive," the situation has obviously become critical. The editorial demands an "end to the schizophrenic two-faced policy" in the Federal Republic and asks the legislators to "clean up the plague-ridden ministries by using the instrument of the investigative powers." [9] Apparently the feeling is that Adenauer has shown himself unwilling to press for the necessary reform.

These warning voices, coming from leading conservative circles, should no longer be ignored in America. If past records and present performances have any meaning, we should pause to consider whether we have correctly evaluated the potential of our ally and whether our foreign policy in regard to the German Federal Republic is pointed in the right direction.

The time is not far off when we shall see the results of our German experiment. In the meantime the debate will go on between those who say that "Nazism is dead and buried" and those who point to the fact that many Nazis are again in key positions of power. It seems clear that if we continue to ignore the facts, if we continue to rely on a policy that is misled by a façade, then "our deeds today will haunt our children tomorrow."

References

Chapter 5

1 *Deutsche Zeitung*, Stuttgart, June 11, 1958.
2 *Christian Science Monitor*, March 22, 1956.
3 New York *Times*, January 8, 1961.
4 *Time*, July 11, 1955.
5 *Die Weltwoche*, Zurich, August 6, 1954.
6 *Frankfurter Allgemeine Zeitung*, May 27, 1959.
7 Gerald Reitlinger, *The Final Solution* (New York: The Beechhurst Press, 1953), p. 72.
8 *Der Spiegel*, February 20, 1957.
9 New York *Post*, April 2-12, 1956: series of ten articles by Theodore Kaghan.
10 Delbert Clark, *Again the Goose Step* (New York: The Bobbs-Merrill Co., Inc., 1949), pp. 29 and 130.
11 New York *Times*, April 26, 1946.
12 *Frankfurter Rundschau*, March 19, 1958.
13 *Die Zeit*, May 6, 1954; also a report in the *Frankfurter Rundschau*, April 8, 1954.
14 Wilhelm Roepke, *The Solution of the German Problem* (New York: G. P. Putnam's Sons, 1947), p. 196.
15 Brian Connell, *A Watcher on the Rhine* (New York: William Morrow & Co., Inc., 1957), p. 221.
16 *Der Spiegel*, October 19, 1955.
17 *Der Spiegel*, August 17, 1955.
18 *Monatshefte* (official monthly of the NSDAP), October 1939.

Chapter 6

1 Clark, *Again the Goose Step,* pp. 289 ff.

2 *Deutsche Zeitung,* Stuttgart, November 15, 1952.

3 *Die Zeit,* October 13, 1955.

4 *Frankfurter Rundschau,* October 1, 1952.

5 *Die Zeit,* October 13, 1955.

6 *Frankfurter Allgemeine Zeitung,* April 4, 1955.

7 John D. Montgomery, *Forced To Be Free* (Chicago: University of Chicago Press, 1957), pp. 145, 79.

8 *Ibid.,* p. 81.

9 Paul Weymar, *Adenauer: His Authorized Biography* (New York: E. P. Dutton & Co., Inc., 1957), p. 240.

10 *Die Gegenwart,* May 7, 1955.

11 *Prevent World War III* (pub. by the Society for the Prevention of World War III), No. 43 (1953).

12 New York *Times,* September 8, 1953.

13 *Frankfurter Allgemeine Zeitung,* October 16, 1956.

14 *Freisoziale Presse,* Hagen, August 13, 1954.

15 From an official press dispatch in the *Frankfurter Rundschau,* May 5, 1958.

Chapter 7

1 Wilhelm Hoettl, *The Secret Front* (New York: Frederick A. Praeger, Inc., 1954), p. 222.

2 *Die Nation,* Berne, February 13, 1952; *Basler Nachrichten,* January 29, 1952; *Der Aufbau,* New York, March 7, 1952.

3 "Hitler's Hidden Treasure," in *United Nations World,* April 1952; "Rebirth of the Nazi International," in the *Nation,* April 5, 1952.

4 *Deutsche Soldaten Zeitung,* No. 9, June 1959.

5 "Middle East Caldron," in *Prevent World War III,* No. 47 (1955).

6 *Der Spiegel,* October 26, 1955.

7 *Der Spiegel,* October 22, 1958.

8 *Frankfurter Allgemeine Zeitung,* February 4, 1959.

9 *Der Sonntag,* Limburg, January 25, 1959.

10 Other significant articles, containing details about neo-Nazi groups and their leaders, appeared in the following papers: *Deutsche Zeitung,* Stuttgart, May 21 and October 29, 1958; *Rheinischer Merkur,* September 6 and December 6, 1957; *Frankfurter Rundschau,* January 31, 1956, and May 21, 1958; *Sueddeutsche Zeitung,* April 19, 1959. See also the penetrating study, *Rightist*

Radicalism in Postwar Germany (Frankfurt A.M.: Franz Vahlen Verlag, 1958), 309 pp.

11 *Frankfurter Rundschau,* October 13, 1952.

12 "Alles fuer Deutschland," *Der Spiegel,* October 15, 1952.

13 *Time,* May 21, 1951.

14 "Putsch Through the Back Door," *Welt am Sontag,* May 10, 1953.

15 "Den Gegner Sturmreif Schiessen," *Neue Zeitung,* Munich, November 22, 1952.

16 *Frankfurter Rundschau,* January 31, 1956.

17 Report on the "Old Fighters," *Frankfurter Rundschau,* May 21, 1958.

18 "The Democratic Fire Department," *Stuttgarten Nachrichten,* May 25, 1956.

19 "Germans Expose Pro-Nazi Writing," New York *Times,* June 17, 1956.

20 New York *Times,* January 18, 1954; also letter by Stuart E. Colie in New York *Times,* February 1, 1953.

21 Montgomery, *Forced To Be Free,* p. 34.

22 Quoted in *Der Fortschritt,* January 16, 1958.

23 *Die Zeit,* May 22, 1958.

24 New York *Times,* November 28, 1954.

25 *Frankfurter Rundschau,* September 9, 1957.

26 *Die Zeit,* March 27, 1958.

Chapter 8

1 *Newsweek,* November 10, 1952.

2 Leon Poliakov, *Bréviaire de la haine* (Paris, 1952); Reitlinger, *The Final Solution.*

3 Victor H. Bernstein, *Final Judgment* (New York: Boni and Gaer, 1947), pp. 19 and 20.

4 *Ibid.,* pp. 152 and 153.

5 Olga Lengyel, *Five Chimneys* (New York: Ziff Davis Co., 1947), p. 70.

6 Reitlinger, *The Final Solution,* pp. 138 and 150.

7 Bernstein, *Final Judgment,* p. 118.

8 *Ibid.,* p. 140.

9 *Ibid.,* p. 139.

10 Gerald Reitlinger, *The SS: Alibi of a Nation* (London: Wm. Heinemann, Ltd., 1956).

11 Alexander Mitscherlich, *Doctors of Infamy* (report about the Nuremberg "Doctors' Trial") (New York: Henry Schuman, 1949), p. xviii.

12 Reitlinger, *The Final Solution,* p. 504.

13 *Deutsche Soldaten Zeitung,* No. 10, October 1958.

Chapter 9

1   Reitlinger, *The Final Solution,* p. 198.
2   *Ibid.,* p. 197.
3   Exchange of letters with the New York *Times* in *Prevent World War III,* No. 54 (1959).
4   *Frankfurter Rundschau,* May 17, 1953.
5   *Frankfurter Allgemeine Zeitung,* July 30, 1951.
6   *Report of the U. S. High Commission,* December 1951.
7   *DSZ,* No. 7, May 1959: "The Sudetenland Is German."
8   *DSZ,* No. 8, August 1957.
9   *DSZ,* No. 12, December 1956.
10 *Die Welt,* August 4, 1958.
11 *Frankfurter Allgemeine Zeitung,* May 19, 1959.
12 *DSZ,* No. 10, October 1958; also New York *Times,* September 15, 1958.
13 *Der Aufbau,* New York, September 16, 1955.
14 *Stuttgarter Nachrichten,* June 14, 1955.
15 *Abend-Zeitung,* Munich. The article appeared as a reprint in the Social Democratic *Vorwaerts,* Cologne, June 24, 1955.

Chapter 10

1   *Der Spiegel,* June 3, 1959.
2   *Frankfurter Rundschau,* April 11, 1957.
3   Foreign Minister von Brentano in the Bundestag on January 31, 1957.
4   The figures were taken from the 1942 volume of the Nazi paper *Bruenner Tagblatt* and published by *Die Oesterreichische Nation,* July 1959.
5   Letter by Jan Papanek in the New York *Times,* August 2, 1957: "The Role of the Sudeten Germans." Papanek, an anti-Communist, was formerly head of the Czechoslovakian delegation to the U.N.
6   *Documents Relating to the Administration of the Occupied Countries of Eastern Europe, No. 8: Extermination of the Polish People,* issued by the Polish Information Center (New York, 1941).
7   Statement by Cardinal Hlond, Primate of Poland, in *La Nation Belge,* February 28, 1940.
8   Bulletin of the Federal Government, Bonn, April 3, 1953.
9   The full text of the document was published in T. H. Tetens, *Germany Plots with the Kremlin* (New York: Henry Schuman, 1953).
10 Alistair Horne, *Return to Power* (New York: Frederick A. Praeger, Inc., 1956), p. 236.
11 *Rheinischer Merkur,* June 22, 1952.

12 *Rheinischer Merkur*, January 8, 1953.
13 New York *Herald Tribune*, August 4, 1954.
14 *The Economist*, London, December 12, 1953.
15 London *Daily Express*, January 16, 1957.
16 *Frankfurter Rundschau*, July 28, 1959.
17 *Volksbote*, Munich, July 4, 1959.
18 "The Old Guard of the Nazi Party," *Sueddeutsche Zeitung*, April 19, 1959; *Der Spiegel*, June 24, 1959.
19 "The Price of Defeat," translated in the *Frankfurter Allgemeine Zeitung*, January 7, 1959.
20 *Volksbote*, January 17, 1959.
21 *Frankfurter Rundschau*, March 28, 1959.
22 *Christian Science Monitor*, May 13, 14, 18, 19, and 21, 1959.
23 *Die Welt*, Hamburg, August 3 and 17, 1959.
24 *Sudeten Bulletin*, July-August 1955; also *Volksbote*, November 5, 1955.
25 *Volksbote*, August 10, 1957.
26 *Volksbote*, August 15, 1959.
27 *Volksbote*, March 1, 8, and 15, 1958; also New York *Staats Zeitung*, March 8, 1958.
28 *Frankfurter Allgemeine Zeitung*, May 4, 1959.

Chapter 11

1 "Crystal Night in Koeppern," *Frankfurter Rundschau*, December 20, 1958, and January 22, 1959.
2 *The Churchman*, New York, October 1, 1956.
3 New York *Times*, February 26, 1959.
4 *Die Welt*, January 8, 1959.
5 *Frankfurter Rundschau*, January 7, 9, and 12, 1959.
6 *Rheinischer Merkur*, February 7, 1958.
7 *Der Aufbau*, New York, April 24, 1959.
8 *Die Zeit*, January 16, 1959.
9 *Allgemeine Wochenzeitung der Juden*, March 27, 1959.
10 New York *Times*, January 23, 1959.
11 Editorial in the *Frankfurter Rundschau*, January 10, 1959.
12 *Allgemeine Wochenzeitung der Juden*, March 6, 1959.
13 *Newsweek*, February 2, 1959.
14 "The Sin of Anti-Semitism," *Sueddeutsche Zeitung*, January 18, 1959; "Do We Have a New Anti-Semitism?," *Die Zeit*, April 10, 1959; "German Anti-Semitism Today," *Der Monat*, May and June 1959.
15 New York *Times*, March 16, 1959.
16 *Sueddeutsche Zeitung*, January 20, 1959.
17 *Die Welt*, January 8, 1959.
18 *Frankfurter Rundschau*, February 5, 1959.

19 *Der Aufbau*, New York, February 13, 1959.
20 *Sueddeutsche Zeitung*, February 5, 1959.
21 *Allgemeine Wochenzeitung der Juden*, February 27, 1959.
22 *Deutsche Zeitung*, July 17, 1959.
23 *Frankfurter Rundschau*, August 24, 1959.
24 *Sueddeutsche Zeitung*, May 19, 1957.
25 New York *Times*, March 7, 1959.
26 *Der Aufbau*, New York, October 2, 1959.
27 *Frankfurter Allgemeine Zeitung*, January 22, 1959.
28 *Sueddeutsche Zeitung*, May 15, 1959; also *Frankfurter Allgemeine Zeitung*, May 23, 1959.
29 *Frankfurter Rundschau*, February 12 and 21, 1958.
30 *Die Welt*, May 20, 1959.
31 *Congress Bi-Weekly* (pub. by American Jewish Congress), October 19, 1959.
32 *Frankfurter Rundschau*, February 17, 1958.
33 *Sueddeutsche Zeitung*, January 17, 1959.
34 New York *Times*, December 27, 1959.
35 *Die Welt*, January 4, 1960.
36 *Rheinischer Merkur*, January 8, 1960.
37 "Swastika Over Germany," New York *Post*, January 15, 1960.
38 *Christian Science Monitor*, January 23, 1960.
39 *Frankfurter Rundschau*, January 20, 1960.
40 New York *Herald Tribune*, January 5, 1960.
41 UPI report in Newark *Sunday News*, October 2, 1960.
42 *Congress Bi-Weekly*, October 19, 1959.

Chapter 12

1 Heine, *Zur Geschichte der Religion und Philosophie in Deutschland.*
2 Roepke, *The Solution of the German Problem*, pp. 48 ff.
3 *Neue Zeitung*, Munich, August 27, 1949.
4 *Frankfurter Allgemeine Zeitung*, January 22, 1959.
5 *Frankfurter Rundschau*, June 22, September 4, 16, 26, and November 20, 1959.

Chapter 13

1 *Die Welt, Frankfurter Rundschau*, and *Sueddeutsche Zeitung*, all for January 10, 1959.
2 "Der Hamburger Fehlentscheid," *Die Welt*, January 12, 1959.
3 Harold Zink (Chief Historian of the Office of the U. S. High Commission

for Germany), *The United States in Germany* (Princeton: D. Van Nostrand Co., Inc., 1957), p. 309.

4   Connell, *A Watcher on the Rhine,* pp. 119-120.

5   *Die Welt,* September 16, 1958.

6   *Die Zeit,* Hamburg, published four long articles about the failure of the courts in the Weimar Republic and the legacy of the Nazi period (February 6, 13, 20, and 27, 1959).

7   *Manchester Guardian Weekly,* April 7, 1960.

8   *Deutsche Volkszeitung,* April 25, 1959.

9   *Sueddeutsche Zeitung,* December 13, 1959.

10   Hubert Schorn (until recently a high-ranking judge in the Bonn Republic), *Judges in the Third Reich* (Frankfurt, 1959).

11   Erich J. Gumbel, *Four Years of Political Murder* (Berlin, 1922).

12   Roepke, *The Solution of the German Problem,* pp. 56 and 57.

Chapter 14

1   *Frankfurter Rundschau,* October 7, 1959.

2   New York *Post,* October 16, 1959.

3   *Sueddeutsche Zeitung,* March 16, 1959.

4   *Frankfurter Allgemeine Zeitung,* August 22, 1952.

5   *Sueddeutsche Zeitung,* January 29, 1960.

6   *Frankfurter Rundschau,* May 1, 1959.

7   *Die Welt,* July 28, 1959.

8   *Der Aufbau,* New York, May 29, 1959.

9   *Der Aufbau,* New York, November 20, 1959.

10   *Sueddeutsche Zeitung,* January 28, 1960.

11   *Deutsche Zeitung,* April 4, 1960.

12   New York *Times,* April 15, 1960.

13   *Sueddeutsche Zeitung,* November 6, 1959.

14   New York *Post,* February 5, 1960.

15   *Die Welt,* January 19, 1959.

16   *Christian Science Monitor,* March 10, 1960.

17   *Hamburger Echo,* August 6, 1954.

18   *Frankfurter Allgemeine Zeitung,* December 6, 1958.

19   *Die Welt,* July 11, 1958; *Frankfurter Rundschau,* July 16, 1958; *Deutsche Zeitung,* July 19, 1958.

20   *Frankfurter Allgemeine Zeitung,* December 16, 1959.

21   *Die Welt,* December 1, 1959; *Frankfurter Allgemeine Zeitung,* December 2, 1959.

22   *Frankfurter Rundschau,* November 20, 1959.

23   *Frankfurter Allgemeine Zeitung,* November 20, 1959; *Die Welt,* December 16, 1959.

24 *Frankfurter Rundschau,* November 14, 1959.
25 New York *Herald Tribune,* December 9, 1960.
26 *Rheinischer Merkur,* September 16, 1960.

Chapter 15

1 *Frankfurter Rundschau,* September 25 and 26, 1958; *Frankfurter Allgemeine Zeitung,* December 12, 1958; *Sueddeutsche Zeitung,* December 20, 1958.
2 *Der Spiegel,* March 9, 1960, published a two-page statement, "The Massacres of Lemberg," by a survivor, Moritz Gruenbart.
3 *Rheinischer Merkur,* November 27, 1959.
4 *Der Spiegel,* January 27, 1960.
5 *Frankfurter Allgemeine Zeitung,* August 6, 1959.
6 *Frankfurter Allgemeine Zeitung,* August 4 and 30, 1958.
7 *Frankfurter Allgemeine Zeitung,* December 2, 1959.

Chapter 16

1 *Frankfurter Rundschau,* December 15, 1952.
2 *Frankfurter Allgemeine Zeitung,* November 8 and 12, 1954; *Deutsche Zeitung,* November 13, 1954.
3 Karl Lachmann, "A German Diplomat's Road to War Crime," in *Corps Diplomatique,* Washington, D.C., September 1, 1946.
4 *Stuttgarter Nachrichten,* October 10, 1955.
5 *Newsweek,* October 24, 1955.
6 *Staats Zeitung,* New York, October 13 and November 2, 1948.
7 New York *Times,* April 26, 1951.
8 "An Extraordinary Spasm of Criminality," report by Arthur Krock, New York *Times,* April 26, 1951. The report is based on the official minutes made in the High Commissioner's office.
9 *Der Spiegel,* January 31, 1951.
10 Charles W. Thayer, *The Unquiet Germans* (New York: Harper & Brothers, 1957), pp. 233 and 234.

Chapter 17

1 Weymar, *Adenauer: His Authorized Biography,* p. 411.
2 Social Democratic [party] Press Service, March 19, 1953.
3 *Sueddeutsche Zeitung,* September 13 and 27, 1959.
4 *The German Dilemma,* p. 51.

5   *Der Aufbau*, New York, December 30, 1955.
6   *Sueddeutsche Zeitung*, January 14, 1959.
7   *Frankfurter Rundschau*, December 24, 1958; also "The Nazi Guinea Pigs," in *Look*, March 17, 1959.
8   Quoted in *Prevent World War III*, No. 48 (1956).
9   *Frankfurter Rundschau*, January 30, 1960.
10   New York *Post*, February 2, 1960.
11   *Sueddeutsche Zeitung*, January 9, 1959.
12   Overseas News Agency, June 12, 1953.
13   *U. S. News and World Report*, March 27, 1953.
14   *Frankfurter Rundschau*, July 30, 1958.
15   *Der Aufbau*, New York, January 10, 1958.
16   *Sueddeutsche Zeitung*, May 14, 1959.

Chapter 18

1   New York *Times*, May 6, 1959; *Die Welt*, May 27 and June 13, 1959.
2   "The Unpleasant Past," *Allgemeine Wochenzeitung der Juden*, February 27, 1959.
3   "What German Youth Knows About Hitler," New York *Times* Magazine, June 7, 1959.
4   *Die Welt*, June 27, 1959.
5   *The German Dilemma*, p. 45.
6   *Frankfurter Rundschau*, February 20, 1960.
7   *Deutsche Volkszeitung*, January 8, 1960.
8   *Deutsche Zeitung*, June 7, 1960.
9   *Frankfurter Allgemeine Zeitung*, August 5, 1959.
10   *The German Dilemma*, p. 39.
11   *Ibid.*, p. 40.
12   *Sueddeutsche Zeitung*, February 7, 1960.
13   *Die Welt*, May 16, 1959.
14   *Die Welt*, May 27, 1959.
15   *Frankfurter Allgemeine*, May 21, 1959.
16   *Die Welt*, June 3, 1959.
17   *Frankfurter Allgemeine Zeitung*, October 22, 1958.
18   New York *Herald Tribune*, July 26, 1959.
19   *Sueddeutsche Zeitung*, February 10, 1960.
20   Editorial in the *Journal for German High School Teachers*, Tuebingen, March 4, 1959.
21   New York *Times* Magazine, June 7, 1959.
22   New York *Herald Tribune*, November 20, 1960.
23   *Deutsche Zeitung*, February 3, 1960.

Chapter 19

1 New York *Times*, September 16, 1955.

2 "Youths Mistrust World War II Foes," New York *Journal American*, October 9, 1958.

3 Clark, *Again the Goose Step*, p. 105.

4 Connell, *A Watcher on the Rhine*, p. 269.

5 Lucius D. Clay, *Decision in Germany*, (New York: Doubleday & Company, Inc., 1950).

6 Weymar, *Adenauer: His Authorized Biography*, p. 462.

7 *Neue Woche*, Saarbruecken, April 16, 1953.

8 Dr. Adenauer speaking before the National Press Club in Washington, D.C., reported in the New York *Herald Tribune*, April 9, 1953.

9 London *Times*, March 14, 1960.

10 *Aussenpolitik*, June 1960, p. 376.

11 *Deutsche Zeitung*, June 25, 1960.

12 New York *Times*, March 22, 1959.

13 *Deutsche Zeitung*, May 31, 1960.

14 *Frankfurter Rundschau*, May 6, 1960.

15 Connell, *A Watcher on the Rhine*, p. 267.

16 Weymar, *Adenauer: His Authorized Biography*, pp. 342-346.

17 Thayer, *The Unquiet Germans*, p. 125.

Chapter 20

1 *Review of Foreign Policy*, 1958, p. 804: Hearings before the Committee on Foreign Relations, United States Senate, Eighty-Fifth Congress, June 3-6, 1958.

2 Edward Hallett Carr, *German-Soviet Relations Between the Two World Wars* (New York, 1951); Gerold Freund, *Unholy Alliance: Russian-German Relations from the Treaty of Brest-Litovsk to the Treaty of Berlin* (New York, 1957).

3 A great deal of documentary evidence is presented in Tetens, *Germany Plots with the Kremlin*.

4 Horne, *Return to Power*, p. 395.

5 New York *Times*, August 17, 1949.

6 *Frankfurter Allgemeine Zeitung*, April 3 and June 23, 1952.

7 New York *Times*, September 15, 1955.

8 New York *Times*, September 18, 1955.

9 *Oesterreichische Nation*, July 1955, p. 98.

10 "Nazi Dream Still Lingers in Europe," *Christian Science Monitor*, January 8, 1960.

11 *Christian Science Monitor*, March 31, 1960.

Chapter 21

1   *Deutsche Zeitung*, March 7, 1960.
2   "Bonn's Generals Ask Atom Arms," New York *Times*, August 20, 1960.
3   Thayer, *The Unquiet Germans*, p. 157.
4   "The Germans Wait Only for a Leader," *Collier's*, October 1, 1949.
5   *Rheinischer Merkur*, April 5, 1953.
6   *Christian Science Monitor*, July 10, 1954.
7   *Rheinischer Merkur*, January 8, 15, 22, and 29, 1960.
8   *Rheinischer Merkur*, July 15, 1960.
9   P. W. Wenger, "Die N.S. Selbstfahrlafette," *Rheinischer Merkur*, January 29, 1960.

Index

ABOUT THE AUTHOR

T. H. TETENS, a leading expert on German geo-politics, was born in Berlin and worked in Germany during the 1920's as an economist and newspaper editor. For more than thirty years he has studied the Pan-German movement, the Nazi party, and the strategic theories of German geopolitics. When Hitler came to power Mr. Tetens was put in a concentration camp. He escaped to Switzerland in 1934. There, in pamphlet and newspaper articles, he foretold the coming German assault on Europe.

In 1938 Mr. Tetens came to the United States. He undertook research work on German problems for government agencies and private organizations. From 1946 to 1947 he served with the U. S. War Crimes Commission in Washington.

Mr. Tetens is the director of the Library on Germanic and Related International Problems. He has written several books on the German question, the most recent being *Germany Plots with the Kremlin*.

EX-NAZIS SCREAM ABUSE AT ALLIES

6,000 SS men cheer Ramcke's rabble-rousing speech

Eichmann, Globk

Dokumentarschau in München. Masse

im Bü

14.IX.33

Die Zinds sind unter uns

Schlußfolgerungen aus dem Offenburger Prozeß / Von Paul No

fenbur

Adenauer Official Helped

374

J. fm. 12.V.61.

Eichmann, Trial Informed

Nov. 1

Adenauer Aide Wrot

Die Waffen-SS marschier

Fallschirmjäger